Connecting Policy

to Practice in the

Human Services

Second Edition

Brian Wharf and Brad McKenzie

OXFORD
UNIVERSITY PRESS

1904 ✹ 2004

100 YEARS OF
CANADIAN PUBLISHING

3uyca) MIC

OXFORD
UNIVERSITY PRESS

70 Wynford Drive, Don Mills, Ontario M3C 1J9
www.oup.com/ca

Oxford University Press is a department of the University of Oxford.
It furthers the University's objective of excellence in research, scholarship,
and education by publishing worldwide in

Oxford   New York

Auckland   Cape Town Dar es Salaam   Hong Kong   Karachi
Kuala Lumpur   Madrid   Melbourne   Mexico City   Nairobi
New Dilhi   Shanghai   Taipei   Toronto

With offices in

Argentina   Austria   Brazil   Czech Republic   France   Greece
Guatemala   Hungary   Italy   Japan   Poland   Portugal   Singapore
South Korea   Switzerland   Thailand   Turkey   Ukraine   Vietnam

Oxford is a trade mark of Oxford University Press
in the UK and in certain other countries

Published in Canada
by Oxford University Press

National Library of Canada Cataloguing in Publication Data
Wharf, Brian
Connecting policy to practice in the human services /
Brian Wharf and Brad McKenzie.—2nd ed.

Includes bibliographical references and index.
ISBN-10: 0-19-541859-X   ISBN-13: 978-0-19-541859-0

1. Canada—Social policy. 2. Social planning—Canada.
I. McKenzie, B.D.(Bradley Douglas) II. Title.

HN107.W533 2003   361.6'1'0971   C2003-904624-9

3 4 – 07 06

This book is printed on permanent (acid-free) paper ∞.

Table of Contents

Acknowledgements

Our first note of appreciation goes to Megan Mueller, acquisitions editor at Oxford University Press, who suggested that a revised edition of *Connecting Policy to Practice* would be timely. Megan supported our work in many ways, including in her willingness to extend deadlines and to coordinate a helpful review process on the first edition. We profited as well from the suggestions and ideas of a very comprehensive review conducted by Ernie Lightman of the Faculty of Social Work, University of Toronto. We also benefited from an earlier review of the first edition completed by Lyn Ferguson of the Faculty of Social Work, University of Manitoba.

We want to acknowledge the help of Steve Kerstetter and Joanne Roulston, the former and present directors of the National Council of Welfare; Ken Battle, the president of the Caledon Institute; and Laurel Rothman, national coordinator of Campaign 2000 who took the time to respond to our request for information on strategies to influence government policies.

A huge thank you goes to Claudette Cormier, Faculty of Social Work, University of Manitoba. Claudette collected and formatted files, compiled references, and acted as the overall coordinator of the project.

Brad thanks his wife, Madeline McKenzie for her helpful reviews of his chapters. Marilyn Callahan provided insightful critiques on Brian's chapters and, in addition to being his wife, continues to be his most astute and helpful colleague.

Our perspective on the need to connect policy to practice in an inclusive manner has been shaped in a major way by our interactions with service users, students, practitioners, and enlightened policy-makers over the years. We hope this book does justice to some of those views.

Preface

The objective in this second edition of *Connecting Policy to Practice* remains the same as in the first: to argue the case for inclusive approaches to policy-making. We present many of these approaches in the chapters that follow: shared decision-making, policy communities, community governance, the vertical slice model, and family group conferences. The underlying rationale for this objective is that inclusive approaches will result in better policy outcomes. Services and programs for service users will be improved, and the work environment of first-line practitioners will be conducive to effective practice. This rationale is supported by evidence. For example, the shared decision-making approach discussed in Chapter 6 was successful in resolving contentious land use disputes in BC. Community governance has allowed services to be tuned to the needs of many local communities as illustrated in Chapters 5, 6, and 7, and family group conferences have shown to be effective in many research studies. These strategies do not always work; nevertheless, the evidence of success is sufficiently persuasive to suggest that inclusive approaches should be adopted and evaluated.

This second edition is substantially different from the first. In the earlier edition, separate chapters were devoted to shared decision-making, community governance, and policy communities. In this edition, these approaches are combined and considered within the overall context of citizen participation. We deal more comprehensively with strategies to connect policy to practice here, and new content has been added to meet this objective. We have added a chapter on the experiences of Aboriginal people, and Marilyn Callahan has contributed a chapter on feminist approaches to policy-making. We have also included a chapter on the strategies used by social movements, advocacy groups, and whistle-blowers to influence and change public policies. As well, we have included two supplementary resources as appendices. The first appendix provides a number of questions that may be used as study questions. The second appendix identifies a number of websites useful in applied policy analysis and selected Canadian journals that cover social policy issues.

Another difference from the first edition is our attempt to connect our work with that of writers like Carniol and Mullaly who have documented the structural inequities in Canadian society. These writers contend that the profession of social work must confront and change these structural flaws, and we have outlined some of the ways we think this could be done. That said, we acknowledge that there are formidable challenges. The policies of many provincial governments have been mean-spirited and oppressive, both for service users and for first-line practitioners. Indeed, many in these groups have neither the time nor the energy to respond to issues that are not related to either a crisis or basic survival. Nevertheless, we remain hopeful and point to the efforts being made by many of those included in the examples cited in this book. It is our belief that better policies and programs for service users will occur if reform-minded practitioners and policy-makers adopt more of the strategies identified in this text.

Introduction

The primary objectives of this book are to present traditional approaches to policy-making and critique these methods, to argue that the policy-making process should include insights from practitioners and those who receive services, and to examine some inclusive approaches to policy-making. Including the knowledge and experiences of practitioners and service users will require changes in the structures and approaches to policy-making that are currently in place both in organizations and in the larger political arena. Thus, we suggest that inclusive policy groups be established in organizations and that new approaches to policy-making, such as shared decision-making, policy communities, and community governance, be developed and supported, particularly by federal and provincial governments. These new approaches are discussed in detail in Chapter 6.

We are well aware that the changes we suggest will not be welcomed by many who now occupy key roles in the policy-making process. Since our proposals will increase the number of people in the policy process, they will be seen as further complicating an often lengthy and complex process. We suggest three rejoinders to this criticism. First, those affected by a policy have a right to participate in its development. Second, their participation will eliminate or reduce many of the problems that currently plague the implementation stage of the policy process. Third, the outcomes will be improved if the policy process includes a diversity of views and perspectives.

We are also aware that certain language can hinder effective communication and with this in mind we have tried to limit the use of professional jargon, whether it stems from policy-makers or from practitioners. In addition, we are sensitive to some language that, while in common usage, stigmatizes those who receive services. One example is to refer to these individuals as 'cases' and to professionals as 'case managers'. In our view, the usual labels of 'client', 'patient', 'case', and even 'consumer' are demeaning and inappropriate, and we have discarded them. As much as possible, we refer to 'clients' as individuals or people who receive services (i.e., service users) or as those with whom professionals work. Although the phrasing may seem clumsy on first reading, our intent is to replace demeaning labels with respectful language. While we regard the term 'consumer' as the least objectionable of these labels, we have tried to minimize the use of this term as well.

Given our audience of students, practitioners, and individuals who receive services, it seems appropriate to begin the book with a story from practice. The story describes an incident that occurred in a project designed to challenge child welfare workers to change their practice—the Empowering Women Project (Callahan and Lumb, 1995). During one of the regular group sessions with single mothers who were receiving services from a local child welfare office in BC, a child welfare worker commented that she and her co-workers were 'stressed out' because of the demands of new legislation that required seemingly endless training courses, a new computer system, and increasing workloads. Indeed, she noted that no less than five workers were currently on stress leave. When she finished speaking, a young mother in the group exploded: '*You're* stressed out— what a bunch of crap! You have a well-paying job, a nice house and furniture, a car and holidays, and you probably have a husband and kids at home. I have nothing—no job, I'm on welfare, my kids have been taken away by you lot, and you think you have problems!'

The group sat in silence for a while as the woman cried and then tried to compose herself. The coordinator of the project asked her if she would like the group to get involved in her struggles. The woman nodded and in a most supportive manner the other single parents began to ask questions: Why had her children been apprehended? Why was she on welfare? To some answers they nodded understanding. To others they indicated that their experiences differed, and based on these experiences they proffered suggestions for action. For example, one woman noted that she had relied initially on her child welfare worker to develop plans but decided eventually that this reliance was inappropriate and insufficient. She assumed some leadership and had suggested specific steps she could take related to employment and counselling. To her surprise she found the worker receptive, and together they developed plans designed to ensure the return of her children.

The lessons from this example are not new to those steeped in and committed to group work and mutual aid: the lived experience of the single-parent women in the group made their questions and their suggestions legitimate and respectful. Therefore, their support was well received. Parenthetically, we might add that some child welfare workers who were attending the session for the first time were surprised by the spirited discussion that included very direct criticism of child welfare practice. Indeed, to staff used to seeing individuals on a one-on-one basis, this group-work approach to practice was novel and quite disconcerting.

There are key questions raised by this example. If this strategy works in practice—if people being served can contribute to the resolution of the issues facing them—why can't the same process work in the policy arena? Why can't practitioners and those who use services contribute their knowledge of the problems they encounter to the policy-making process? We argue throughout the book that the policy-making process, as currently organized, largely excludes those who are most affected by the outcomes of the process. In a very real sense, policies are initiated, planned, and implemented by people who will be unaffected by the programs or services. Some examples include policies for First Nations people, for children who are neglected and abused, for the unemployed and the poor, for the elderly who are poor, and for people with disabilities. Only in the last-remaining universal policy arenas of health and education do policy-makers and providers have a stake in the outcomes of their work, but even here some escape avenues can be found in private schools, nursing homes, and medical clinics.

In attempting to unravel the reasons for this state of affairs we note first that policy-makers, whether in their roles of legislators or senior bureaucrats, are usually men, while practitioners who implement policy and those who receive services are usually women (Wharf and Callahan, 1984). Indeed, the predominantly male policy-makers are also middle-aged and prosperous. Although some may have begun their careers as practitioners, others have never experienced the stresses and challenges faced in practice. In addition, and even more importantly, most policy-makers have grown up in and continue to live in comfortable middle- or upper-class homes and have only the faintest knowledge of and sympathy with the poverty-ridden lives of those who receive services. Therefore, the knowledge and experience gap between those who make policy and those who must live with the consequences is enormous.

A second step in the unravelling process can be found by examining the organizational structure of government. The fundamental premise of representative democratic government is that authority is rooted in the office of the prime minister or premier, in Cabinet, and in the legislature. Thus, a minister is in charge of his/her ministry and all actions are undertaken in the minister's name. In order to ensure that this occurs, governments have established hierarchical organizations in which authority is delegated from the minister to a deputy minister, to associate or assistant deputies, to regional directors and, finally, to the staff who actually carry out the legislation and the policies. And as ministries have grown in size and complexity, so has the challenge of ensuring compliance with the will of the legislature.

In most jurisdictions in Canada, attempts to meet this challenge have taken the form of developing ways to control and inspect the work of first-line staff. Control mechanisms include regulations and procedures that specify how the work should be carried out. Ensuring compliance with the rules demands the presence of supervisors, inspectors, and audit teams. Thus, at one time in BC the work of first-line staff in the Ministry for Children and Families was inspected by the local supervisor, the specialist in charge of child protection, ministry audit teams, and the Office of the Child Commissioner. Comments from a recent review of the work of first-line staff sum up the view from the field:

> We have analysts and bureaucrats in head office who live to make up policies that they think will help me in the field. Most of them have never been here and don't know what's going on. . . . The field office perception is that head office people value rules more highly than they value people. (Carroll and Siegel, 1999, p. 138)

This approach to organizing work has become known as the corporate style of management. Whether intended or not, this style has effectively divided practitioners and their immediate supervisors from senior managers and policy-makers. It has resulted in the 'industrialization of social work practice' (Fabricant, 1985), whereby practitioners are stripped of their professional judgment and discretion and are expected to conform to a highly routinized work environment.

Another way of understanding the corporate style of management is afforded by the analysis of Kouzes and Mico (1979). These authors identified three domains within organizations: *policy, management,* and *practice*. The policy domain is occupied by politicians and senior bureaucrats, such as deputy ministers. The primary concern of this domain is to develop policies and programs that will enhance the image of the political party in power. Will new programs or the elimination of existing programs win the favour of the electorate? On the other hand, most practitioners are dedicated to their profession, to its standards, and to the needs of those with whom they work. For its part, the management domain is caught in the middle, trying to assure the policy-makers that programs are being efficiently run while at the same time responding to the demands of practitioners for additional resources.

The differences among these three domains can become so large that 'the result of the interactions of these domains is an organization that is internally disjunctive and discordant' (Kouzes and Mico, 1979, p. 456). However, it is important to add that this analysis, while helpful, does not include those receiving services, and, in fact, too many of these individuals fail to receive the services they want or need. To add this fourth domain would strengthen the claim that public sector organizations are severely flawed.

Although our views may not be widely shared, we believe that those we serve can make valuable contributions in identifying the circumstances that make their lives difficult and in pointing to ways of overcoming these difficulties. This view sets us apart from those who hold that professionals have the knowledge and skill to both identify problems and to prescribe solutions. It also sets us apart from those who advocate that the remedies to today's problems lie in a return to patterns of the past; for example, women should return to home and hearth, divorce should be made more difficult, and social services provided by the state and/or by voluntary agencies should be available only as a last resort. For those who hold these neo-conservative views, it is not particularly important to find ways of including the excluded: if service users cannot take care of their own affairs, it is argued, they can scarcely contribute to the complex business of planning and governing programs.

Here is the conundrum: we believe that the excluded should be included in policy-making, but we recognize that it is exceedingly difficult for both first-line practitioners and service users to take part in the policy-making process within human service organizations and in the larger political arena. In a very real way, these public sector agencies, organized in a hierarchical fashion and enmeshed by rules and regulations, are part of the problem. They transform those receiving service from citizens into 'cases' and they diminish the capacity of first-line staff to participate in policy-making. We note here some confirming evidence from a national study on the human service workplace:

> A landmark study of 31,500 employees in health, education and other social services work the hardest and longest but feel the least appreciated and believe they are unfairly blamed for mismanaged systems. . . . In fact the survey suggests that what makes Canada's health care and education workers stressed and unhappy has more to do with the system than their work with patients and students.

For their part, service users do not participate in policy-making for some practical reasons: they are busy people; they often do not receive a welcoming or personal invitation to participate; and for them, meetings—the customary means of soliciting input—are boring and held in inconvenient locations at inconvenient times. In addition, they do not participate because they do not feel they have the right to do so—they feel like second-class citizens who have nothing to contribute. Thus, while the practical issues related to meetings can be resolved, the pervasive feeling of being a second-class citizen is much more difficult to address. The literature on citizen participation is voluminous and is unanimous in the conclusion that participation is largely confined to the 'well off, the well spoken and the well educated' (Wharf Higgins, 1997, p. 280).

The concept of 'citizen' in Western democracies seems to be reserved for those who are working, earning a wage, and thus paying their way, or for those who have worked or are deserving of help for clearly recognizable reasons, for example, the elderly or people with disabilities. The feeling of loss of citizenship is experienced most acutely by those who are unemployed and who are dependent on society for a living. This is no wonder, since as a society we are at our meanest when it comes to dealing with the long-term unemployed, with street youth, with single mothers, and with those addicted to alcohol or drugs.

In a classic text on community action, Marris and Rein (1967) highlight the issue in the following fashion:

> The dilemma of community change arises whenever the restoration of individual dignity is taken as a psychological problem inherent in those who are demoralized, rather than as a moral problem inherent in the society which demoralizes them. We derive our sense of worth from the whole context of relationships which define a social being. To restore dignity we must above all treat people with respect. The poor need the respect of employers, nurses, social workers, policemen and public officials. And this means not only politeness but an honesty of purpose which does not disguise the shortcomings of the services offered. (p. 189)

Treating people with respect applies to the policy-making process, to the management of agencies, and to practice. It is a view that replaces suspicion with trust. It replaces regulations to be obeyed and inspection of these regulations, with support and a valuing of first-line practitioners. This view is identified and supported by writers such as Peters and Waterman (1982), Brodtrick (1991), and Mintzberg (1983). Although practised in a few business organizations, it is rarely found in the public sector.

An intriguing example of this view comes from the voluntary sector. Gary MacCarthy, a former long-time director of the Vancouver United Way, claims that one of the characteristics of successful United Way organizations is that they value and support their member agencies. Should an agency experience problems either in management or in service delivery, the United Way will offer assistance to overcome the problem. The essential point is that the agency is seen as having a problem and not seen as a 'problem agency'. According to MacCarthy, less successful United Way organizations treat their member agencies with suspicion, believing that they are mismanaged or that there is an excessive duplication of services.

Replacing suspicion with respect at all levels of the human service enterprise is a challenge we have yet to meet. Writers such as John McKnight have advocated the creation of caring communities where networks of support provide a context for relationships that enhance self-worth (McKnight, 1995). Research by Cameron (1995), Fuchs (1995), and Callahan and Lumb (1995) has demonstrated the efficacy of social support networks in neighbourhoods and among single-parent women.

The concept of the caring community has much to commend it. But if caring stops at the community level, if it is taken to mean that nothing beyond the boundaries of the community matters; then communities can become closed. To use Montgomery's phrase, they can become subject to 'acute localitis' whereby an élite controls the affairs of the community (Montgomery, 1979). Even more importantly, acute localitis can lead to values and behaviours characterized by prejudice and fear. The gated communities now becoming popular in the United States provide an apt example of this point.

Hierarchically organized structures and corporate management practices continue to dominate the public sector, and only occasionally do some signs of change emerge. These changes reflect interesting innovations rather than established directions; however, they need to be examined closely for their potential to contribute to more inclusive policy-making. One of the most important of these is community governance, and this is examined more closely in Chapter 6.

To conclude this introductory chapter, we emphasize again that our vision of the policy-making process is one that includes those affected by policy outcomes and that is characterized by an openness and an attitude of respect towards first-line staff and service users.

Recommended Reading

1. For a review of the literature on citizen participation, see J. Wharf Higgins, 'Who Participates: Citizen Participation in Health Reform in B.C.', in B. Wharf and M. Clague, eds, *Community Organizing: Canadian Experiences* (Toronto: Oxford, 1997) and J. Wharf Higgins, J. Cossom, and B. Wharf, 'Citizen Participation in Social Policy', in A. Westhues, ed., *Canadian Social Policy* (Waterloo, ON: Wilfrid Laurier University Press, 2003).

2. For a discussion of recent trends in public administration, see O. Dwivedi and G. Gow, *From Bureaucracy to Public Management* (Peterborough, ON: Broadview Press, 1999).

Chapter One

Policy: What Is It and Who Makes It?

What Is Policy?

The objectives of this chapter are to outline our understanding of what policy is, to describe general characteristics of the policy-making environment, and to identify who makes policy in Canada. The first step is to come to grips with an understanding of just what social policy is. Some definitions are both abstract and all encompassing. Thus, MacBeath defines social policy as the 'right ordering of relationships between men and women who live together in society' (MacBeath, 1957, p. 3). Similarly, Gil views social policies as 'guiding principles for ways of life, motivated by basic and perceived human needs' (Gil, 1990, p. 23). According to these views, social policy is synonymous with public policy and encompasses all the actions of governments in their continuing but not always consistent attempts to regulate social and economic structures and citizens' quality of life.

The distinction between *grand* and *ordinary* issues is useful in clarifying the meaning of social policy. Grand issues are those pertaining to the fundamental structure of political and economic life. These grand issues include those on the distribution of income and wealth, on the distribution of political power, and on corporate prerogatives (Lindblom, 1979, p. 523).

The *grand issues* are dealt with on a national and, increasingly, on an international level. They represent the major economic and fiscal challenges that confront all levels of government but particularly the federal government. While many social commentators have argued that these challenges should be resolved by doing what is best for the well-being of all citizens, the reality is that economic and fiscal matters take precedence over social concerns in Canada. The prevailing assumption is that if the economy flourishes, then all will benefit, and enough resources will be available for health and social service programs.

To an extent this assumption is valid. Certainly all citizens benefit from full employment and a healthy economic climate. But if the grand issues are dealt with by exporting jobs to other countries with lower rates of pay, by eliminating jobs, by a regressive income tax structure, and by a failure to develop and retain adequate and universally available programs in income security, health, and education, then many citizens are relegated to poor-paying jobs or to a life of poverty.

In contrast, the *ordinary issues* concern more personal matters, such as the provision of health and social services and planning for the development of cities and neighbourhoods. Although the grand issues set the context for ordinary matters and exert considerable influence on them, there is considerable scope and slack available to policy-makers concerning the nature of services and how best to provide these services. For example, Canada has followed the lead of the United States in dealing with the grand issues involving the economy (McQuaig, 1991), but the traditional Canadian path with regard to policies for health and social services has deviated from the American model in some fundamental ways. Thus, Canada has a universal health care system, although it must be noted that this program is under considerable threat in the current social policy climate.

For most citizens on a day-to-day basis, the ordinary issues assume great significance. Given our interest in connecting the efforts of social workers and other human service practitioners with the policies that govern their practice, we focus more extensively on the ordinary issues of social policy in this book. Thus, we have selected the following definition of social policy: 'Social policy is all about social purposes and the choices between them. These choices and the conflicts between them have continuously to be made at the governmental level, the community level, and the individual level. At each level by acting or not acting, by voting or not voting, by opting in or contracting out, we can influence the direction in which choices are made' (Titmuss, 1974, p. 131).

The relevant parts of this definition are *purpose*, *choice*, and *level*. Policy is all about choosing directions—in situations in which choices are clouded by conflicting values and where facts and information cannot be marshalled to establish clearly that one choice is superior to all others. Thus, the term 'policy-making' is reserved here for wrestling with and deciding among various difficult choices. The choices are made at a variety of levels: for example, the federal government struggling with the thorny issue of unemployment; a provincial ministry of health plagued by uncertainties surrounding the delegation of responsibility to communities; and the dilemma facing a settlement house trying to decide if a demonstration held to protest the income assistance policies of a provincial government will jeopardize future funding.

Although the topic is not often posed in these terms, we argue that 'policy' choices also confront practitioners in their work. Should nurses working with senior citizens opt for home support or long-term care? Should child welfare workers dealing with a situation of child neglect recommend apprehension of the children or the provision of a range of support services to the family? The choices facing practitioners are just as difficult and perplexing as those that baffle policy-makers. Furthermore, these choices have to be made in a context that involves people in a highly immediate and compelling fashion and in which the consequences of these choices are of immense significance to people's lives.

It is important to emphasize that all these struggles in policy-making and in practice are surrounded and complicated by firmly held ideologies and beliefs. Indeed, decisions are framed by ideologies and personal experience, and while research and information can complete and round out the frame, they rarely alter it to any significant extent. We deal with the notion of framing in the discussion of the initiation stage of policy-making in Chapter 4, but we need to establish at the outset the intimate connection between ideologies and politics.

We note throughout the book that the policies of governments are suffused by partisan politics. The actions of politicians and political parties are guided by ideologies that represent firmly held views of the appropriate role for the state, and these ideologies have a significant impact on social policies. The most significant ideologies in contemporary times are *neo-conservative, liberal,* and *socialist.* It is of course presumptuous to present these views in a brief and condensed fashion, given that a voluminous literature exists on each, and we have no intention of trying to summarize the work of the main theorists in this area. However, it is important to recognize the general relationship between these ideologies and social policy. Table 1.1 sets out the key points of this relationship.

Two other ideologies are often referred to in popular discourse: neo-liberal and social democratic. The latter term includes contemporary advocates of democratic socialism and others whose social policy stance includes support for a more comprehensive welfare state. The neo-liberal label is primarily used to describe the agenda of fiscal restraint that has dominated public policy in the past two decades, including restraints on public spending, user fees for public goods, and the dismantling of welfare state programs. We are aware that governments of all stripes, including the NDP, can adopt a neo-liberal agenda, but the label tends to gloss over the policy differences and contradictions that do exist between different governments. For example, the Ontario government under the leadership of Mike Harris was more extreme in its approach to people on welfare than the governments in a number of other provinces. As well, there are sharp differences between Alberta and the federal government on the issue of privatization in health care even though both governments have imposed cutbacks on social spending in some sectors. For this reason, we retain the use of the terms 'neo-conservative' and 'liberal' in this book. In so doing, we note an important qualification. We use the terms to refer to a policy orientation that is shaped by ideology rather than political parties that may carry labels such as Conservative or Liberal. Thus a Liberal government may adopt neo-conservative policies, and one Conservative government may advance a neo-conservative agenda that differs substantially from another Conservative government in a different province or from a different era.

The differences among these political philosophies are substantial and the consequences for citizens and social programs are profound. Although they deal with equity and fairness issues in different ways, only the socialist philosophy is

Table 1.1 The Relationship Between Ideologies and Social Policy

IDEOLOGY	SELECTED PROPONENTS	RELATIONSHIP TO SOCIAL POLICY
Neo-conservative	George W. Bush Margaret Thatcher Mike Harris	A residual approach based on the 'Charity Model' is advocated, reflecting the belief that social programs destroy individual initiative. Public spending restraints and the provision of social programs only as a last resort are advocated.
Liberal	W.L. Mackenzie King Pierre Trudeau René Levesque	Public social programs are important in addressing general risks to well-being, but these are subservient to economic issues.
Democratic Socialist	J.S. Woodsworth* David Lewis Tommy Douglas	Advocates commitment to universal social programs and stipulates that social policy should be equal to economic policy. Social provision should be based on need.

*J.S. Woodsworth was the first leader of the federal Co-operative Commonwealth Federation (CCF), the predecessor of the New Democratic Party (NDP). David Lewis was a leader of the federal NDP. Tommy Douglas was the NDP premier of Saskatchewan at the time medicare was introduced in that province and later, leader of the federal NDP.

centrally concerned with these issues and none address gender and racial inequalities as an overriding priority.

Policies set the context for practice in some significant ways. For example, British Columbia's *Family and Child Service Act* (1980), which was enacted by a neo-conservative government, contained no provisions for support and preventive services. At a later point, some of these services were established, but, in keeping with an overall government policy of privatization, the services were assigned to voluntary agencies. Ministry staff were assigned two roles: as investigators of complaints of child neglect and abuse, and as case managers of the services provided by voluntary agencies. Missing were the long-standing social work roles of counsellor and advocate for clients. This policy has had a lasting and far from positive impact on the culture of the ministry and its reputation in communities. Indeed, the report of a community panel established to inquire into the state of child welfare in British Columbia in 1992 commented that for many citizens the predominant image of child welfare workers was that of 'social cops' (Report of the Community Panel, 1992, p. 124).

The 1990s preoccupation with 'bashing the poor', led by neo-conservative governments in Alberta and Ontario, provides another example. Welfare benefits were cut by 16 per cent in Alberta, and 21 per cent in Ontario in the mid-90s, and workfare requirements have made it more difficult to qualify for income support.

The discussion outlined above highlights the impact of policy on practice and the need for practitioners to alter the negative effects of policies on service users. Perhaps if more attention was paid to the perspectives of practitioners and service users we could also avoid some of the more punitive aspects of many social policies that are adopted.

The Current Policy Environment: Inequality in Canada

We turn first to the current social policy environment in Canada, and the unacceptable level of inequality that exists. The well-to-do in Canada control both the distribution of income through employment and the redistribution of income through the tax system. Although the latter has had a very modest redistributive effect, the share of the market income of the top quintile of the Canadian population has been in the range of 42 to 50 per cent, whereas the share of the bottom quintile has fluctuated between 2 and 3 per cent (Kitchen et al., 1991; Torjman and Battle, 1995; Lightman, 2003).

A disturbing trend is the marked trend towards greater inequality in income profiles. For example, Lightman (2003, p. 8) notes that the share of total market income for the lowest quintile declined from 2.6 per cent in 1989 to 1.8 per cent in 1998, whereas the share of total market income for the highest quintile increased from 46.3 per cent to 50.1 per cent over this nine-year period. The inclusion of transfer payments did little to alter these trends; total income (market income plus transfer payments) declined for the lowest quintile from 5.0 per cent in 1989 to 4.3 per cent in 1998, and during the same time period the share of total income for the highest quintile increased from 42.5 per cent to 45.5 per cent.

A recent report by Kerstetter (2002), published by the Canadian Centre on Policy Alternatives, documents wealth inequality in Canada and the growing gap between the rich and the poor based on Statistics Canada data for 1999. Among the key findings are the following:

- the wealthiest 10 per cent of family units held 53 per cent of the wealth in 1999; the wealthiest 50 per cent of family units had 94.4 per cent of the wealth, leaving only 5.6 per cent to the bottom 50 per cent;
- the average wealth of the poorest 20 per cent of households fell from $1,474 in 1970 to a paltry $150 in 1999 after adjustments for inflation;
- the poorest 10 per cent of family units had more debts than assets in 1999, and their average wealth declined by 28 per cent between 1970 and 1999;
- the average wealth, adjusted for inflation, for the richest 10 per cent of family units increased by 122 per cent—from $442,468 in 1970 to $980,903 in 1999. (p. 4)

Most governments in Canada were preoccupied with their annual operating deficit (as a first step in addressing the public debt) as a single-minded agenda during the 1990s.[1] Public spending cuts, particularly to social programs, coupled with monetarist policies, increased tax revenues, and low interest rates, led to balanced federal budgets beginning in 1997–8.[2] But the erosion of social programs has placed many programs, including medicare, under severe stress. Modest efforts to restore some of the cuts to social transfers to the provinces have occurred, but the report of the *Romanow Commission on the Future of Health Care in Canada* released in 2002 recommended an additional $15 billion in health care funding alone by the federal government over four years (Little, 2002, pp. A1, A10). Another government response has been to reduce benefits or make it more difficult to qualify for benefits. As noted earlier, several provinces have cut welfare benefits, but they are not alone. For example, the federal government made major cuts to unemployment insurance beginning in 1994. The new Employment Insurance (EI) program, introduced in 1996, extended these measures by lengthening qualifying periods and reducing benefit levels for frequent recipients of EI. In 1989, 77 per cent of men and 70 per cent of women who were unemployed were covered by unemployment insurance. By 1998, only 41 per cent of unemployed men and 30 per cent of unemployed women were receiving EI benefits. In the same year the federal government collected $8 billion more in premiums from employees and employers than it paid out (Canadian Centre for Policy Alternatives website, 2002).

The official rate of unemployment declined from a high of 11.9 per cent in 1992 to 7.4 per cent in January 2003. However, an analysis of unemployment rates at the end of 1998 demonstrates that the official rate of unemployment significantly underestimates the true rate of unemployment (Robinson, 1999). For example, at the end of 1998, the official rate of unemployment was 8.3 per cent. But, to be officially out of work, one not only has to be out of a job, but also actively looking for work in the week prior to the Statistics Canada survey. Thus, those who have given up searching are not counted. If these discouraged workers were counted, the 1998 rate of unemployment would have been 10.9 per cent, a rate that is 31 per cent higher than the officially reported one. This still excludes those who are working part-time but would prefer full-time work and the differences in lost hours of work. According to Robinson, when these people are considered, the estimated rate of unemployment at the end of 1998 was 13.9 per cent. In addition, these calculations exclude First Nations reserves where the unemployment rate often exceeds 90 per cent (McKenzie and Morrissette, 2003, p. 253).

Poverty rates, using the Statistics Canada *Low Income Cut-Off* (LICO) increased slightly between 1990 and 1999 (from 15.3 per cent to 16.2 per cent) (Canadian Council on Social Development website, 2002). A higher proportion of young people, older persons over 65, and females were poor. While the rate of female lone-parent families living in poverty declined somewhat between 1990 and 1999, 55.8 per cent of these families were living on income below the LICO. Child poverty rates declined modestly from a high of 21 per cent in 1996 to 16.5 per cent in 2000; however, in 2000 more than 1.1 million children in Canada were living in poverty (Campaign 2000 website, 2002). Again this information underestimates the number of poor children because data excludes children living on First Nations reserves, Yukon, Northwest Territories, and Nunavut.

These examples demonstrate the failure of the federal and provincial governments to respond to social justice objectives, including narrowing the inequality gap and alleviating poverty. But this is not simply our observation. Indeed, these issues were highlighted by the United Nations Committee on Economic, Social, and Cultural Rights that criticized Canada for its failure to do more to address problems of poverty and inequality (Canadian Centre for Policy Alternatives, 1999, p. 24).

This failure is not just a question of resources. Cutbacks in social programs are currently justified on moral as well as economic grounds. It has become popular to advance the view that what the poor need most is more hardship and more stigmatization, not improved opportunities, to help them rise out of poverty! Why has this argument achieved so much currency in a society with a historical commitment to the values of caring and sharing? In his populist book *Shakedown*, Reid (1996) defines this change as a transition from the 'spend and share' era of the 1960s through the 1980s, to the current 'sink or swim' era defined by shrinking incomes, corporate downsizing, and declining government services. While the top 20 per cent of Canadians get richer, the bottom 80 per cent get poorer. Technology and globalization, Reid argues, are killing more jobs than they are creating.

We turn now to a brief examination of the impact of globalization on Canadian social policy.

The Effects of Globalization on Social Policy

Of particular importance to policy-making in the human services is the growing strength of the neo-conservative agenda focused on the market model, reduced social expenditures, and economic globalization. Economic globalization with its emphasis on free trade and the mobility of capital is endorsed by neo-conservatives because it reflects good business, defined openly as higher profits for those large corporate structures able to compete in the global marketplace. But how does globalization affect social policy and the well-being of citizens living in specific nation states?

Several authors have examined the topic of globalization and its impact on social policy. For example, Teeple (2000) argues that globalization and its enabling framework, through instruments such as the World Bank and the International Monetary Fund, have contributed to a decline in social reform. Dobbin (2001) discusses the power of transnational corporations (TNCs) that can move their operations to countries where labour is the cheapest and environmental laws the most lax. There are more than four thousand transnational corporations controlling 33 per cent of the world's assets while employing only 5 per cent of the world's workforce (Council of Canadians, 1997, p. 11). Rice and Prince (2000, p. 21) note that two hundred of these corporations control a quarter of the world's economic activity. The state is increasingly unable to regulate the activities and tax the surplus of globalized capital, leading to a reduction in the powers of national governments. Trade deals like the North American Free Trade Agreement (NAFTA) and treaties developed by the World Trade Organization (WTO)[3] give these companies more leverage because they allow them to take legal action against national governments on matters they view as creating unfair competition, even when those actions are designed to protect the environment or the local economy. For example, the Ethyl Corporation, a giant American chemical firm, threatened to sue Canada in 1998 for banning the highly toxic gasoline additive MMT. Despite the fact that MMT is banned in Europe and several American states, the Canadian government was forced to settle out of court, paying Ethyl $20 million and removing the ban. Similarly, S.D. Myers Inc., an American chemical firm that recycles PCBs, won an $8 million suit against Canada because the government tried to uphold an international environmental agreement banning the export of toxic waste (Barlow, 2002, p. 2).

Economic globalization may be an inescapable reality but stringent international controls are required if the public interest both in Canada and other countries is to be protected. As it is currently structured, economic globalization produces negative and insidious effects on social policy in both the developed and developing world.

In developing societies, working people are at risk of losing employment through plant closings or the transfer of production to non-union, low-wage sites. Technological advances reduce the need for human labour and workers are transferred from permanent jobs to short-term employment in order to reduce wage and benefit packages. Meanwhile, one-fifth of the world's population (some 1.2 billion people) were living on less than $1 per day in 2000, and 100 million children were estimated to be living or working on the streets (United Nations 2000 Human Development Report quoted in Canadian Centre for Policy Alternatives, 2000, p. 3).

The International Monetary Fund (IMF) and the World Bank have contributed to the impoverishment of many countries by lending money that could not be repaid. Structural adjustment programs (SAPs), designed by the IMF and supported by the World Bank, are imposed on nations that apply to the IMF for refinancing because they have fallen behind in their payments. Structural adjustment programs require debtor nations requesting refinancing to foster trade by eliminating restrictions on imports and exports, privatizing national resources and public utilities, cutting back in public services such as health and education, devaluing currency, and making loan payments a national priority (Prigoff, 2000). While these 'adjustments' are supposed to make these countries competitive in a global market, the social costs of adjustment have been extensive, especially for women and children. In addition, Ismi (2002) links these IMF imposed SAPs to wars and millions of deaths in Africa alone. Only recently has the World Bank acknowledged some of these adverse effects and responded by allocating some resources for social investment.

These developments also affect Canadian social policy. First, because they give priority to countries characterized by low wages and few benefits, TNCs impede the development of progressive social policies. This strategy can also be observed within Canada in that companies may play off one provincial government against another. These tactics limit the power of governments to establish fair labour practices or rates of taxation, and they also restrict the power of unions at the bargaining table in trying to establish a fair wage rate or related social benefits like pensions.

Second, in determining where they will establish their enterprises, TNCs place pressure on governments to provide tax holidays or incentives that restrict government revenues that could be used for social programs. In addition, they often exert influence on government to reduce the level of benefits in income support programs like welfare and Employment Insurance to ensure a ready supply of cheap labour, and to relax protective legislation such as minimum wage laws or environmental protection legislation. While companies may place direct pressure on governments regarding such changes, the influence is also exerted through comparisons with other jurisdictions that are being considered as a place to locate. The result is that there is enormous pressure to design policies to serve the interests of the market economy rather than the needs of people. The influence of various instruments of globalization is widespread, and it is of interest to note that in November 2002 the IMF warned the Canadian government not to increase health care spending just prior to the release of the report of the *Romanow Commission on the Future of Health Care*. This report, along with the Senate report on the same topic, recommended a major infusion of federal spending on medicare.

Perhaps one of the most important effects of globalization is its influence on civil society. Civil society is a concept that is frequently identified in relation to community capacity-building and the development of local democracy. In our view, one of the essential attributes of a civil society is the ability to hold others, including institutions, accountable for their actions. This may occur through informal actions, formal complaints, the influence of public opinion, redress through the legal system, or elections to replace those in power. Although accountability mechanisms are often imperfect, they do exist even in the case of elected officials. When some of the power normally vested in government and local institutions are transferred to TNCs that are accountable not to the citizens of the country where they are located but to international shareholders primarily concerned with profits, this equation is altered. While globalization is not the only reason that people often feel unable to influence the policies that affect their lives, it contributes to the weakening of civil society, particularly in relation to social policy, by placing the authority for these decisions out of reach by local citizens.

Two possible scenarios related to diminished state power are identified by Marchak (1991). First, decreasing state power may lead to the mobilization of actions to promote policy reform on a more global scale. One example was the mobilization of support to defeat the Multilateral Agreement on Investment, a proposal by the 29 richest countries in the world designed to ease the movement of capital across international boundaries, in 1998. The growing international resistance to the concentration of power among transnational corporations is also reflected in protests that occur at all major meetings of groups such as the WTO. In addition, groups like the Council of Canadians are active in coordinating

Canadian opposition to the social costs of globalization. A second possibility is that social policy will adapt to an environment characterized by a diminished state role, particularly with respect to the state's capacity to regulate the national economy. If the latter scenario prevails, we will become increasingly less able to rely on government to protect the health and social programs we have come to value in Canada.

What Can Be Done?

Marchak (1991) notes that the new right stands in opposition to the welfare state and in favour of completely free markets untrammelled by state intervention. She suggests that the rise of this political ideology parallels the failure of the state to provide social services free of debt even though Canada's debt is primarily attributed to causes other than social spending. Cameron and Finn (1996) have noted that government spending on social services since the 1970s was responsible for only about 6 per cent of the federal debt. Moreover, Canada spends less on social programs compared to 13 other developed countries, including Greece and Spain, and social spending, at present, is growing more slowly compared to all other spending in the economy. Despite these trends, the presence of a significant public debt has led to an increased demand to privatize public programs, including the social services.

Neo-conservative arguments do resonate with the concerns of many people. It must be recognized that ideology does not exist independently from people's lives; rather, daily life reflects and shapes one's ideological commitments. Citizens are faced with rising taxes, declining incomes, poorer services, the past failures of social programs, and concern about the debt. In addition, the media in Canada, which is dominated by a right-wing orientation, is always ready to highlight these concerns. These experiences influence the views of the public on social spending. For example, the fact that federal and provincial governments were able to reduce social spending in the 1990s, including major cuts to welfare rates, without major protests demonstrates a hardening of public attitudes in the late twentieth and early twenty-first century. And while there may be growing support for increased social investment in programs like medicare, there is less concern for those regarded as the undeserving poor (e.g., the homeless and those welfare recipients regarded as employable).

Policy-making in the health and social service sector today cannot ignore broader questions about the Canadian political economy. But it is not a matter of learning to accept less. Three arguments support a more activist stance. First, public awareness about issues such as health care, child welfare, and child poverty can be increased, and concerns about these issues will have a significant impact in shaping future policies in these areas. For example, concerns about child poverty have remained on the policy agenda of the federal government because of public and interest group advocacy, despite the government's rather inadequate efforts to deal with this pressing social problem. It is also of interest to note that in the annual *Maclean's* poll at the end of 2002, 37 per cent of Canadians (more than twice the rate for any other answer) identified health care, education, and social services as the most important issues facing Canada (Gregg, 2002). Advocacy and social action groups have an important role to play in shaping positive responses to these problems. Second, smaller-scale policy initiatives make a difference to the people served by these policies, while providing program models or options that can contribute to larger and more comprehensive changes. Initially, shelters for abused women were developed on a very small scale, but a network of these resources now spans the country. Finally, governments play an important role in facilitating new and potentially beneficial policies even in times characterized by political and fiscal conservatism, and progressive policy-making is all about how to influence and shape more of these kinds of policies.

Who Makes Policy?

In our view, the grand issues of social policy are controlled primarily by a relatively few men in business and in the federal government. Often, in fact, they exchange positions, serving for a time as a politician or senior bureaucrat and then assuming responsibilities in the business world. Our view of who rules is supported by numerous studies dating back to the groundbreaking research of Porter (1965) and continuing through the work of Clement (1975 and 1983), Panitch (1977), and Newman (1975 and 1981). These studies consistently found that a relatively few men, largely of Euro-Canadian descent, have prospered under the existing structures and values of Canadian society and enjoy a disproportionate amount of influence in maintaining these structures and values.

Compelling accounts of who rules, and in whose interests, are provided in a series of best-selling books by Linda McQuaig. The series began with an examination of the tax system in Canada (*Behind Closed Doors*, 1987), followed by an inquiry into free trade and the GST (*The Quick and the Dead*, 1991). McQuaig's analysis continued with an investigation into the decline of support for health and social security programs (*The Wealthy Banker's Wife*, 1993), and the reasons for the national debt (*Shooting the Hippo*, 1995). In these books some consistent themes emerge: the growth of multinational corporations, the unequal distribution of power and wealth, the unfairness of the tax system (see Box 1.1), and the declining support for health and social programs.

One aspect of élite rule is that élites are so confident of their position that they seldom bother to challenge the analyses of their critics. Indeed, they have not only camouflaged their privileged position, but they have also convinced Canadians that spending on social programs is responsible for the deficit. Contrary and compelling evidence for the fallacy of the claim that the debt was caused by spending on social programs comes from none other than Statistics Canada's own journal, the *Canadian Economic Observer*: 'It was not explosive growth in program spending that caused the increase in the deficit after 1975 but a drop in federal revenues relative to the growth in the Gross National Product . . . and the biggest drop was in the amount paid by corporate taxes' (Mimoto and Cross, 1991). An interesting footnote to this study is provided in McQuaig's *Shooting the Hippo* (1995). She reports that the accuracy of these conclusions was verified by

Box 1.1 Corporate Tax Evasion

In 1994, 81,462 corporations made $17.1 billion in profit but paid no corpo-
rate taxes. Eighty per cent of the $17.1 billion of untaxed profits was earned
by corporations making more than $1 million in profits in 1994, and 46 per
cent of these untaxed profits was earned by corporations making more than
$25 million in profits. The finance sector which includes banks, trust, and
insurance companies accounted for nearly one third of the corporate profits
that went untaxed and in 1993 and 1994 untaxed profits in this sector alone
exceeded $5 billion.

(From *The 1997 Annual Federal Budget Framework in Brief*, Canadian Centre for Policy Alternatives, 1997)

a number of reliable sources, including staff of the Economic Council of Canada,
but they were a source of embarrassment to senior officials within the Ministry of
Finance. The finance department was determined to cast blame for the deficit on
excessive spending on social programs and wanted to turn a blind eye to evidence that diminished this claim. In response, the associate deputy minister of
finance ordered Statistics Canada to repudiate and retract the study's findings.
While Statistics Canada did not go this far, the August 1991 issue of the *Canadian
Economic Observer* included a mild disclaimer that regretted any inconvenience
the article may have caused (McQuaig, 1995, p. 62).

The same attitudes are evident in the actions of corporations and business
firms that lay off workers in the interests of increasing efficiency and profits and
then expect social programs such as unemployment insurance and social assistance to assume responsibility for providing financial support to these workers.
To compound the irony, business leaders then criticize social programs for being
too generous and for being responsible for the deficit. Yet the excessive remuner-
ation paid to business executives is, in that community, a cause for celebration.
Each year the *Globe and Mail* publishes the salaries (including other compensation components such as stock options) for the best paid Chief Executive Officers
(CEOs) of Canadian companies. In 2001, fifty CEOs made between $6.5 million
and $58.2 million (*Globe and Mail, Report on Business Magazine* Website, 2002).
At the top of the heap in 2001 was Frank Stronach, chairman of Magna International Inc., and in the entire list there was not one woman. And despite significant losses in the stock market between 1999 and 2002, these CEOs did not suffer.
Between 1998 and 2001, the average compensation package for the richest CEOs
in Canada increased by a whopping 82.5 per cent!

We should note here that the findings of studies of power at the national level
in Canada are paralleled by similar studies in the United States (among others in
a voluminous literature, see Mills, 1956; Domhoff, 1967 and 1971; Lundberg,

1968; and Lapham, 1988). The conclusions of these studies are summarized in a book excerpt that appeared in *Harpers Magazine*:

[T]he people who run big business bear a remarkable resemblance to the people who run big labour, who in turn might be mistaken for the people in charge of the media and the universities. They are the same people. . . . Almost exclusively white, disproportionately mainline Protestant or Jewish, most of the members of the American élite went to a dozen Ivy League colleges or top state universities.

. . . Not only do the comfortable members of the overclass single out the weakest and least influential of their fellow citizens as the cause of all their sorrows, but they routinely and preposterously treat the genuine pathologies of the ghetto—high levels of violence and illegitimacy—as the major problems facing a country with uncontrollable trade and fiscal deficits, a low savings rate, an obsolete military strategy, an anachronistic and corrupt electoral system, the worst system of primary education in the First World and the bulk of its population facing long-term economic decline. (Lind, 1995, p. 38)

Although we have summarized information supporting the influential role played by élites in society, there are dissenting voices. One interesting challenge to the position that the élite rule in their own interests, without any counterbalancing of their power, is provided by a series of case studies of policy communities in Canada. These case studies are collected in a book that examines the influence of policy communities on public policies (Coleman and Skogstad, 1990). The case studies and the conclusions are interesting not only because they suggest some modifications to the élite view of power, but also because they provide some useful information on policy communities. We deal with the latter in Chapter 6, but we comment below on the conclusions about the exercise of power.

The case studies examine a number of policy communities including the East Coast fisheries, farming communities in Ontario and Quebec, the banking industry, forestry, the women's movement, the poverty community, the occupational health industry in Quebec, and labour. All the cases consider the extent to which policy communities influence or alter the autonomy and the capacity of the state. 'Autonomy' is defined as the ability to act in an independent fashion, while 'capacity' refers to the ability of the state to marshal the resources it requires to translate its intentions into outcomes. Following their analysis of the case studies, the editors come to the following conclusions:

We reject the societal-centred argument that public policy is a function of the preferences and influence of social forces or interest groups and that state officials or institutions have little autonomy to shape public policy in their own vision. Equally we do not accept that characteristics of the state alone—its institutional structures and/or the capacities and goals of political officials within it—can explain policy outcomes. Rather, explanatory import is enhanced by examining closely the interaction between state and societal actors. (Coleman and Skogstad, 1990, pp. 313–14)

The authors reach this conclusion about the interaction between state and societal actors in the exercise of power and influence despite the fact that the case studies dealing with the two least-developed and weakest communities—the women's movement and the poverty community—reveal quite clearly that these groups had little impact on the social policies of the federal government. On the other hand, and as one might expect, the policy communities in banking and forestry did influence the actions of government, and it is no accident that the memberships of these policy communities consist primarily of wealthy and influential individuals. This reinforces rather than weakens our argument that élites exercise a disproportionate amount of influence in Canadian society, particularly in relation to the grand issues of public policy.

Since the grand policies established at the international and national levels set the overall direction for Canadian society and determine the resources for health and social programs, examining who rules at the provincial and local levels may seem relatively unimportant. Yet the consequences of grand policies affect people in their local communities—on their streets, playgrounds, schools, and workplaces. And despite the pervasive influence of the grand issues and the limited mandate of local governments, these and other local governing structures do have an important part to play. For example, the policies of school boards and of individual schools shape and influence the quality of education in communities. Similarly, the actions of municipal governments with respect to land use, social planning, recreation, and neighbourhood organizations affect a number of important services, and in many provinces the emergence of regional health boards will play a major role in determining the quality of health care. While we recognize that grand policies are very significant in determining the overall issues of power and income distribution, we are primarily concerned with the ordinary issues of social policy. For example, we are concerned with who makes policy in child welfare and how the products of this process affect the lives of children.

Literature on the participation of citizens in the governance of health, education, recreation, and social services demonstrates that those who govern the ordinary issues of policy are primarily middle-class, professional, and/or businessmen. While the membership of women has increased over the years, few poor people, and members of ethnic minorities take part in the decisions that affect them. Research demonstrates that opening up opportunities for participation usually results in these opportunities being seized by professionals and middle-class citizens. Thus, a study of participants in the community resources boards established by an NDP government in British Columbia in the mid-1970s revealed that 44 per cent directly employed in the human services; 18 per cent were lawyers and businessmen; 14 per cent came from the trades and clerical sector, and retired citizens and housewives predominated in the remaining 34 per cent (Clague et al., 1984).[4] Low-income citizens and users of services were noticeable by their absence. Similarly, when child welfare services were decentralized to six agencies governed by community boards in Winnipeg in 1985, the boards were dominated by white, middle-class professionals.

In fact, this finding should come as no surprise. In the first place, individuals receiving services are busy people struggling to eke out an existence with inadequate incomes, and they often move frequently in search of employment or because of low incomes. Ironically, their busy lives are created in part because of the complicated pattern of human service agencies. Most service users do not own their own cars and have to travel by public transit from agency to agency, each having its own intake and service requirements. In the second place, most of us accept invitations to participate in a group only if the invitation interests us, if we believe that we can make a difference, and if we think we will be welcomed by and will feel comfortable with the people issuing the invitation. To date, human service organizations have failed to address all these necessary aspects of participation in ways that would enable greater participation by service users.

A study of citizen participation in the New Directions health reform in British Columbia confirms the above observations. After noting that members of low-income, disability, and other marginalized groups were conspicuous by their absence, Wharf Higgins contacted these groups and asked whether they were uninterested in health issues and why they had not accepted the invitation to participate. The responses are illuminating:

> Their experiences suggest that as a result of circumstances beyond their control—a mental illness, a physical disability, the inability to live at home, their ethnicity—their rights as a citizen in society had gradually, systematically been stripped away. Validation as a taxpayer, a person, a citizen had expired. The First Nations groups spoke of their long history with colonization and the mistrust of government. The single parents and youths referred to the medical community's disdainful treatment of them as patients. (Wharf Higgins, 1997, p. 290)

We return to some of the conclusions and recommendations of this study later in the book.

In summary it is our contention that, regardless of the policy arena, the élite members dominate the policy process. Thus, within health and social service organizations the pattern of governance is repeated. Health policies are set by physicians and administrators who are usually men, and these policies are implemented by nurses, social workers, physiotherapists, and speech therapists, most of whom are women. In the social services, men have assumed most of the policy-making roles, and women have assumed most of the responsibility for implementation (see Callahan, 1993; Swift, 1995a and 1995b). In our view, this unequal distribution of power is detrimental to the overall purpose and outcomes of child welfare and other fields in the health and social services. The consequences of this inequality, and some possible ways to change this distribution of power, are explored in subsequent chapters.

Recommended Reading

1. See S. Kerstetter, *Rags and Riches* (Ottawa: Canadian Centre for Policy Alternatives, 2002) for a discussion on wealth inequality in Canada.

2. Gary Teeple provides an excellent discussion on globalization in *Globalization and the Decline of Social Reform into the Twenty-First Century* (Aurora, ON: Garamond, 2000).

3. Ernie Lightman provides extensive treatment of social policy and its relationship to the market in *Social Policy in Canada* (Toronto: Oxford University Press, 2003).

Notes

1. One needs to distinguish between the operating deficit of a government in its annual budgeting cycle and the 'public debt' that represents the accumulated debt resulting from annual deficits over a period of time. Government borrows money from both Canadian and international sources to finance a deficit in any given year and pays interest on these amounts. These are often referred to as the cost of 'servicing the debt'. It is normal for government to carry a certain amount of debt that is related to infrastructure investment for future use; however, there is an ongoing debate about whether or not the amount of debt in Canada is a major policy concern. When budget surpluses occur, governments are faced with determining how much emphasis should be placed on three public policy choices: paying down the debt, investing in new public programs, and reducing taxes.

2. 'Monetarist policies' refer to actions taken by the central bank, acting on behalf of the national government, to control the money supply. Monetarism is generally associated with neo-conservatism (also referred to as neo-liberalism) because it is designed to ensure the full play of market forces. The major goal is to control inflation, primarily through adjustments in interest rates. It is argued that if inflation is low, prices will be determined competitively through supply and demand, and in this environment capitalism will flourish. These policies, which have been popular since the mid-1980s in many countries, can be contrasted with Keynesian policies that support government or state intervention, particularly in recessions, to stimulate the economy by injecting demand (e.g., new employment programs or new money) into the system. While Keynesian policies create or sustain employment, they increase the amount of money relative to available goods and services and can increase inflation. Keynesian policies are associated with the development of the welfare state because they support state intervention to modify the free play of market forces in order to redistribute income and opportunities. Monetarist policies generally oppose state intervention or investment, and are less concerned with problems such as high unemployment. Because they are associated with a reduced role for government in managing the economy, these policies also support the expansion of a global economy based on free market principles. According to monetarists, the problem of high unemployment will be addressed as the benefits of new investment, encouraged by low inflation and a free market, increase economic growth and new jobs 'trickle down' to those currently out of work.

3. The World Trade Organization was established in 1995 as a successor of the General Agreement on Trade and Tariffs (GATT). The GATT was one of the earlier treaties regulating international trade and the imposition of protective tariffs on imported goods.

4. These percentages add up to 110. The error is in the original source and, therefore, cannot be corrected here.

Chapter Two

Policy-Making Models and Their Connection to Practice

The policy-making process outlined in this chapter introduces five different models. Three commonly identified approaches are the *rational* or *synoptic approach*, *incrementalism*, and *mixed scanning*. These models are frequently referred to in the literature; in effect, they have stood the test of time, although each has its limitations. A fourth, the *value criteria model*, incorporates values as an explicit component of the policy-making process. This model is an adaptation of the rational model and was developed by the Institute for the Study of Child and Family Policy at North Carolina (Dobelstein, 1990; Moroney, 1991). Rein (1970) and Titmuss (1968) were early advocates of the need to explicitly examine values in the policy-making process.

A final model summarized in this chapter is an adaptation of the *garbage can model* originally coined by Cohen, March, and Olsen (1972) in their study of universities, and later adapted by Kingdon (1995) to explain how policies are developed by the state. This model identifies the importance of both problems and solutions as major ingredients in the policy-making process; however, it also explicitly recognizes the central role of politics, a somewhat neglected attribute of other models. This model places more emphasis on the actual process of policy-making and can be used to explain why, in the real world, good plans don't always get adopted. We have selected these models for inclusion because they can be adapted to planning and policy-making at both the organizational and governmental levels. The characteristics of each of these models are identified below. But first we note some of the variables that confound the task of describing these models. First, as discussed in the previous chapter, the policy environment at a provincial, national, and, more recently, global level affects the development of policy in some significant ways. This environment is shaped by ideological, technical, and socioeconomic factors, and these largely determine the resources governments are prepared to commit to new policy initiatives, particularly in the health and social service sectors. Second, the arena or level within which policy-making occurs can influence the process. For example, somewhat different models or approaches may be adopted by an organization trying to develop policies to deal with adolescent offenders in its catchment area, compared to the models adopted by the federal government concerned with social security reform. Because of its intimate knowledge of the problem and its limited resources, a local organization may adopt an incremental approach whereas the federal government may utilize a comprehensive approach in reforming social security. Finally, policy-making remains difficult to classify because each situation is unique and the process is adapted, to some extent at least, to that particular situation. One important consideration is whether the government wishes to act quickly without bothering with studies or analyses of any kind. As we noted in Chapter 1, a government with a cause may be impatient with any kind of process, and the absence of process is particularly evident when governments decide to reduce funding or eliminate programs.

The Rational Model

The rational or synoptic approach is based almost entirely on the analysis of objective data in an orderly sequence. This approach to policy-making is anchored in systems theory and the analysis of factual or observable data using the scientific method. While the irrationality of the policy process may be acknowledged, proponents of this model are more likely to attribute this irrationality to the unwarranted interference of politics, politicians, and political agendas. The preferred role for the planner is that of the expert technician who coordinates the complex tasks associated with policy-making.

The development of the rational model is often associated with Herbert Simon, a consultant with the Rand Corporation during the 1950s, and its popularity with the government of the United States coincided with the appointment of Robert MacNamara as the Secretary of Defense in John F. Kennedy's administration in the early 1960s. Fresh from his success as the chief executive officer of the Ford Motor Company, MacNamara was determined to transfer business techniques to the public policy field. Analytical tools such as benefit-cost analysis and program policy budgeting systems (PPBS) were adopted. Both reflected a goal-oriented approach to policy development in which goals and measurable objectives would be clearly identified, and options would be evaluated in terms of benefits and costs. The rational model features five general steps (Carley, 1980):

1. Define the problem in objective (behavioural) terms.
2. Develop a list of all feasible alternatives that would resolve the problem under prescribed circumstances.
3. Project the general consequences that are likely to flow from each strategy and the probability of those consequences occurring.
4. Collect and examine data appropriate to each alternative and determine the relationship of predicted outcomes to policy objectives and the relative benefit-cost ratio of each alternative strategy.
5. Select a strategy that best approximates identified goals and objectives and achieves the best benefit-cost ratio.

Several problems have been identified with the rational model. One is the difficulty of identifying and analyzing all feasible alternatives in determining the single best solution. In social policy development, this can be characterized as an information- or knowledge-related problem in that most policy decisions involve situations or circumstances that are somewhat unique; the consequences cannot be adequately predicted; and only a limited number of variables can be considered (Moroney, 1991). A second issue is that of values. Although a rational model may incorporate value considerations, the assumption is that once values are clarified, they can be ranked and dealt with in the same ways as other types of information. In effect, the policy-maker is assumed to play a neutral or value-free role. Thus, policy-making within the rational model stresses technical rationality where the focus is on examining the most efficient means to achieve a predetermined end. However, the focus on means often results in inadequate attention being given to outcomes and we are then left with policies that may work on technical grounds but that are nonetheless 'bad policies'. Finally, the rational model often assumes that implementation follows logically from policy initiation and formulation and thus pays inadequate attention to the implementation phase.

Although the comprehensive version of the rational model calls for an analysis of all possible alternatives, a later modification of the model ended the consideration of alternatives once a satisfactory one was located. The result was policy development within a framework of 'limited rationality'. While this modification addressed questions of feasibility, it sacrificed the appeal of finding the most desirable policy choice following a comprehensive search for alternatives. A major problem with either the limited or comprehensive rational approach is the lack of attention to values or to whether the 'ends' of policies can be justified. As noted earlier, a new policy may be designed to carry out a stated goal efficiently and effectively, but with insufficient attention to values a rational model of policy-making may result in the adoption of undesirable policies. Moreover, the rational model allows policy-makers to evaluate alternatives according to their own values because they remain in complete control of the process.

In social policy sectors such as child welfare, policy development often begins with a data collection phase. The complexity of problems facing policy-makers is such that they often feel overwhelmed. Sometimes task forces, Royal Commissions, or special inquiries will be mandated to outline a policy direction after gathering information, hearing from stakeholders, and initiating special studies. These strategies reflect a rational approach to policy development, and such groups can perform a useful role in policy-making in some circumstances. (See Box 2.1 for an example of a rational approach to legislative change.) However, the appointment of such bodies by governments or other decision-makers can also be used as a method to avoid taking action on controversial, complex, or costly issues while appearing to give these matters serious attention.

Despite these limitations, the rational model—or some of its major aspects—is widely used by human service practitioners. The medical model that begins with diagnosis, then the identification of optional treatment approaches, and finally

Box 2.1 New Child Welfare Legislation in BC: A Rational Approach to Policy-Making

By late 1991 a number of factors converged to produce the required impetus for major change to British Columbia's child welfare legislation. These included increased criticism of the reliance on statutory authority within the 1980 *Family and Child Service Act*; the election of a new NDP government that espoused a commitment to more family support services and a willingness to consult with the public; and the death of an adolescent in a government-funded youth facility that led to a highly criticized report from the provincial ombudsman. The government appointed a community panel composed of a mix of government and community members, and Aboriginal members formed a separate Aboriginal panel that held hearings in Aboriginal communities. These panels consulted widely; they held public meetings, received written briefs, conducted research, organized several day-long round-table discussions on special topics, and met with professional groups and organizations. This comprehensive rational approach to policy-making included a strong commitment to public participation. For example, the main panel heard 550 presentations in more than 23 communities and received over 600 briefs from individuals and groups. A broad approach to examining the needs of children and families was taken, and issues such as poverty, service integration, and the adversarial relationship between child welfare agencies and families were addressed. After several months, two major panel reports were published, each outlining broad recommendations for new legislation and a new, more preventive approach to dealing with communities, families, and children. Many of the more radical recommendations of the panel reports—such as the inclusion of a provision stating that no child would be apprehended due to a lack of family resources—were rejected. Nevertheless, the reports were accepted by the ministry as a framework for drafting new legislation. A Legislative Review Group was appointed to draft legislation, and in the spring of 1993 an implementation Steering Committee was formed to begin preparing the various regions for change. The Legislative Review Group consulted with a variety of groups, including regional staff, and in 1993 a White Paper, *Making Changes: Next Steps*, was released. Work continued on developing a policy paper to outline proposed legislation and this paper was approved by Cabinet in December, 1993. Under the guidance of a new minister, drafting of the new Act was completed in the spring of 1994. In June 1994 the legislature passed the new *Child, Family and Community Service Act*, and its companion legislation, the *Child, Youth and Family Advocacy Act*.

(Adapted from Durie and Armitage, 1996)

selection of the most appropriate intervention is a common approach to practice, particularly in health and mental health settings. Similarly, the planned change model found in many frameworks for social work practice stresses an orderly, systematic approach to change. The terms applied to the various steps may differ from the medical model but the process is essentially the same. Professionals are cast in the roles of the expert or change agent working *on* rather than *with* a patient or client, who is considered to be a largely passive recipient of services.

Incrementalism

If the rational model of policy-making is seen as too isolated from the real world of politics and policy-making, a second model, incrementalism, has been criticized for being too closely associated with the status quo. Incrementalism is commonly associated with Charles Lindblom (1959, 1968, and 1979), who referred to the process as 'the science of muddling through'. Lindblom argued that change is most likely to occur when one calculates the marginal benefits of small adaptations from current approaches.

Advocates of incrementalism suggest several benefits. First, small-scale changes avoid major disruptions and the possibility of avoiding unanticipated negative outcomes that often result from large-scale changes. If a small change results in positive effects, it can be accelerated; if it leads to adverse effects, it can be halted and reversed without causing major problems. Second, incremental changes can usually be incorporated within existing organizational arrangements. Third, the approach accounts for political and normative realities by incorporating these considerations into discussions of alternatives during the change process. Furthermore, such discussions can include the views of those who make policy, those who implement it, and those who are affected by it.

Incrementalism generally accepts that existing structures, service mandates, and power structures within service organizations are legitimate and appropriate. Thus, it adopts an essentially conservative approach to change (see Box 2.2 for an example of an incremental approach to legislative change). Boulding captures the limitations of incrementalism aptly in the following phrase: 'We stagger through history like a drunk, putting one disjointed incremental foot after another' (Boulding, 1964, p. 931).

Mixed Scanning

Mixed scanning was advanced by Etzioni (1967 and 1976) in an attempt to integrate the best aspects of the rational and incremental models. Mixed scanning suggests that situational factors will determine when each approach should be emphasized. It advocates an approach to policy development that begins with a comprehensive scan of the existing policy, including problem analysis and alternatives, and then adopts an incremental approach to the implementation of new policies.

Mixed scanning is a cumbersome term for a model that captures what happens

Box 2.2 Legislative Reform in Manitoba: Incrementalism in Action

In the summer of 1996 the Manitoba government launched a process to update its 1985 *Child and Family Services Act*. However, a very limited approach to reform was undertaken. The public consultation process was limited to a mere few weeks' duration, with only a few presentation dates in approximately six centres throughout the province. Furthermore, presenters were directed to confine their recommendations to a series of specific and quite limited policy questions published in a 'consultation workbook'. These included questions such as whether grandparents should have a right to apply for access to children who are apprehended, whether birth parents under eighteen should be able to consent to private adoption, whether private practitioners arranging for adoptions should be licensed, whether teenaged dads should be required to pay child support, and whether child welfare workers should be required to have a minimum level of training. No comments on larger issues related to the general orientation of existing legislation or problems in the current service delivery system were invited. While presenters at public hearings did not necessarily confine themselves to this narrow set of questions, their views on broader policy issues were not stressed in the final report published by the panel. The report of the panel then made recommendations on the limited issues identified at the outset, and some of these recommendations were incorporated as amendments to the Act in the spring of 1997. However, these relatively minor changes did not alter the general thrust or philosophy of the existing Act.

on many occasions. Policy-making often takes place in an incremental fashion, yet the use of comprehensive approaches, including task forces and commissions, to scan the broad policy environment, attests to the influence of the rational model.

There are a number of similarities between mixed scanning at a macro level and strategic planning, which has been widely adopted within human service organizations at the agency and operational level of planning over the past ten years. Although strategic planning has been a popular approach to policy-making at the organizational level, it requires continued organizational investment to realize potential benefits. It is also plagued by two of the difficulties associated with many forms of policy-making: it is difficult to predict consequences, particularly in a policy environment where so much lies outside the effective control of organizations; and, most importantly, service users and first-line staff are frequently excluded from or underrepresented in the planning process. We return to the discussion of strategic planning in chapter 3.

The Value Criteria Model

There are different versions of the value criteria model, sometimes referred to as the value-analytic model (Gallagher and Haskins, 1984), but they are similar in their overall approach to policy-making. First, the problem is defined and available alternatives for dealing with it are identified. Although responses to a problem may represent only a limited range of alternatives, the problem analysis stage can direct attention to key normative elements of the problem, including causality. For example, the conventional child welfare system has all too often separated First Nations children from their families, communities, and culture. Identifying and analyzing the negative consequences of this approach can spur a consideration of alternatives such as First Nations control over child welfare services, the development of more community-based foster care resources, and the development of more culturally appropriate services.

A second step is the development of value criteria for evaluating alternatives. These value criteria should include both universal and selective criteria. *Universal criteria* may represent general value considerations such as effectiveness, efficiency, and feasibility, whereas *selective criteria* represent those values that are more specific to the problem or issue being considered. In the example above concerning First Nations child welfare, selective criteria may include self-determination, community responsibility, and cultural appropriateness. The third step involves the gathering of data required to assess each alternative, and the analysis of each alternative according to value criteria. In the final step, the alternative that maximizes the greatest number of values, including efficiency, is recommended or a range of alternatives with identified strengths and weaknesses are discussed.

Although this model has considerable appeal to policy development in the human services because of its explicit consideration of values, it is apparent that conflicts can arise over the criteria that ought to guide final policy selection. For example, if a particular policy choice maximizes more of the selected values but also requires higher costs, how is this conflict to be resolved? And who sets the key values to be used in policy selection—the decision-maker, the policy researcher, the service user, or others?

The selection of value criteria is the most controversial stage of this policy model but it should be recognized that other policy-making models incorporate values even if this is done implicitly. In the value criteria model, values are explicitly identified and at the very least, they become more visible and open to debate. While the selection of value criteria depends on the nature of the policy being considered, this step is the point at which an ethical framework for policy-making can be proposed. Therefore, it is important to identify guidelines for the development of value criteria. Saleebey (1990) has identified some broad philosophical cornerstones relevant to policy-making in the human services. These are as follows:

a) beginning with an ethic of indignation about the denial of human dignity and opportunities;
b) incorporating humane inquiry and understanding based on dialogue;
c) a focus on compassion and caring; and
d) a quest for social justice.

These four cornerstones foster empowerment and social change to promote equity.

In a discussion of criteria for theory evaluation in social work research, Witkin and Gottschalk (1988) arrive at similar conclusions. As adapted to our purposes, the steps in developing value criteria for policy-making are as follows:

1. the approach should be explicitly critical in considering historical, cultural, political, and economic factors;
2. people must be recognized as active agents in shaping as well as reacting to their environment;
3. the life experiences of service users must be considered; and
4. solutions should promote social justice.

The term 'social justice' is frequently evoked, yet it is open to various interpretations. We adopt the position advanced by Rawls (1971), who argued persuasively that social and economic inequalities created in society should be adjusted to provide the greatest benefit to the least advantaged. Social justice, then, is about redressing problems of inequality.

Box 2.3 provides an example of how value criteria have been used to shape policy development in a First Nations child and family services agency.

The Garbage Can Model

The modified garbage can model of policy-making developed by Kingdon (1995, pp. 86–8) represents an attempt to describe policy-making as it unfolds in the day-to-day life of governments and organizations. Three 'families' of processes are observed to exist in setting governmental agendas: *problems*, *policies*, and *politics*. These are likened to separate streams that often operate quite independently of each other. First, there is a 'stream of problems' that captures the attention of policy-makers in a government or an organization. Second, there is a policy community of specialists, which may include people inside or outside the organization, that concentrates on generating policy proposals. These individuals or groups advance a 'stream of solutions'. Some of these ideas and solutions are taken seriously, while others are not. The third ingredient, the 'political stream', is composed of elements such as public opinion, election results, changes in administration, ideological shifts, and interest group campaigns. Participants in the policy-making process may be active in all three process streams at the same time or they may be active in only one or two of these streams.

Each of the actors and processes associated with these streams can function as

Box 2.3 An Example of the Value Criteria Model of Policy-Making

The development of West Region Child and Family Services in Manitoba illustrates how the value criteria model can be used to develop policies that shape an agency's overall orientation to practice and program development. Growing awareness of the child welfare system's colonizing effects in First Nations communities in the late 1970s and early 1980s led to the signing of a Master Agreement by Manitoba First Nations, the government of Manitoba, and the government of Canada in 1982. This Agreement paved the way for the transfer of administrative control of child welfare services to tribal council authorities in the province, and in 1985 West Region Child and Family Services, serving nine First Nations reserves, became a fully mandated child and family service agency. This agency paid special attention to assessing the impact of the conventional child welfare system on family and community life, an impact represented by the loss of hundreds of children from their families and communities, and by the presence of powerlessness within many of these families and communities. This led to the adoption of four key philosophical principles by the new agency that are used as guidelines for policy development. These principles, which may be expressed as value criteria, are Aboriginal control, cultural relevancy, community-based services, and a comprehensive team-oriented approach to service delivery. Thus, a service model has been adopted that relies on local staff working with local child and family service committees that have considerable authority. Specialized service teams have also been developed to provide support and back-up services to local staff. In addition, the agency adopts a broad approach to child and family services by undertaking initiatives in day care, family violence intervention, and community development.

Cultural relevancy shapes policy development through such things as an emphasis on hiring Aboriginal staff, providing culturally relevant staff training, and incorporating the wisdom of elders. Furthermore, the agency has played a leadership role in developing culturally appropriate foster homes, including the widespread use of extended family care. The agency is managed by a Board of Chiefs, but there are also extensive efforts to incorporate a broader level of community participation in policy development. For example, an Operational Planning Workshop is held every two years in which representatives from each community engage with agency staff in identifying new service needs and priorities. Today, very few children now require care outside their community or their culture, and an external evaluations have demonstrated that the agency provides both a high standard of service quality and a supportive, sustaining work environment for its staff.

(Adapted from McKenzie, 1994; 1999)

either an impetus or a constraint to change. Although there may be some overlap and some connection between the streams, they are largely separate from each other, governed by different considerations and styles. For example, key problems with feasible solutions may not emerge on the policy agenda because of an absence of political support. The lack of political interest in a feasible solution may be due to the fact that the solution has emanated from a think-tank with a different ideology from that of government, and we address this issue further in Chapter 9. In addition, feasible solutions may not gain acceptance if governments fear that public support will not be forthcoming.

Although these streams usually operate independently, they do connect at times. This opens a 'policy window' that can lead to problem recognition, agenda setting, and the creation of new policies or programs. However, if these opportunities are missed (e.g., if no action is taken or if the political mood shifts), then the policy window will close and the opportunity will be lost, at least for the time being.

A key stage in the process is problem recognition and definition. Recognition, according to Kingdon, generally occurs through three mechanisms. The first is a change in indicators such as unemployment rates, economic growth, interest rates, or the rate of children in care. A second mechanism is a focusing event that directs attention and sometimes action in response to an issue. The third mechanism is normal feedback from the operation of programs including the role of evaluation in influencing policy development.

Pal (1992, p. 135) elaborates on Kingdon's list of mechanisms leading to problem recognition by identifying criteria that can be used to determine when a problem becomes a *public* problem. In order to define something as a public problem, he suggests that it must affect a substantial proportion of the public, offend or affront widely held public views or mores, or be the direct result of previous public policies. The example of changes to the Canada Pension Plan illustrates the argument. Actuarial information in the mid-nineties indicated that without substantial changes, the plan would not be able to meet future benefit payments for retiring Canadians. In addition, the crisis was intensified by previous government policies that resulted in benefit payouts to beneficiaries that were in excess of the value of their contributions. In this case, the problem affected a wide number of Canadians, and resulted, in part, from the failure of previous policies. After a great deal of debate around the relative merits of public versus private pension plans, the federal government decided in favour of the former and raised the premiums paid by contributors to the plan.

It is often difficult to predict which issue will be defined as a public problem. Its recognition depends on a combination of objective data and the subjective perception that change is required. Indeed, in some cases, subjective perceptions become more important than objective data. Youth violence in Winnipeg provides one example. In recent years there has been growing concern about high levels of juvenile crime, particularly within the inner city. However, the actual rate of youth crime did not change significantly during the 1990s. This has not prevented a growing perception among the public that youth crime is increasing, a perception fuelled by increasingly intense media attention on the operation of organized street gangs. In turn, this perception has led to heightened demands for a more punitive approach to the problem of youth crime.

Issues can remain on the policy agenda for some time, although the weighting of certain issues may vary at different times depending on how the three streams interact. Furthermore, items can fall off the policy agenda because they cannot be sustained or because the problem may appear to be solved. For example, in the 1980s the need for a national daycare strategy was widely recognized, and the federal Conservative government made a commitment at that time to launch such an initiative. However, the government retreated from this commitment and the daycare issue received very little attention in the federal policy arena over the next two decades. It is of interest to note that policy advocates are trying to ensure that child care is returned to the federal policy agenda; and in January 2003, the Child Care Advocacy Association of Canada and the Canadian Child Care Federation released a poll of 1,200 Canadians showing that 90 per cent of respondents support a nationally coordinated child care plan (Child Care Advocacy Association of Canada, 2003).

The garbage can model provides useful insights into the policy-making process, and it directs attention to the political environment that plays such a significant role both in determining how the process unfolds, and ultimately, in the outcomes that emerge.

A summary of the policy-making steps in each of the models is provided in Table 2.1, although we stress that these steps rarely follow each other in a linear fashion. We have also presented the models as discrete approaches, but in the real world of policy-making, a mix of more than one approach can often be identified.

To some extent, the major approaches to policy-making outlined above oversimplify the policy development process. In fact, policy-making is a process of trying to decide what to do in situations in which values and opinions often conflict and where the final choice is heavily shaped by differing ideologies. Given this reality, it follows that the product will reflect the values of those who are in pivotal positions. Policy-making is about recognizing the legitimacy of a social problem, establishing the feasibility of a particular solution, and garnering support for the adoption of a preferred solution. As we noted in Chapter 1, it is not surprising that those with power wield a disproportionate amount of influence over the policies that are eventually adopted.

It is essential to emphasize that regardless of the approach—whether rational or incremental—social policy is permeated by politics. In the last analysis, the major decisions are made by politicians and governments whose pre-eminent concern is to meet enough of the people's needs to be re-elected. Thus, all-important policies will be assessed through the political lens of votes: Will this initiative help or hinder a party's chances of being re-elected? But government, and organizations for that matter, do not *always* follow the most politically expedient route. As we noted earlier, they are sometimes driven by causes that reflect a deeply held conviction or ideological commitment, and policy directions under

Table 2.1 Models of Policy-Making: A Summary

A.   The Rational Model[1]

1. Define the problem in objective terms and classify goals.
2. Develop a comprehensive list of alternatives to address the problem.
3. Project possible consequences and the probability of occurrence for each set of alternatives.
4. Examine data for each strategy in relation to goals and benefit-cost calculations.
5. Select a strategy to maximize goals and to achieve the best benefit-cost ratio.

B.   Incrementalism[2]

1. Calculate the marginal benefits of current choices for addressing the problem.
2. Initiate small choices toward a solution that would achieve marginal benefits.
3. Increase the emphasis on choices that produce positive results; reduce the emphasis on choices leading to negative results.
4. Policy emerges from a combination of choices that work.

C.   Mixed Scanning[3]

1. Define the problem and classify goals.
2. Conduct a comprehensive scan of alternatives.
3. Select alternatives for detailed analysis based on potential for goal achievement and feasibility.
4. Collect data and select the alternative best able to maximize goals and feasibility considerations.
5. Project incremental incorporation of policy choice.

D.   The Value Criteria Model[4]

1. Define the problem and identify policy alternatives available to deal with the problem.
2. Establish universal and selective criteria (values) for evaluating alternatives.
3. Gather data related to each alternative, and assess each alternative relative to value criteria.
4. Recommend the alternative that maximizes the value criteria, or offer a range of alternatives that maximize different criteria in different ways.

E.   The Garbage Can Model[5]

1. Three types of processes exist in agenda setting for policy-making. These are characterized as streams of problems, solutions, and politics.

2. These streams exist somewhat independently of each other, but from time to time a window of opportunity opens when these three streams come together. A key stage is public recognition of a problem and three mechanisms can contribute to this stage. These are a change in economic or social indicators, an unpredictable event, or feedback from program operations.

3. Once a policy window opens, problems, solutions, and political opportunity are combined in a 'garbage can' and the outcome will depend on characteristics associated with the problems, alternatives, and participants included in this mix.

4. If the opportunity is missed or if no action is taken, the policy window closes, and one must wait for the next opportunity. Issues can also sit on the policy agenda although they may be weighted differently at different times. In addition, items can fall off the policy agenda because interest cannot be sustained or because the problem appears to be resolved.

[1] (Adapted from Carley, 1980, p. 11)

[2] (Adapted from Lindblom, 1959)

[3] (Adapted from Etzioni, 1976)

[4] (Adapted from Dobelstein, 1990, p. 71)

[5] (Adapted from Kingdon, 1995, pp. 86–8)

these circumstances are not easily compromised. For example, the Saskatchewan NDP government, led by Tommy Douglas, withstood significant public pressure in 1961 when it adopted Canada's first medicare program. On the other side of the political spectrum, the Conservative government in Ontario in the 1990s followed its ideological principles when it enacted changes that resulted in widespread hardship to the province's poorest citizens:

> Directly through the 22 per cent cut in their monthly payments and indirectly through the cancellation of the Jobs Ontario program, the poorest of all Ontarians have been hit grossly disproportionately. Indeed, reduced spending on welfare recipients will account for a full one-third of the $1.4 billion in cuts that Eves [then finance minister and later premier] announced. This move was necessary, the finance minister said, to head off a 'spending crisis'. In fact Eve's motive here was ideological rather than financial. . . . It is those on welfare who are paying for the ideological convictions of the Harris government. (Gwyn, 1995, p. 4)

Connecting Models to the Work of First-Line Practitioners

We now consider how the policy-making models policy connect to the work of practitioners in the human services. At the outset we acknowledge the difference in purpose between policy and practice, a difference that often creates a gap between the two that is difficult to bridge. Policies represent an overall course of action to deal with a need or problem that affects a large number of individuals, whereas practice is concerned about what should be done *in a specific situation.* Too often policies, when rigidly adopted, fail to consider the specific circumstances or needs of individuals or communities, which are, in fact, the primary concerns of practitioners. One way of closing the gap between policy and practice is to include service users and practitioners in the development of policy. Moreover, if policies in the human services retain some elements of flexibility, practitioners will be able to adapt these to the particular needs of individuals, families, and communities. We give special attention to inclusive models of policy development in Chapter 6.

Do any of the policy-making models ensure that the wisdom of practitioners and service users will be combined with that of policy-makers? The rational approach is primarily a top-down process that clearly assigns a primary role to policy analysts who are responsible for drafting new policies or legislation. It is an élite approach to planning in which pre-eminent roles are assigned to policy experts, and even when this approach incorporates far-reaching consultations, the eventual choices are made by a select few.

As the name suggests, incrementalism is a more informal process that may well facilitate partnerships between policy-makers and practitioners. Although a series of small steps can eventually lead to substantial changes, it is more likely that these steps will continue in a well-established direction, and will not significantly challenge accepted ways of doing things, whether in policy or practice. For example, in child welfare, incrementalism might result in the addition of new resources and programs, but it would not reframe the mission of child welfare in a fundamental fashion. Incrementalism is unlikely to lead to reforms in governance structures or to establish care-giving work as work requiring an equitable salary from the public purse. Indeed, incrementalism promotes an environment in which policy becomes routinized and practitioners become its caretakers. Although incrementalism allows for some limited contributions from practitioners, opportunities are not usually extended to service users. Like the rational approach, it is not seen here as the approach of choice. And since mixed scanning represents a combination of both the rational and the incremental approaches, it, too, represents a limited approach to connecting policy and practice.

The value criteria model is an adaptation of the rational model; however, it incorporates the explicit treatment of values. This is its most important strength, but its ability to serve as a useful tool in connecting policy and practice is highly dependent on what values are selected for consideration and on how the process of value analysis is conducted. For example, if the value criteria used in policy selection incorporate the concerns of practitioners and service users, the potential for meaningful connections between policy and practice is enhanced. However, if values reflect the concerns of centralized policy-makers who remain distant from the day-to-day concerns of first-line staff and service users, this model will also fail to integrate these two domains.

The garbage can model of policy-making incorporates political processes as a consideration in policy adoption. This model also recognizes a role for policy communities that contribute to the stream of solutions by recommending particular policies. Although practitioners and service users may be involved in these policy communities, their involvement is often quite limited. One of the reasons is that policy communities must usually sustain their efforts over a relatively long period of time to obtain relatively modest gains. Such long-term commitments are often difficult for practitioners and service users.

Each of these approaches may be adapted to be more inclusive in ways that increase the potential of connecting policy and practice; however, none insist on inclusiveness. The value criteria model comes closest to realizing this potential in that it allows for the specification of value criteria that can include consultation and/or decision-making input from practitioners and service users. Clearly, this policy-making model must adopt the central principle of inclusiveness if it is to succeed in connecting policy and practice concerns. But in order to achieve this principle, policy-making must be transformed from a process in which decisions are made in secret at the highest level of the organization, and then packaged within this arena for marketing to an apparently resistant and largely uninformed group of practitioners and service users. As indicated by the example in Box 2.4, policy-makers seem to demonstrate an all-too-frequent pattern of failing to include those who will be most directly affected by the adoption of new policies.

It will be apparent to many that the arguments that swirl around the pros and cons of the policy-making models also occur within the practice domain. As noted above, the rational approach is based on systems theory and the scientific method, while other approaches depart from these traditions to varying degrees. The differences in the various approaches are to a large extent mirrored by the debate surrounding the use of research and the scientific method in social work practice. The opposing positions in this debate are espoused by two eminent social work educators. The position that social work practice should be based on empirical research is expressed by Edward Mullen in relation to the problem of AIDS. He argues that:

> [the] scientific method requires that the practitioner determine what has already been found out through prior study to be effective ways for helping people deal with impending depression and what is known about these methods with people with AIDS. Scientific criteria also require that social workers systematically evaluate their own attempts to help people with AIDS cope with impending depression. (Mullen, 1992, p. 111)

The opposing position is expressed by Howard Goldstein, who believes that the scientific method is too rigid and too confining as a template for social work practice:

Box 2.4 Policy-Making and the Failure to Consult with Those Affected

In March 1997 a high-level policy forum on gang crime was convened in Winnipeg to discuss the growing problem of inner-city youth gangs dominated by Aboriginal young people. While two federal cabinet ministers, provincial Cabinet ministers, policy officials, the mayor of Winnipeg, and other leaders met at an inner-city location, dozens of Aboriginal people were barred from entry. Only after arguing with security staff for some time were a small group of representatives from the Native Youth Movement allowed in, and then only on the condition that they keep quiet. After about an hour, at the moderator's invitation, two representatives delivered an impassioned presentation to community leaders who responded with an enthusiastic ovation at the end of the presentation. One of the presenters argued that the focus must be to rebuild the social structure and the family unit within the Aboriginal community to resemble the structures that existed before colonization. The other Aboriginal young person allowed to speak urged participants to bring young people to the table. (Adapted from Nairne, 1997)

Professor Mullen perpetuates the seductive myth of the scientific method and its promises of professional status and respectability. It defines social work as a technology that can discover the causes of human suffering and despair, devise precise interventions and predict outcomes. Our heritage and practice prove that social work is not a technology, but rather a humanistic endeavour in which artistry, creativity, intuitiveness and interpersonal talents are hallmarks of our professional competencies. (Goldstein, 1992, p. 113)

It is not difficult to identify with some of the ideas and beliefs associated with both of these positions. One solution is to try to identify the best in both positions. However, in the field of social policy we are inclined to agree with Rittel and Webber (1973, p. 158), who state:

As distinguished from problems in the natural sciences which are definable and separable and may have solutions that are findable, the problems of governmental planning—and especially those of social or policy planning—are ill defined: and they rely on elusive political judgment for resolution. (Not 'solution'. Social problems are never solved. At best they are only re-solved—over and over again.)

The next chapter extends the discussion of policy-making by describing the structures within which policy-making processes occur.

Recommended Reading

1. To appreciate the work of a social policy legend, read Richard Titmuss, *Social Policy* (London: George Allen and Unwin, 1974).

2. For a careful examination of the policy process, particularly in relation to political context, see J. Kingdon, *Agendas, Alternatives, and Public Policies*, 2nd edn (New York: Harper Collins, 1995).

3. For a more in-depth examination of the public policy process, see M. Howlett and M. Ramesh, *Studying Public Policy* (Don Mills, ON: Oxford University Press, 1995).

Chapter Three

Making Social Policy in Canada: Institutional and Political Factors

This chapter focuses on policy-making structures, and although we include a discussion of the structures in the federal government, primary attention is given to the provincial government level because of its key role in the development of Canadian social policy. We include a discussion of organizational structures, but pay only limited attention to the cities and municipalities because they play a less significant role in social policy in Canada. This may differ somewhat in Aboriginal communities where local or regional government structures may have more significant control over social policy initiatives or their management. Examples of policy-making in different Aboriginal contexts are addressed in detail in Chapter 8.

Social Policy and the Federal Government

The federal government's role in social policy is overshadowed by the role of provincial governments. This is a function of arrangements established in the *British North America Act, 1867* and later confirmed in *The Constitution Act, 1982,* which ceded responsibility for local affairs, including social policy, to provincial governments. At the nation-building stage, state involvement in social welfare was relatively minor. A strong central government role was regarded as important, but the key areas of responsibility were defined as foreign policy, taxation, and trade. Over time the strength of provincial governments has increased as they have demanded more power and as expenditures on health, education, and social welfare have grown. The growing power of provincial governments has produced a more decentralized and fragmented state system. For example, each province and territory in Canada has its own child welfare legislation, whereas legislation and related policies pertaining to child welfare are the responsibility of the central government in many European countries including the United Kingdom. Whether the relatively weak role of the federal government in matters of social policy is good or bad is an often-debated policy issue. On the one hand, the ability to establish national policies and standards is restricted; on the other hand, citizens have somewhat more access to provincial governments and theoretically, at least, it is easier to influence this level of government.

This is not to imply that the federal government role in social policy is unimportant. First, it has responsibility for social policies that are national in scope, such as the Child Tax Benefit, the Canada Pension Plan, Old Age Security, and Employment Insurance. These programs were developed as a result of federal-provincial agreements that transferred responsibility to the federal government on these matters. Second, the federal government provides funding to provincial governments for health, education, and social services. Federal funding for these programs has a significant impact on the adequacy and effectiveness of services in these areas of social policy. As well, the transfer of funding, as in the case of medicare, can be tied to standards or principles that influence the ways in which these funds can be spent. Unfortunately, the federal share of funding for these programs has declined as a percentage of overall costs over the past two decades. In addition, the federal government has relaxed national standards in a number of these areas. This has allowed provinces to establish their own standards and spending priorities. Although this can be beneficial in some cases, it can also create problems. This is particularly evident in income support programs (welfare); in several provinces welfare rates have been slashed and restrictive policies on eligibility have been established. Third, the federal government is primarily responsible for policy development and funding for services to members of First Nations living on reserves, the Inuit, and others who qualify for federal services under the *Indian Act*. Finally, the federal government provides targeted funding for certain initiatives, including research, that reflect social policy objectives. Examples include the First Nations and Inuit Child Care strategy, the Community Action Program for Children (CAPC), and the National Children's Agenda (NCA). CAPC addresses the health and social development needs of children from birth to six years of age living in conditions of risk whereas the NCA is a broad framework that is used to organize research and development efforts designed to promote the well-being of children. One example of a specific program under the NCA is the Early Childhood Development Agreement, a partnership arrangement among federal, provincial, and territorial governments, which invests in initiatives to promote healthy child development.

All organizations create formal mechanisms—referred to here as 'structures'—for developing policies, and we turn now to a brief review of these structures at the federal government level. Canada inherited a British parliamentary system, often referred to as the Westminster model, where power centres on ministers who are responsible to the House of Commons or provincial legislatures for the policy and programs initiated by government. This model of government is based on the principle of unity among government and opposition parties that results in most members of a political party adhering to the 'party line' on policy matters. This also produces a highly adversarial style of debate where government members are expected to speak in support of government policy and opposition members are expected to speak against government policy. The Cabinet is the key policy-making authority, although policy-making is often more centralized in the Prime Minister's Office (PMO) and other structures created to manage overall government policy.

Milne (2000) describes the federal policy-making process as a 'policy market-place', and the following summary draws some information from his description of how this system operates. Power flows from the prime minister (PM), and although Cabinet is influential, it is secondary to the prime minister on major policy issues. For example, Cabinet does not vote on issues; instead the PM is able to declare Cabinet consensus on issues, even if only a few ministers support his or her view. In theory, government is held accountable in Parliament through 'question period' and procedures that require parliamentary approval. In fact, most policy-making occurs in the bureaucracy, at the Cabinet level, or through the actions of the PM. The PM's influence is significant because of the powers attached to this office. For example, the PM makes all appointments to Cabinet, the Senate, and other senior level posts in government, including the governor of the Bank of Canada. Of course, this is not done alone. These responsibilities are supported by a politically appointed staff of approximately one hundred advisors in the Prime Minister's Office (PMO). As well, there are several hundred other senior staff in the Privy Council Office (PCO) with primary responsibility for managing the affairs of Cabinet and its various committees.

There are key Cabinet committees that review and recommend proposals from ministers that require full Cabinet approval. Although the number of these committees varies, the key committees in the present government are Social Union (concerned with new initiatives in the social sector), Economic Union (concerned with initiatives in the economic sector), Treasury Board (which approves all expenditures), Special Committee of Council (which reviews Orders-in-Council), and Communications (government public relations). Orders-in-Council include decisions that may be made by Cabinet rather than Parliament before they can be implemented. These include a wide range of appointments and regulatory items that ensure that the machinery of government continues to operate. Treasury Board is the only Cabinet committee created by law and it is chaired by the president of the Treasury Board. It is supported by a large group of staff known as the Treasury Board Secretariat. In addition to standing committees, the PM or Cabinet may establish ad hoc committees to deal with special issues that arise.

There are about 20 to 30 ministers in a Cabinet, and about 10 junior ministers or secretaries of state whose responsibilities lie within the portfolio of another minister. Each minister will also have his or her own political staff that are in addition to the career bureaucrats working in the department itself. Central agencies like the PMO, the PCO, Treasury Board Secretariat, and the Department of Finance are very powerful and exert significant influence on major policy issues or the general direction of government policy at the federal level. For example, the Department of Finance, with the support of the PMO, was primarily responsible for the budget-cutting exercise of the 1990s, which had a significant impact on federal expenditures related to health and social policy during that decade. With the exception of the Department of Finance, which holds consultation meetings on the budget, none of these central agencies consults in an ongoing or formal manner with the public or interest groups on policy priorities.

Over the past two decades the PMO has become more influential in shaping government response, particularly on major policy issues. However, federal policy-making takes place at different levels and not all matters are dealt with by the PMO or even Cabinet. Much of the policy-making occurs at the departmental level or across departments and the interplay among ministers, and between ministers and senior department staff, complicates the process of policy-making enormously. And we have not yet considered the relative influence of individual actors and interest groups outside government who advocate for or against particular policy options!

There is a wide spectrum of interest groups (business, labour, and social development groups), paid lobbyists, and political cronies who attempt to influence ministers and other government officials on policy matters of concern to them. National interest groups, such as the Canadian Council of Chief Executives or the Canadian Taxpayers' Association often focus primarily on lobbying. Others, such as the Canadian Council on Social Development (CCSD), the National Council of Welfare, the C.D. Howe Institute, the Institute for Research on Public Policy, and the Canadian Centre on Policy Alternatives focus more on research, whereas the Council of Canadians and the Fraser Institute combine research with an active advocacy role.

In the past two decades, a curious contradiction has developed. Although policy-making authority has become somewhat more decentralized with provinces demanding more control, policy-making within the federal government has become more centralized. For example, those members of the government who are not Cabinet ministers have very little influence over policy development. And while more attention to federal-provincial partnerships might help to establish more relevant and effective policies, these partnerships appear exceedingly difficult to establish in a climate marked by political posturing and bureaucratic controls that get in the way of more collaborative initiatives.

Social Policy and the Provincial Government
Key Policy-Making Structures at the Provincial Level

The dominant role of provincial and territorial governments in the development of social policy requires us to pay more attention to this level of government. Although the processes and structures vary somewhat from province to province, there is sufficient similarity to warrant using one province as an example. The Manitoba government in 2002 is selected as an illustrative example in the following discussion, and readers from other provinces are encouraged to locate additional information on the governmental structure that exists in their province or territory.

As noted in our discussion of the federal government, Cabinet is regarded as the central policy-making authority even though other structures are created to mediate its role. At the federal government level we noted the extensive control exercised by the PMO, and provincial premiers will have a staff complement headed by someone who occupies a role such as a chief of staff. The premier and his/her chief of staff will exert a great deal of control over policy initiatives that are politically sensitive. Beyond this, the level of control is somewhat dependent on whether a premier operates in a more centralized fashion or relies on Cabinet debate and discussion to shape policy.

In Manitoba, the structures of government are relatively simple. There is a Policy Management Secretariat made up of staff that provide support to Cabinet and some support to the three standing committees of Cabinet. These standing committees are Treasury Board, Community Economic Development, and Healthy Child Manitoba. Although Treasury Board is common to all governments, the nature and role of other standing committees can differ. Indeed, the title and focus of these committees can often reveal a good deal about the philosophical orientation of the government in power. Standing committees will have their own complement of staff, but in Manitoba it is the staff from the Policy Management Secretariat that links the work of these committees to Cabinet. Standing committees are comprised of ministers of the government and in Manitoba, Treasury Board is chaired by the Minister of Finance. Whereas the staff of standing committees are likely to be career civil servants, staff of the Policy Management Secretariat are appointed by the party in power. These staff are essentially political appointments and a change in government will likely lead to staff changes at this level of government.

All major government policy initiatives in Manitoba are first considered by one of the standing committees of Cabinet. For example, a major social policy initiative launched by government focusing on children might be developed by staff from the Healthy Child Manitoba Committee, but then it would be reviewed by the political arm of this committee (i.e., ministers and senior staff from several departments) before it is forwarded to Cabinet. Treasury Board is a key structure because this committee must review and approve all expenditures, and therefore it exerts considerable control over policy development. Treasury Board can be an obstacle to new initiatives if it tries to micro-manage the development of new policies; if this posture is assumed, it will often delay new initiatives by referring these back to committees for more information.

One other structure that has become increasingly important to governments over the years is the mechanism used to manage information flow and communication with the public. In Manitoba, this responsibility is carried by the Cabinet Communications Committee. This committee designs communication strategies in an effort to put a positive spin on government initiatives in a way that connects with the public. For example, in 2002 the Kyoto Accord on greenhouse gases was being hotly debated across the country and the Manitoba government had come out in support of this treaty. As a means of connecting with the public, a communications strategy was designed to draw attention to the effects of inaction on the ecosystem of polar bears. Why polar bears? First, almost everyone likes the image conveyed by polar bears. And second, it was seen as a way of simplifying and packaging a very complicated issue so that it would garner the support of the general population.

Governments are often slow in adopting major innovations in social policy, at least of the progressive variety, and new policies are often prompted by initiatives initially developed in the non-governmental social service sector or by the advocacy efforts of policy networks and lobby groups. There are several reasons for this. First, government is risk-aversive; it always has one eye on how the public will react and how this might play in the next election. Because new social policies generally require new public spending, there is bound to be some level of public resistance. This tends to make governments more conservative, particularly in their approach to social spending. Second, as described above, government operates like a bureaucratic machine with layers of decision-making structures, each with its own set of requirements that serve to slow down the policy-making process. Finally, the available financial resources to government are often more restricted than it might appear. For example, the ongoing operations of government departments might require up to 95 per cent of the revenues available to the government, leaving relatively small amounts for new initiatives. While internal reallocation or expenditure cuts can increase the amount of resources available for new investments somewhat, there is always intense competition among departments for new money.

Despite the foregoing, provincial governments play an important role in policy-making. The state, through its general ability to create legislation and policy affecting the general population and to direct expenditures and other resources, has a major influence over policy development. However, while individual ministers of departments may have significant influence over matters in their own department, their influence over general government policy is much more limited. And those who are not members of Cabinet have even less influence.

How New Policies Are Developed Inside Government

New policies are developed in response to problems that appear on the agenda of governments. This agenda is shaped by issues that arise because of the cycle of government planning or the influence of interest groups. Issues that appear on the government's agenda may be foreshadowed in items such as departmental priorities, throne speeches, or the budget; in these circumstances 'policy windows' or opportunities for new initiatives may exist. Usually governments undertake more new initiatives in the first two years after being elected than they do in the last two years of their mandate. Policy windows can also be triggered by unexpected events such as a crisis, results from an inquest, or the exposure of an issue by the media or pressure groups.

Developing policy in response to policy windows has become increasingly complex as governments engage in efforts to coordinate policies across departments or other levels of government. Policy specialists, skilled in being able to manage policy-making in these types of environments, play an important role in determining the success of these endeavours. Another important resource is the policy and planning branches of larger government departments (sometimes labelled research and planning branches). These units are instrumental in generating planning options and advising the minister of the department.

Three different types of policy-making within government are identified here. One type of policy-making is confined to the bureaucratic structures of the department. Indeed many of the activities carried out at the departmental level will receive only limited attention from the minister.[1] New policy directives, regulations, policy manuals, and protocols for service delivery may be established within departments without any significant discussion at the ministerial level and without ever entering the radar screen of Cabinet.

A second type of policy-making concerns an issue that requires political attention. This may come to the department because of external pressure or because it has been referred to the department by another level of government. Departments of government are usually composed of divisions (program areas) that might be headed by assistant deputy ministers. These individuals are accountable to a deputy minister who is the chief staff member to the minister. Detailed policy changes may be developed by staff within program divisions. For example, an income assistance division might draft policies related to a change in eligibility requirements for social assistance. These might then be forwarded to a senior departmental level, such as the policy and planning branch, which reports more directly to the deputy minister and minister.

If a new issue or opportunity emerges and becomes a policy priority for government, a process like that depicted in Figure 3.1 may unfold. At an early stage, there may be efforts to educate others about the need for a policy response or to advocate for a particular solution. In some cases, research may be undertaken or a demonstration project may be launched. If the need for a particular policy response is substantiated, it will be brought forward to the political level of the department (i.e., the minister) by champions and/or legitimizers who try to establish the credibility of a recommended policy response. Policy champions and legitimizers may be from inside government, from outside government, or be a combination of insiders and outsiders. If the minister is convinced that a policy response is required, three possible actions may be taken. First, where the minister has the required authority s/he will initiate the policy response leading to an outcome. Second, if the minister decides that sanction for a policy response must come from central government, the matter will be referred to the Cabinet. Third, in some cases collaboration with other departments or governments may be required. While collaboration with another department may be initiated by the minister directly, Cabinet may also demand this. Collaborative efforts with other levels of government are usually sanctioned by Cabinet or the premier's office.

The third type of policy-making within government unfolds more directly at the political level (i.e., Cabinet). In this case an issue or opportunity is viewed as important enough to require the immediate attention of Cabinet, a number of departments, and staff from the Policy Management Secretariat. In these matters policy is led by central government (Cabinet, the Premier's Office and the Policy Management Secretariat) which assumes the role of the policy making authority even though matters may be referred back to various departments for action. As indicated in Figure 3.2, policy is coordinated from the centre in these circumstances. One example was the development of the *Aboriginal Justice Inquiry Child Welfare Initiative* in Manitoba. This initiative involves the transfer of responsibility for all child welfare services provided to Aboriginal people in the province to newly created Aboriginal authorities. Because implications transcend several departments and the issue is politically sensitive, the government's

Figure 3.1 Government Policy Process in Response to
an Issue Beginning at the Departmental Level

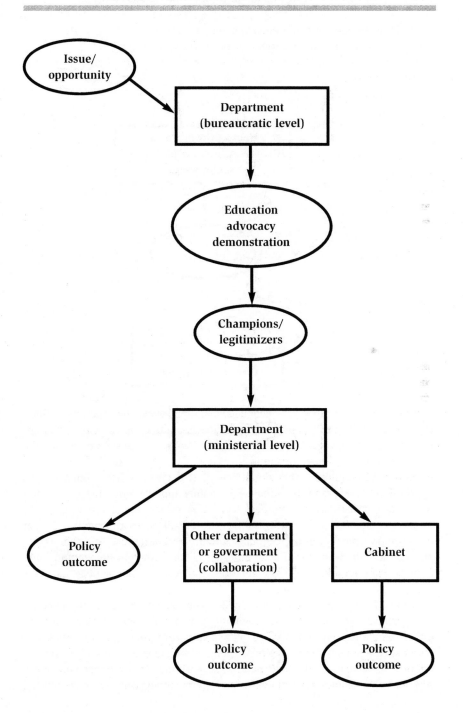

general response has been developed centrally with more specific actions assigned primarily to the Department of Family Services and Housing.

Figure 3.2 Government Policy Process in Response to an Issue Beginning with Central Government

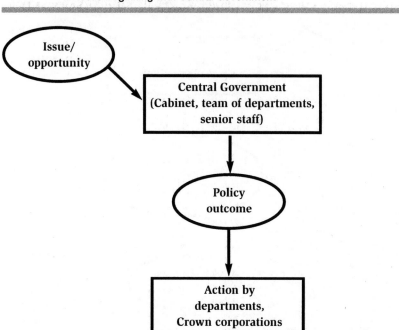

Policy-making within government occurs at three levels: the department, Cabinet, or the legislature. Matters that require the assent of Cabinet are referred to as Orders-in-Council whereas the budget and changes in legislation require the approval of the Legislative Assembly.

Documents submitted to Cabinet are of two types: those requiring final approval by Cabinet and those that seek Cabinet approval but must also be presented to the legislature (i.e., new legislation or requests for new expenditures). Documents submitted to Cabinet are organized in a prescribed format that contain information on the policy/program request, cost, and the service and political implications of the requested change. Matters that require only Cabinet level approval include regulations for new policies or bills that have been approved by the legislature, a wide range of other matters that are considered to be within the government's policy and expenditure plan approved by the legislature, and proposals for new initiatives, such as the creation of a committee to hold hearings on changes to child welfare legislation. Quite often governments try to shift the authority for making decisions from the legislature to Cabinet to avoid public and opposition scrutiny of controversial issues. Although this enables government to manage sensitive issues more effectively, it often contributes to a policy-making process that contradicts the essential principles of transparency and accountability.

The Canadian parliamentary system has a well-entrenched protocol that must be followed when changes in legislation are required. Although bills may be introduced by any member of the legislature, private member bills require unanimous approval if they are to be further considered. Because this occurs only on rare occasions, most changes to existing legislation or new bills are introduced by government through the respective ministers responsible for the issue to be addressed.

Legislation is normally introduced into the legislature in the form of public bills. These bills result from a process that may have included policy review and development, the minister's approval, Cabinet approval, the drafting of the bill, and detailed approval of the bill for introduction to the legislature by the Cabinet or a committee of government. Once a government bill is introduced to the legislature, government members are expected to support the bill, thus ensuring its passage if the governing party holds a majority of seats. In Manitoba, a new bill requires two days' advance notice, although the House (i.e., the legislature) may give unanimous consent to shortening the notice period or waiving it entirely.

The minister's first introduction of a new bill is known as 'first reading'. Although a brief explanation of the purpose of the bill is specified at first reading, no detailed statement is given, and debate is not permitted at this stage. The vote that takes place on first reading simply signifies the approval of the House to consider the bill and to approve printing.

The bill is printed after the first reading and distributed to all members of the legislature, although in practice, printing may have occurred prior to first reading. This speeds up the process and allows for the distribution of the bill soon after first reading.

'Second reading' normally cannot occur until at least two days after the bill has been distributed. Debate is permitted at this stage, and this is initiated by the minister's motion that the bill be given second reading. Debate occurs in the legislature and ends after a vote is taken. If the motion passes, the bill is considered to have been given second reading.

After second reading, normally the bill is referred to a standing or special committee for review. On rare occasions, such as when emergency legislation is being considered, the bill may be simply referred to the Committee of the Whole (i.e., the legislature). Both government and opposition members sit on standing and special committees. The purpose of the committee stage is to allow members of the committee to receive representation from the public about the bill. Following public presentations, the bill is considered 'clause by clause' by the committee. Each clause is voted on, and it is at this stage that amendments can be moved by the minister and by Opposition members.

On completion of the committee review, the chairperson of the committee reports to the House on the committee's deliberations, including any proposed amendments. After these amendments are considered by the legislature, the bill is given 'third reading'. Before it becomes a statute it must receive royal assent by the lieutenant-governor. The bill has the force of law once it is given royal assent unless the bill contains a provision that indicates it comes into force on a specified date or on a date fixed by proclamation. Legislation that is complex or requires the development of new regulations, forms, and procedures is often not proclaimed until some time after royal assent. This gives departmental staff the opportunity to develop new regulations and procedures. If no fixed day of proclamation is specified, an Order-in-Council must be passed by Cabinet directing the lieutenant-governor to issue a proclamation that the statute comes into force on the date specified by Cabinet.

Almost all government bills contain a provision authorizing government to develop regulations that guide the specific implementation process of a new policy. Regulations set out the details of the policy, yet they do not come under the scrutiny of the legislature or require its approval. In this regard, the legislature is prevented from holding government accountable for the detailed interpretation of policy or the intended steps in implementation.

A final aspect of provincial policy-making concerns the nature of issues that become part of the government's policy agenda. Some of these emerge as a result of information generated by the normal operating phases of a department. For example, persistent overexpenditures by Winnipeg Child and Family Services, a voluntary child welfare agency in Manitoba, resulted in the government's decision to assume direct control of the agency in the fall of 2001. Other issues are established as part of the government's policy agenda because of pre-election commitments, or they are established as initiatives that are identified in the Speech from the Throne when a new legislative session commences. Finally, issues or policy proposals may be proposed by policy advocates from outside government.

As we note elsewhere, issues or policy proposals that are presented to government by advocates from outside government may be incorporated as part of the government's policy agenda or rejected. If a proposal responds to a particular problem in a way that is consistent with existing government philosophy, adoption is more likely. However, even a good proposal may be rejected if it conflicts with the ideology or publicly stated position of the governing political party. For example, a policy initiative that might call for the expansion of publicly provided services is likely to be viewed unfavourably by a government committed to privatization. Prevailing government philosophy, then, can inhibit the capacity to innovate or respond to advocacy efforts. At the same time, there are often differing perspectives among members of government, even within Cabinet, and over time the general policy stance of the government can shift in response to public pressure or other changes. In addition, ministers who want to be more creative may get around the general policy commitments of government by creating exceptions or framing a new initiative in a way that avoids any direct conflict with the overall philosophy of the government. This approach relies on finding 'wiggle room' between a new initiative and prevailing government policy that might appear to be in conflict with the new policy proposal.

Political will is an important variable in policy-making and its influence is difficult to predict. In Chapter 2, we provided examples of how a government with a cause may pursue a particular policy agenda even if there will be significant political costs to bear. This approach reflects political will, defined here as the willingness of a government to take some risks with public opinion by developing a policy response in conditions of uncertainty or where there is a strong ideological commitment to action. Political will can lead one government to follow a social justice agenda and restore welfare benefits to recipients who are unable to survive on existing allowances. Conversely, a neo-conservative government may impose severe public sector cutbacks despite widespread public disapproval.

Organizational Policy-Making
Policy-Making Structures in Organizations

Agencies, particularly those in the voluntary sector, will have their own policy-making structures. These are much simpler than those found in government. For example, the board of directors may approve particular policies but policy development may occur through a subcommittee of the board, a joint staff-board committee, or a senior management committee of staff. When major programs or policy changes are contemplated, an agency may establish a committee composed of a cross-section of direct service staff, senior staff, and board members, and, depending on the relative commitment of the agency to inclusiveness, client representatives to develop or frame the new policy. Such 'vertical slices' represent a greater commitment to a participatory approach in the development of new policies. Forms of strategic planning are also used in government and small-scale community policy-making initiatives, and we include a brief discussion of small-scale policy-making in the next section.

Although it is easier to incorporate an inclusive approach to policy-making within organizations than governments, there is no guarantee that this will be the case. Organizations characterized by an elitist, centralized approach to management can ignore the voices of first-line staff and service users in ways that are characteristic of some government policy-making bodies.

Even more so than in government, organizational policy-making is heavily influenced by the values and style of the person in the primary leadership position. The approach of this individual will have a major impact on whether planning at the third level becomes more inclusive or whether a more traditional, centralized model will be adopted.

First Nations communities and other Aboriginal organizations are gaining greater policy-making authority in the areas of health, education, and social services. Structures are usually community-based if authority is assumed at the community level or regionally-based if authority is vested in a regional structure that serves several communities. The structures that are established in these circumstances may resemble miniature versions of those that exist at a governmental level. For example, in a First Nations community, one of the councillors may have a portfolio that includes health and social services. However, the approaches to policy-making are much less complex than those that exist at a provincial or federal government level, and in this regard the structures and policy-making processes are more like those that exist within organizations. As in organizations, the approach to policy-making can vary a great deal. Some may adopt a more centralized approach to policy development whereas others will attempt to foster a more inclusive, collaborative approach.

Small-Scale Policy-Making

Our discussion of policy-making has focused on policies and programs that are developed at the governmental or organizational level. But ordinary issues in policy-making can also include small-scale innovations launched by a single staff person or a small team within an organization or by a community group. These types of initiatives can have a profound effect on the lives of those who receive services, even if the number of service users is relatively small. For example, the expansion of a program that provides mentoring support to pregnant women with substance abuse problems to include a public education prevention component can make a difference to those who don't have access to important information on the effects of FAS/FAE or available community resources. What model of policy-making is appropriate in these circumstances?

The process of small-scale policy-making draws on a number of common steps associated with some of the policy-making models outlined in Chapter 2, and these steps are discussed in more detail in the next chapter. An important consideration is the initiation stage of a new small-scale innovation. The individual or group launching the initiative has more control over these processes than in large-scale programs, yet they must take the time to develop a consensus about the need for action with those who are responsible for approving the project. A particularly important consideration is whether other programs provide services that might be defined as similar or related to those that are being proposed. The potential for community partnerships may need to be explored, particularly if one is developing a new proposal that will require external funding.

A strategic planning approach is often used to launch a new initiative. If it is pursued as a participatory exercise that engages key stakeholders in developing the innovation, it can help to resolve any value differences and reach a consensus on key components of the new policy or program. Although the steps followed in strategic planning vary somewhat, the following tasks are usually covered in some form:

- *Understand the historical context of the agency or problem.* This involves an examination of general information on trends, critical events, and any ideals that characterize the agency or sponsoring group.
- *Establish a vision or idealized image of the service or program three or more years into the future.* This helps to identify any tensions that may need to be resolved and highlight general goals, essential in establishing a mission statement for the new initiative.
- *Complete a situational assessment that involves an analysis of both the*

internal and external environment affecting the agency or sponsoring group. The strengths and weaknesses of the internal environment are identified along with the opportunities and threats in the external environment.

- *Identify the issues for which there are yet no obvious solutions.* Strategic issues may emerge from tensions that surfaced during the visioning stage or from the situational assessment.

- *Develop strategic options and select the preferred alternative to address each major unresolved issue.* The activities involved here are similar to those involved in the formulation stage of policy-making. Alternatives are first identified and then assessed for their ability to meet the general goals of the new initiative.

- *Assess feasibility, including general implementation challenges that may need to be considered.* At this stage one should consider the views of service users as well as political, financial, and legal implications of proposed changes. Other considerations include an assessment of key stakeholders and the likelihood of obtaining their support for the new initiative. Strategies will need to be designed to deal with those likely to oppose the new initiative if these individuals will be influential in whether the new policy is adopted. One also needs to consider both the material and non-material resources required to implement the new strategy and possible sources of these resources.

Strategic planning can be useful in resolving differences about general strategies to be adopted and in setting the general direction for a new program or initiative; however, results lack the specificity required for implementing a new program initiative. This stage requires attention to 'action planning', or what is sometimes referred to as 'implementation planning'. Action planning requires clarity about goals and objectives. Goal statements are defined here as general statements of program outcomes or what will be accomplished, whereas outcome objectives are more specific and measurable changes that will be experienced by service users. Each goal may have several outcome objectives. In developing outcome objectives, one should also give attention to performance indicators that will help assess whether the new initiative is effective at various stages of the implementation process. While outcome objectives are important in focusing on the anticipated benefits that will emerge from the project, process objectives can be specified to outline things that must be done to build the operating capacity of the project. For example, a new innovation may require the formation of a management structure and a staff-training program.

Once objectives are clarified, action plans can be specified for each objective. Action plans are sets of activities that explain how changes will be accomplished. Each action plan may involve a number of action steps or tasks that must be carried out in the implementation stage.

Action plans may need to be established to identify some of the following tasks associated with the development of a new innovation:

- Developing the governance and management structure for the new initiative.
- Developing an outreach strategy to recruit and select service users or the target population.
- Designing a staff orientation and training strategy.
- Developing the service model or technology to be used.
- Specifying the approach to be used in evaluating success and monitoring implementation.
- Delivering the service.

Action planning can become quite detailed and it is important to establish a timeline where activities are sequenced and integrated within a general policy-making framework. In small programs this can be accomplished by specifying beginning and ending dates for various activities; in larger programs computer modelling can be used to help establish a timeline for program implementation. However, even in small initiatives it is advisable to establish an action-monitoring plan. An action-monitoring plan might include the following:

- A list of the general set of activities or action plans to be carried out along with information on the resources required, those resources that are available and what must be done to secure needed resource shortfalls.
- A list of the action steps or tasks for each action plan.
- Information on who is responsible for each task and requirements for accountability. In small group initiatives, accountability may be to the group; in larger initiatives a coordinator may be identified and written reports may be required.
- A timeline for tasks that specifies the start and completion dates for different tasks.

In small-scale policy-making the development of detailed action plans may follow formal approval of the new initiative, and such plans will guide the implementation process.

The Centralizing Trend in Government Policy-Making

In our discussion of policy-making at the federal government level we referred to the trend towards centralization where the prime minister and senior staff have assumed more and more control over key government policy decisions. This trend is also apparent at the provincial level, particularly among neo-conservative provincial governments. In these circumstances, the premier's office exercises enormous influence over policy development with almost no attention to a review of alternatives or how the implementation process can be managed. This approach to policy-making in Ontario, under Mike Harris, led to some well-publicized policy disasters, including the tainted water scandal at Walkerton that resulted in several deaths. In Ontario, during the Harris era, policy-making was driven by a narrow ideological agenda that included cuts in taxes, reduced social and other public services, and efforts to dramatically curtail the influence of more localized organizational structures such as unions, school boards, and municipal governments. In such circumstances, policy-making may be described as 'policy by ideological imperative from the centre'. Although a great deal of policy-making at the federal level under Chrétien occurred from the Prime Minister's Office, this example of centralization might be labelled 'policy by ad hoc imperative from the centre'.[2] The term 'ad hoc' is used here because the policies of the federal government, while generally conservative in orientation, lack the extreme right-wing qualities of those found in Ontario under Mike Harris or in British Columbia under Gordon Campbell. The centralization of the policy-making apparatus within various governments means that these decisions are seldom a reflection of the needs and concerns of practitioners and service users. In addition, the role of citizens in shaping government policy is largely restricted to casting a vote during elections.

The centralizing trend in government policy-making at the federal level and in a number of provincial governments, a trend often referred to as the 'democratic deficit', makes the job of connecting policy to practice in a more inclusive manner that much more difficult. As well, it contributes to a general cynicism about government and the role of active citizenship in having any meaningful influence in policy processes. Phillips and Orsini address this problem in a general way and recommend a number of reforms designed to enhance the role of the citizens in political and public sector institutions. These authors identify eight dimensions of citizen involvement in policy processes, and we note some of the most important below:

- mobilizing interest: creates interest and debate on an issue;
- claims-making: allows individuals and organizations to make claims, express positions and values on policy issues;
- knowledge acquisition: provides information and knowledge to enable informed debate;
- community capacity-building: enables the development of social capital, leadership and collective action at the community level; and
- transparency and feedback: demonstrates how public input was used and how it makes a difference. (Phillips and Orsini, 2002, p. 9)

Although these authors are somewhat pessimistic about reversing the centralizing trend at the top of the policy-making pyramid at the federal government level, a number of changes to promote more citizen involvement in policy-making are recommended. One involves reform to both the political party system and Parliament that would promote increased policy-oriented discussions between elected political officials and citizens. This might include an increased capacity for parliamentary or legislative committees to conduct research and public consultations as well as greater autonomy in developing policy options. Second, more attention to the creation of a civic forum for engaging a broader cross-section of the public in policy debates and discussion is recommended. Third, a change in the culture of governments is required to ensure that citizen involvement begins to be seen as an integral part of the policy process. Indicators of such a shift would include the willingness of governments to provide more access to information and resources to support such a process. Finally, greater investment in promoting civil society is required. This includes such things as relaxing the rules on charitable organizations so they can speak out on issues without fear of losing their funding, and promoting the responsibility of public and community institutions to build approaches that involve service users and community members in policy design.

Conclusion

General strategies to promote inclusive policy-making are discussed in more depth in the second half of the book; however, there is much that can be done to utilize existing opportunities and to promote the development of small-scale reforms to the policy-making process. How can staff on the first-line of service delivery promote this transition in the human services? At the outset, it is important to note the contradiction between the centralizing trend among some governments and the demand for more input and participation that emerges from commitments to diversity and minority rights. Perhaps this contradiction can be exposed in building more active social movements that promote social justice causes rather than profits and free market principles.

One level involves the professional work of staff within their employing agencies where there are opportunities to become involved in activities that incorporate connections to the policy making process. This can happen within the practitioner's service organization or through involvement as an agency representative on task groups or coalitions that are related to professional responsibilities.

One can also choose to invest energy in extra-organizational activities related to a professional association, union, political party, or a cultural organization that engages in policy advocacy work. Activities in the political arena can include volunteer work on campaigns and can lead to the development of networks and opportunities to influence the policy process through these networks. For some it can include running for political office and the possibility of participating in government. Active participation in policy networks allows individuals the opportunity to be more influential in that their voices are multiplied through that organization and the efforts that are made to build coalitions around social issues. There are many opportunities for this type of involvement, including human rights organizations, policy-oriented groups like the Council of Canadians, social planning councils, or the Canadian Centre for Policy Alternatives as well as more service-oriented organizations. We bring important knowledge and experience to these organizations that can be invaluable in policy or service advocacy. Finally, one can act individually in lobbying key political or agency stakeholders on policy issues that are important.

In Chapter 4 the stages of the policy-making process are discussed in depth, and a model for policy analysis is outlined.

Recommended Reading

1. For a useful outline of the policy-making process at the federal government level, see G. Milne, *Making Policy: A Guide to the Federal Government's Policy Process*, 8th edn (Ottawa: Author, 2000).
2. For a guide to small-scale policy-making, see B. Schram, *Creating Small Scale Social Programs* (Thousand Oaks, CA: Sage, 1997).

Notes

1. These three types of government policy-making were identified by Tim Sale, the former minister, Department of Family Services and Housing, Government of Manitoba.
2. We are indebted to an anonymous reviewer for drawing our attention to the distinction between the two types of centralization described here.

Chapter Four

The Stages of the Policy-Making Process

Introduction

In this chapter we identify the stages of the policy-making process and note the similarities between these and the stages that occur in practice. Although the stages can be conceptualized as separate and distinct, they should not be viewed as steps in a linear process. On the contrary, in both policy and practice they frequently merge and flow into each other. Nevertheless, clarity and understanding is aided by discussing stages in a discrete fashion. The chapter also includes an extensive discussion of policy analysis.

As Figure 4.1 indicates, there are five stages of the policy process: initiation, formulation, execution, implementation, and evaluation. Analysis should occur throughout the policy-making process; however, it is useful to identify the different ways we apply this concept in the policy-making process. We conceptualize policy analysis in the initiation phase as problem analysis, we reserve the term 'policy analysis' for the formulation stage, and in the final stage analysis is an evaluative activity. The execution stage requires little analysis and, given the close connection between policy and practice in implementation, discussion of this stage is the subject of the following chapter.

We conclude the chapter by presenting an integrated model of policy analysis as a way of emphasizing the commonality of the analytic tasks required in all stages.

Figure 4.1 Corresponding Stages of Policy and Practice Process

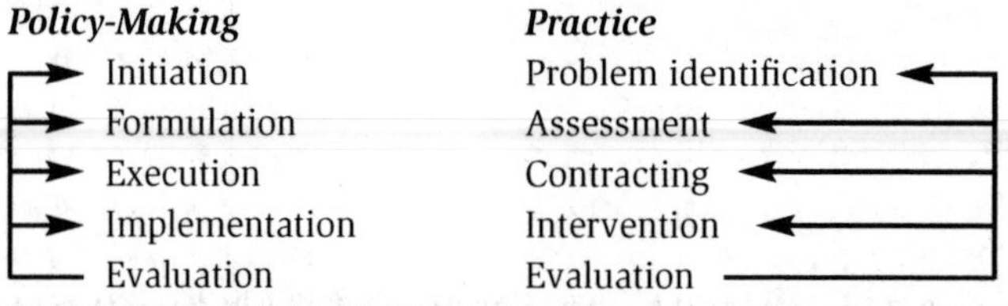

Policy-Making	*Practice*
Initiation	Problem identification
Formulation	Assessment
Execution	Contracting
Implementation	Intervention
Evaluation	Evaluation

Stages in Developing Policy and Practice

Initiation and Problem Identification

In both policy-making and practice, action or change begins at a discernible point. In practice, the beginning point might take the form of a request by a client for assistance, a referral from another agency, or a complaint by a neighbour or another professional. In policy-making, the beginning point might emanate from the pressure created by social movements, the public, or interest groups who have become convinced of the inadequacy of existing policy, or as a government response to a campaign promise.

In all the possible scenarios, a 'convergence of interest' (Sower et al., 1957) or a crisis of some magnitude must occur before action will be initiated. As conceptualized by Sower and his colleagues, a convergence of interest reflects the notion of an idea whose time has come: the perception that something simply has to be done about a particular condition. In the garbage can model of policy development, a convergence of interest is defined as a 'window of opportunity' that occurs when the political stream, the stream of problems, and the stream of policy solutions come together. A convergence of interest is often influenced by the characteristics of the person or organization pushing for change; these characteristics include authority, legitimacy, and commitment. Thus, an agency director may have the authority to propose a change but may lack the confidence of the agency's staff. A change proposed by such a director may be initiated, but it will encounter problems during the change process. Conversely, a long-standing staff member who is highly regarded by colleagues may lack authority, but may nevertheless possess a high degree of legitimacy. Both of these people will need to supplement their proposal with energy and commitment; indeed, causes pursued by a dedicated champion may well succeed despite the absence of other factors usually considered essential in bringing about change.

A convergence of interest that leads to initiation is somewhat more complicated in policy-making than it is in practice, and the notion of convergence of interest is expanded here to include a set of factors that need to be considered in assessing the likelihood of policy initiation. These are evidence of need for the change, availability of resources, the complexity of the change being contemplated, organizational readiness, environmental readiness, the commitment of key actors, and timing (see Table 4.1). Thus, a relatively simple change proposed by and backed by the commitment and resources of a minister of social services or a minister of health in a sympathetic environment will in all likelihood be initiated. However, the scenario will shift if the minister's proposal involves a complex issue about which there is widespread disagreement. As we noted earlier, controversial issues will likely be referred to some type of study group. The prospects of a successful launch are more remote if the proposal for change emanates from a backbencher of a party in opposition or from a professional organization lacking close connections with the minister and the party in power.

Table 4.1 Factors to Consider in Assessing the Likelihood of Policy Initiation

Factors	Key Questions
Need for change	Is the change a political priority or do results from a formal needs assessment support change?
Complexity of issue	How complex is the issue and is action required by several sectors?
Commitment of key actors	Do key decision-makers support the change?
Organizational readiness	Do organizations that must plan and implement the change have the motivation and capacity to do so?
Environmental readiness	Do key stakeholders in the policy environment, including the public, support the change?
Availability of resources	Are sufficient resources available to implement the change?

The explanatory power of the concept of convergence of interest takes a different form in the event of a crisis such as the death of a child. Crises can provoke new unanticipated actions, especially if they can be used to reinforce the agendas of those in positions of power and if resources are available. Thus, the 1992 death of Matthew Vaudreuil in British Columbia was interpreted by the minister and senior staff in charge of child welfare as justification to inquire into the internal working conditions of the department and the practices of the first-line staff. In this example, Judge Gove was appointed to conduct a far-reaching investigation of child welfare practices in the province, and his recommendations led to major organizational and service delivery changes in this field.

In practice, the initiation stage begins with a complaint or a referral that is accepted by the agency. Again, the likelihood of acceptance is much greater if the request comes from a respectable and well-known source. When faced with referrals from unknown or poorly regarded sources and requests from service users who have earned a reputation for being difficult, rude, or antagonistic, staff might delay responses or ignore the request. Again, a crisis often spurs a prompt response regardless of the source of the referral or the reputation of the client. Other factors that may influence the acceptance of a referral include the agency's mandate or service priorities. Once accepted, the problem identification phase commences. In cases where a service user wants a particular service, the problem definition phase proceeds through mutual dialogue and exploration. However, this is not the case when the person has not requested a particular service or has a significantly different view of their needs than the service provider.

The most perplexing part of the initiation stage revolves around defining the problem to be addressed. Social problems are notoriously difficult to pin down and yet the definition sets the stage for the rest of the policy-making process. Indeed, the very term 'definition' is problematic because it connotes precision and explicitness. We prefer the term 'framing', which outlines the general parameters of the issue being addressed.

Framing provides a sense of direction. It sets out preferences and prescribes limits based on ideologies and experiences, but refrains from the explicitness expected of a definition. Although Rittel and Webber (1973) use 'definition' rather than 'framing', the essence of the latter notion is captured by their description of social problems as 'wicked problems'.

Wicked problems have a number of distinguishing properties, for example:

a) there is no definitive formulation of a wicked problem;
b) wicked problems have no stopping rule: they are resolved over and over again;
c) solutions to wicked problems are not true-false but good or bad—depending on one's values and experience;
d) every solution to a wicked problem is a 'one shot operation'; because there is no opportunity to learn by trial and error every attempt counts significantly;
e) every wicked problem is essentially unique; and
f) every wicked problem is a symptom of another problem (Rittel and Webber, 1973, pp. 167–8).

In our view, framing the problem is the most significant aspect of the initiation stage. Thus, if the problem of poverty is framed as the unwillingness of citizens to work, then the solution would be to force people to work or to provide incentives so that more individuals will find and keep employment. Similarly, if the problem is framed simply as the lack of employment opportunities, then attention would focus on job creation programs. However, if poverty is framed as the consequence of a number of faulty and interlocking public policies, including educational preparation, the availability of work, and the failure to establish a progressive tax system, then the task becomes one of examining the very concept of work, who receives compensation, as well as whether there are sufficient opportunities for employment. Framing the problem in this way implies the need for a more comprehensive and radical examination of options.

Practitioners face similar dilemmas in the problem identification phase of practice. Should a single-parent mother be viewed as a disadvantaged and distressed person with limited resources doing her best to manage under difficult circumstances? If so, then the appropriate response would be to assist her by increasing her resources and reducing her stress. Conversely, the identification of the same person as requiring training in parenting and budgeting skills will result in referrals to suitable training programs.

An example of framing in practice (see Box 4.1) relates to the project touched on in the Introduction.

The example in Box 4.1 illustrates the power of framing in setting the course of the policy-making and practice processes. In fact, the framing of wicked problems is set largely by ideologies. We argued in Chapter 1 that most of those who wielded influence in framing and developing social policies in the 1990s were driven by ideologies that were neo-conservative in nature and reflected a residual

Box 4.1 Framing the Problem in the Empowering Women Project

The Empowering Women Project in British Columbia brought together child welfare workers and their clients and asked them to find ways to meet the needs of clients and to change child welfare practice. The first step was to identify a number of clients interested in the project, to convene a group meeting, and to develop action plans. The coordinator of the project was a former child protection worker. In her previous role her relationship with service users typically began with an investigation of a complaint of neglect or abuse. She acknowledged that her assessments of possible neglect or abuse were, like those of her colleagues, based on pinpointing problems and deficits: Is there evidence of abuse and/or neglect? Are there indications of a poor marital relationship? Are the parents immature? Is the available income adequate? Is the housing satisfactory?

The coordinator of the project now works with service users in a completely different way because her assessments are framed by interactions with a group of motivated women eager to address issues and identify solutions. This frame focuses on strengths: for example, one woman was a carpenter, another was a day-care worker, and a third was an experienced secretary. From the perspective of the people who use services, the opportunity to identify problems, to discuss solutions, and to work with the coordinator as a source of assistance rather than as an investigator also altered the women's framing experience substantially. These women felt validated and motivated to take action in a way that had not occurred to them in the past.

view of state-provided services. Thus health care funding was restricted and directed primarily to hospitals and doctors at the expense of health promotion and early intervention, in turn contributing to a crisis in medicare. Similarly, child welfare programs have focused on child protection rather than early intervention and prevention. Paradoxically, this focus has led to higher numbers of children in care and increased costs. These frames have set the context for practice and a deep and continuing fault line has been created by the gap between the needs of service users and the policies ostensibly designed to serve them. As a result, practitioners have been forced to focus their energy on crisis-oriented responses only or trying to address the gap with too few resources or support to make a real difference.

While the key actors in the initiation stage of policy-making are more likely to be those possessing some degree of formal power, there are occasions where the initiation of change occurs as a direct result of persistent campaigns by those affected either by the absence of a policy or by an inadequate policy. Examples include the efforts of the feminist movement to establish transition houses for battered women and to change hiring practices in the workforce, and the struggle of First Nations people to settle land claims and to achieve self-government.

We should note that when initiation involves issues that are controversial or have significant budgetary implications, the decision to proceed will be made by the governing body: the premier and the Cabinet in the provincial government, the council in a municipal government, and the board of directors in a voluntary agency.

Assessing Problems, Needs, and Resources

The problem analysis phase involves careful consideration of both objective and subjective aspects of the problem. Key issues include how many people are affected by the condition as well as how they feel about and react to the issue. Problem analysis in policy analysis differs from the way problems are defined in traditional research. While one is concerned with who, what, and where issues, it is also important to understand the history and causality of the problem, previous attempts to address the problem, and the community's readiness to deal with the problem. There are a number of common questions that can be posed in completing an analysis of the problem and these are included later in this chapter where we introduce a specific model for policy analysis.

Once problems have been framed and defined, they have to be translated into needs. Problems are closely related to needs, but needs reflect the gap between what the situation is and what it should be. If there is insufficient information available on these needs, it will be necessary to conduct a needs assessment. But *need* is a difficult concept to both define and measure. One can distinguish between *needs* and *wants*; whereas wants are what people are willing to pay for needs are closer to what people are willing to march for. In this context *needs* take on attributes that are closely related to *rights* or what all people should have available to them. Needs also differ in terms of importance, and these are dependent on circumstances. This is illustrated by Maslow's (1954) approach to the definition of needs for individuals. He argued that needs can be conceptualized in a hierarchical fashion. Therefore, a person is primarily concerned with meeting physiological needs first (i.e., food and shelter), safety and security needs later, and then higher level needs such as love and self-actualization. As a person's needs at a more basic level are met, more attention can be paid to higher level needs. This approach can be illustrated by examining the provision of services to abused women and their children in cases of domestic violence. For example, if the abuse is serious the first response will be to refer the woman and her children to a shelter and only after this basic need is met to consider such things as restraining orders (security and safety), counselling services (to help restore self-esteem), and other options, such as employment and alternative housing (autonomy and self sufficiency).

As the previous discussion emphasizes, need is a relative concept that is affected by both values and context. Standards and attitudes of the public change over time. Thus, the commonly accepted definition of a poverty line in Canada (i.e., the Statistics Canada low-income cut-off or LICO) is adjusted annually to reflect changing income and costs. Public attitudes and expectations also change. Accessible transportation for the disabled, which is identified as a need in most urban centres in Canada today, would have likely been defined as a luxury a generation ago. Because of our interest in relating needs to the development of programs, there must also be some expectation that resources can be identified to respond to these needs, and that the technology is available to solve the problem.

Kettner, Moroney, and Martin (1999) summarize four different perspectives on need: normative, perceived, expressed, and relative (see Table 4.2). Each perspective has both advantages and disadvantages. A normative perspective on need suggests that one can measure the existence of need through the use of a commonly accepted standard. The Statistics Canada LICO, which is used to identify the number of people living in poverty, is one such standard. Other standards have been developed to define the adequacy of housing, nutrition, and the ratio of hospital beds to population in a community or region. Although standards are helpful in defining needs, they are not always available for the problem area in question.

Perceived needs are what people think or feel they need. Perceived needs are measured by asking people what they need through survey methods or interviews. But perceived needs are not always a good reflection of who would actually utilize services. For example, estimates of those who are sexually abused are commonly provided to demonstrate the prevalence of sexual abuse, yet not all of these victims would utilize services that might be developed to respond to this need.

Expressed needs can sometimes be confused with perceived needs; however, they are not the same thing. If a need is expressed, there must be some attempt to obtain a service. Wait lists or the number of referrals for service are common methods of measuring expressed needs. Although this approach to needs assessment brings us closer to understanding the demand for a service, this approach also has its flaws. If people know there are long wait lists for family counselling at a family service agency, they may not bother to register because they are not prepared to wait six months for a service they require immediately. Instead, they may seek out a private practitioner or go without this service. As well, people cannot be expected to express a need by registering for a service that does not yet exist!

The final perspective is relative need. Relative need does not begin with the assumption that a standard or criterion exists. Instead the level of need in one area or community is compared with the level in another community to identify differences that may require attention. Comparisons of the unemployment rate in a First Nations community with another community or with the national or provincial average reflects a relative perspective on need. Although a relative approach to needs assessment provides for a wider range of comparisons than might exist if one used a normative perspective, there are potential problems. Comparative studies of child poverty may lead to preoccupation with differences between provinces, and these differences may then divert attention from the substantive issue of child poverty. In the last analysis it is clear that using a number of different perspectives will provide a better picture of the needs pertaining to a particular problem.

A number of different methods may be used to measure needs. The first step is

Table 4.2 Perspectives on Need

Normative need: requires comparison to an accepted standard.

Advantage:

• if needs are greater than existing standard, provides support for action

Disadvantage:

• standards are often not available or accepted

Perceived need: reflects what people think and feel.

Advantage:

• more representative of views of potential target group

Disadvantages:

• may not be indicative of actual demand for service or the number of people who would utilize services

• perceptions change over time

Expressed need: reflects data on numbers of people who actually try to obtain a service.

Advantage:

• good predictor of demand for service or the number of people who might utilize a particular service

Disadvantages:

• may omit people who have given up trying to obtain a service

• is not a useful measure of need where no service exists for a newly identified problem

Relative need: reflects a comparison of data from one area or community with another or with a provincial or national average.

Advantage:

• allows one to measure gaps where standards do not exist

Disadvantage:

• may focus on differences in need rather than the characteristics that reflect the presence of the particular need under consideration

---

to examine what already exists. This might involve a review of such things as social indicator data, including information available through Statistics Canada, local and national research studies, and records on service utilization. New information may be collected through surveys or interviews with service users and providers. More interactive techniques, employing primarily qualitative methods, can also be used. These include community forums, focus groups, and nominal group methods. Public hearings, sometimes organized as a component of special commissions, are an expanded version of a community forum, where an individual or group may present a brief on the issue being examined.

Needs studies also make use of evaluation research methods, particularly in cases where studies can demonstrate a cause and effect relationship. For example, the development of needle exchange programs in Canadian cities was based on evidence linking the multiple use of needles to the spread of HIV. Needs studies are very important in policy analysis because a new policy initiative is seldom undertaken without demonstrable evidence of need.

While needs assessment studies are useful in policy-making, we argue that they reflect a deficit-oriented approach to analysis unless they are combined with an assessment of assets and capacities. Here again, a parallel between policy and practice can be drawn. In the human services, there is a growing awareness of the need to build on strengths at the individual, family, and community level in order to promote change, and this process begins with an identification of existing strengths and resources as an important aspect of the assessment stage. McKnight and Kretzmann (1992) apply a similar approach to policy-making at the community level in suggesting that needs-oriented assessments give us only half the picture. What is required to complete the picture is an identification of strengths and resources—a process described as 'mapping community capacity'.

Using the community as an example, three types or levels of strengths and resources should be considered. First, there are the resources and strengths of individuals and organizations within the community that are largely subject to community control. Next are the assets located within the community that are largely controlled by outsiders. These assets may include both private and public institutions such as hospitals, schools, and social service agencies. Finally, there are potential building blocks that include those resources originating outside the neighbourhood that are controlled by outsiders. These may include actual or potential social transfer payments and capital improvement expenditures. With this kind of information, a policy analyst is in a better position to address existing needs by building both on identified strengths and on potential resources. While the principle of assessing strengths and resources is perhaps easier to apply in the case of a geographic community, it can also be applied to groups linked through affiliation or interest. In order to make a helpful contribution to the policy-making process, conventional approaches to needs assessment must be modified to incorporate procedures that develop an inventory of resources and capacities.

Formulation and Assessment

The second stage of the policy-making process—formulation—involves developing and analyzing alternatives. The methods of policy analysis are particularly relevant to this stage of the planning process and a model for policy analysis is discussed in the next section of this chapter. Policy analysis, as it is applied in the formulation stage of the policy-making process, is concerned with predicting the future consequences of different policy options. This requires a focus on both technical data and the political aspects of decision-making. Because policy analysis makes an effort to predict the anticipated outcomes of policy alternatives, it often considers evaluation studies conducted on similar policies that have been implemented elsewhere. Even though the major thrust or direction for change may have been set by the manner in which the problem has been framed, a number of different potential responses will still need to be considered. Thus, in formulating a 'get tough' response to delinquency, policy-makers may want to consider whether expanding the number of police and probation officers is preferable to an increase in the number of juvenile detention facilities, and, within the latter option, whether wilderness camps are preferred to other forms of confinement.

Formulation is the stage in which techniques from the rational model of planning become most useful. Formulating alternatives may begin in brainstorming sessions in which no suggestion, however improbable, is rejected. Once all possible alternatives have been identified, research may be conducted to anticipate consequences, and criteria may be identified to assist in the selection process. Such criteria might include the anticipated cost, the feasibility of implementation, the benefits to the political party in power, and possible outcomes for beneficiaries. As will be obvious from this beginning list, criteria are not of the same order or importance. Do benefits to the party in power outweigh financial costs? Does the flexibility of a new service take precedence over ease and simplicity in implementation?

Special commissions and task forces are favourite vehicles for dealing with complex issues at the formulation stage. These structures have a number of advantages to those in power: they give the appearance of action while buying time before a decision is required, and they assure everyone that the problem is being studied in depth by experts. While special commissions can be a means of postponing a policy response they can also draw attention to the need for a significant policy response. One example is the *Romanow Commission on the Future of Health Care,* which released its report in November 2002. This raised expectations for both reform of medicare and new investment in health care by the federal government.

The results from special commissions can also be surprising and none was more surprising than the outcomes of the Royal Commission on Taxation (McQuaig, 1987). This commission was established by a Conservative government and the members appointed to the commission were, in terms of background and experience, equally conservative in their views of fiscal policy. The government was confident that, after due course and proper study, the commission would conclude that the existing tax structure was basically sound and that only minor changes were warranted. However, the assignment required that commission members immerse themselves in every aspect of taxation, including country-by-country comparisons, the pros and cons of capital gains and inheritance taxes, deferred arrangements for corporations, and loopholes. This examination led some members, including the influential chair, Kenneth Carter, to fundamentally alter their views and to recommend sweeping changes. Unfortunately most of the Commission's recommendations have been ignored by successive federal governments.

An integral part of special commissions and task forces is inviting the public to attend hearings and to submit briefs. These invitations are often taken up by a large number of individuals and groups. For example, the community panel that reviewed child welfare in British Columbia prior to the formulation of the *Child, Family and Community Service Act* (1994) 'heard 550 presentations in more than 23 communities and received over 600 written briefs from individuals and groups' (Durie and Armitage, 1996, p. 19). In such circumstances a vast amount of information is gathered, organized, and classified according to the themes that have emerged; analyzed to permit the identification of findings and recommendations; and, finally, translated into policy and/or legislation by analysts and legislative drafters.

While governments that follow this approach can claim that they consulted the public prior to making a choice among competing options, there is, nevertheless, no way to assure the public that all views have been represented in the final report in an equal and fair fashion. For example, governments may select those views that are more consistent with their particular perspective. The consultation process itself is open to even more criticism when, as in the case of the 1994–5 review of Canada's social security system, the nature of the inquiry was carefully orchestrated by policy-makers, including the selection of who was to be allowed to present briefs.[1] In this example, the distillation of public input begins with controlling who can provide this input.

One useful way of analyzing the extent of the influence of citizens in the policy-making process is provided by a framework called 'a ladder of citizen participation'. The ladder has eight rungs (see Figure 4.2). The top three rungs—citizen control, delegated power, and partnerships—represent differing degrees of citizen power. The next three, which include placation, consultation, and informing, symbolize degrees of tokenism. Consultation, the middle rung of this group, allows 'the have-nots to hear and have a voice, but . . . they lack the power to ensure that their views will be heeded by the powerful' (Arnstein, 1969, p. 217). The two bottom rungs refer to processes that do not enable participation; they include therapy and manipulation. We refer again to this useful conceptualization in the discussion of community governance in Chapter 6.

Figure 4.2 A Ladder of Citizen Participation

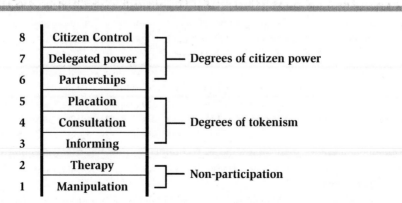

Like their policy counterparts, professionals in direct practice must develop an intervention plan, and tasks undertaken in completing an assessment provide the basis for such a plan. As in policy formulation, this phase may be extensive and elaborate, involving a number of people and generating several alternative strategies. In some cases, the phase may be brief and yield only one plan. The latter is likely to occur when the medical model holds sway and a plan is developed by the practitioner or by an external expert. On the other hand, if a partnership approach exists, intervention plans will be developed jointly by the practitioner and the service user, perhaps with the input of additional experts. In these circumstances, it is more likely that a wider range of options will be considered.

Using Special Lenses in Policy Analysis

Approaches to policy analysis can be distinguished by the relative emphasis placed on content or process issues. A content approach stresses the actual ingredients of a policy, that is, the substance of the policy, its goals and value preferences, and the types of benefits it provides (see Chambers, 1986). The contents of policies are important because these are related to actual or anticipated consequences. However, content approaches do not focus on how policies emerge and why they are developed in a particular fashion. For example, content approaches pay little attention to the political processes that shape policy-making and the trade-offs and compromises that may characterize the policy development stage. As noted in Chapter 2, this is one of the appealing attributes of the garbage can model of policy-making. A pure content approach to policy analysis also tends to reinforce an élitist approach to policy analysis in that the policy expert, as armchair critic, gathers data on the policy issue, subjects these data to critical scrutiny, and draws conclusions about the impact of the policy.

Without minimizing the importance of analyses of policy contents, often developed to stimulate debate and dialogue about the policy, we argue that process considerations must also be included as components in a preferred model for policy analysis. A process approach to policy analysis pays more attention to who influences the development of policies, how action is generated, and who makes decisions (Flynn, 1992). Additional considerations include questions of feasibility and how the implementation stage will affect the contents of a new policy. These considerations demand that policy analysts get out of their offices and discuss some of these issues with service users and staff responsible for delivering new programs. From a process perspective, policy analysis and policy-making are understood as an ongoing set of activities that involves creating and adapting policies and programs. This approach is consistent with efforts to encourage ongoing inclusiveness and connections between practice and policy. As well, process questions such as who influences policy development and how policy provisions are implemented enable the use of this information in trying to influence changes to particular policies or programs.

Process considerations, then, place an emphasis on policy analysis as an exercise in information-sharing as well as information-gathering; in addition, activities may include negotiation and partisan-based advocacy. At the end of the day, any analysis of a policy must be designed to make a contribution to policy-making or policy change. If policy analysis is not undertaken with this goal in mind, it will remain aloof from practice and disconnected from the change process.

One approach that integrates content and process concerns is the identification of a special lens or focus, often framed as a series of questions, to assess the particular impact of a policy on special populations. An example of this approach is the family impact model (Spakes, 1984). In this particular approach, policies are assessed for their impact on the membership function in families, the economic function, and the socialization/nurturance function. A series of questions is identified to guide such an assessment, and two examples follow:

a) Does the policy strengthen or erode the stability of the family?
b) Does the policy provide adequate support to different types of families?

This approach to the identification of particular impacts has broader relevance in focusing policy attention on traditionally neglected aspects of the policy-making process. For example, health and social service policy questions that focus on effects related to women, minority groups, and first-line service providers can be routinely incorporated as components of policy analysis if this approach is adapted to reflect such considerations. Two examples of such frameworks follow.

An Aboriginal framework for social work practice that includes five core elements has been proposed by McKenzie and Morrissette (2003). These are: a) recognition of a distinct Aboriginal worldview; b) recognition of the effects of colonialism; c) recognition of the importance of Aboriginal identity or consciousness; d) appreciation of the value of cultural knowledge and traditions in promoting healing and empowerment; and e) an understanding of the diversity of Aboriginal cultural expression. While these elements reflect guidelines to be used in the development of culturally appropriate approaches to social work practice, they also identify considerations that may be used to develop a cultural lens for policy analysis.

A helpful framework for assessing the impact of a policy on women's equality was developed by the British Columbia Ministry of Women's Equality (1994). This framework identifies two general questions for determining the gender implications of any policy:

a) Does the policy discriminate against women in its outcomes?
b) Does it support full participation and equality for women?

The gender lens framework proposed in these guidelines has two parts. One is an analytical lens that requires analysts to look at what they bring to their work. These include such factors as knowledge, ways of working, information sources and methods, and consultation processes. The analytical lens is reproduced as a series of questions in Table 4.3. These questions are important because they direct attention to process considerations such as the analyst's own frame of reference and whether those women's groups likely to be affected by the policies have been consulted. A second component requires an exploration of the implications of the policy being analyzed according to different factors. Eight factors are identified that represent ways in which discrimination can occur or, conversely, in which equality can be supported. These factors are: a) legal processes; b) life experiences; c) systemic discrimination; d) economic equality; e) independence and dignity; f) violence against women; g) health and social issues; and h) social equality. These factors represent content issues that require special attention in the analysis process. The use of a gender lens receives further attention in Chapter 8.

Execution and Contracting

At the execution stage, choices are reviewed and a decision is made. In federal and provincial policy matters, recommendations involving major changes and/or a substantial increase in resources will be reviewed by analysts in a standing committee of Cabinet and Treasury Board before being forwarded to the premier and the Cabinet for decision. When the policy takes the form of new legislation or changes to existing acts, the Cabinet will review and approve these plans prior to sending the draft bill to the legislature for debate and a decision.

In a voluntary agency, the board of directors will decide whether to proceed with the plans. Prior to doing so, it may refer recommendations made by committees comprising board and staff members to outside consultants or to standing committees of finance and personnel.

The execution stage in practice rests essentially with the practitioner and the service user. This is most often referred to as the contracting stage, in which goals, objectives, tasks, and activities for ongoing work are outlined.

Implementation and Intervention

Implementation is the fourth stage of the policy-making process, and as noted earlier, the next chapter is devoted to this topic.

The parallel stage in practice is intervention. A wide range of intervention models exists in practice. Intervention, like the assessment stage in practice, will be shaped by several factors. These include the following: mandate of the agency; the nature of the problem; guidelines provided in the practice theory used in this particular situation; the service contract that has been established; and the nature of the relationship that evolves between the practitioner and service user.

Two general distinctions can be made and these are largely shaped by the mandate of the agency and the nature of the problem being addressed. In the case of voluntary contracts where the service user exercises a choice to receive service, more mutuality in the working relationship that evolves can be anticipated. In the case of non-voluntary situations where service is a requirement, whether or not the service user agrees, more difficulties in establishing a mutually acceptable approach to intervention may be anticipated. This is often true in fields such as child welfare and corrections although resistance to intervention

Table 4.3 A Gender Lens: Analytical Guidelines

Category	Questions
1. Values Framework	1.1. What personal and professional experiences, values, and circumstances do I bring to this analysis?
	1.2. How have I ensured that the diverse experiences, values, and circumstances of individuals and groups who will be affected by the policy issue are reflected in my analysis?
2. Data and Information Sources	2.1. Have I considered sources of information other than statistics/quantitative data?
	2.2. What are my sources for statistics/quantitative data?
	2.3. Do the statistics used in this analysis include information based on both women's and men's experiences? Are they separated according to gender?
	2.4. Is there literature or research material on this topic that I should read that presents women's perspectives, experiences, or voices?
	2.5. Have I considered qualitative data and information?
3. Consultation and Language	3.1. Have I consulted with women's groups regarding the issue?
	3.2. If I cannot consult women's groups directly, how have I ensured that their concerns are known and reflected in my analysis?
	3.3. Have I avoided using language that perpetuates stereotypes?
	3.4. Is the language used in my document gender-inclusive and respectful of all people?
4. Differences and Diversity	4.1. Have I considered how women from specific groups, such as women of colour, lesbians, poor women, women with disabilities, and Aboriginal women would be affected by this policy?
	4.2. Does this policy approach respect cultural and/or other differences?
	4.3. Does this policy approach consider the needs of women in different regions? Rural and urban?

(From *Gender Lens: A Guide to Gender-Inclusive Policy and Program Development*, reprinted with permission from the BC Ministry of Women's Equality) may characterize other fields of practice as well. On the one hand, the intervention phase in voluntary service contracts may be compared to the implementation phase of policies where there is a high degree of acceptance of these policies by both service users and providers. On the other hand, the intervention phase in non-voluntary service contracts may reflect problems that are somewhat similar to those that arise in the implementation of policies that do not seem to match the particular needs of service users. There are other similarities between policy implementation and practice intervention. For example, resource limitations can adversely affect the success of both.

While this comparison of practice intervention and policy implementation is of interest, one should not underestimate the differences. First, not only is intervention shaped by policies, but also in a very real way it is an extension of the implementation phase of the policy-making process. Second, because policy implementation is generally mediated by a larger number of political and bureaucratic decision-makers, and it is designed to meet the general needs of a target population, there is a greater likelihood that policies may fail to match the specific needs of an individual service user. In these circumstances it is often the ability of the practitioner to modify and adapt policies that will determine the extent to which service users' needs are met.

Analysis as Evaluation

Evaluation is the final stage of the policy-making process, but all stages should be subjected to evaluation in order to improve the process as it unfolds. Evaluation results from policy implementation are particularly important, and this information may cause us to alter our understanding of the problem, to modify goals, or to include new activities in the implementation stage.

It is not always easy to distinguish between program and policy evaluation, and it is important to acknowledge that there is considerable overlap. First, a new policy often leads to one or more programs that may be established to carry out the policy. For example, changes to child welfare legislation which incorporate both mediation and family group conferencing as alternative methods of dealing with child protection concerns will lead to the development of programs to promote these approaches. And even if family group conferencing is identified as a separate policy under a new legislative framework that includes several new policy initiatives, there may be a variety of family group conferencing programs set up across the province. Second, most of the methods used to evaluate programs will be used to evaluate the impact of more general policies. However, the term 'program evaluation' is generally used to refer to measuring the effects from a specific program, whereas 'policy evaluation' is concerned with the broader assessment of a general course of action, a framework or piece of legislation.

A policy study may involve a large-scale study of multiple sites, or a review of program evaluation results from studies of individual programs. In addition, a policy study often involves a review of research or evaluation studies on the topic, which have been conducted in other jurisdictions. As indicated, policy evaluation studies often combine direct research with secondary analysis of research that has been conducted in the area. In the example noted above, a specific program evaluation might be conducted on the family conferencing initiative launched by a particular agency. However, government may be interested in whether family conferencing in general is an important policy initiative and whether it should be expanded to new sites. Thus, a more general policy evaluation of all sites might be commissioned with specific guidelines to examine effectiveness and efficiency on a province-wide basis. As well, specific policy questions pertaining to the feasibility of expanding this policy initiative may be included as part of the evaluation.

The use of research to inform policy development is not the rule in Canada, and we have much to learn from the approach that led to the development of the *Children Act* (1989) in Britain (see Box 4.2). While the use of government-funded research for policy development is not widespread in Canada, evaluation studies are often commissioned to examine specific policy issues (see the example in Box 4.3). From a provincial perspective, Quebec, more so than other provinces, appears to take a more systematic approach to using evaluation research in policy-making in that it funds studies for this purpose in particular fields of practice, such as child sexual abuse. Furthermore, an important requirement is that these studies involve close collaboration between researchers and practitioners.

An important consideration is the extent to which policy is shaped by research and evaluation information about what works. Too often our knowledge about what works in the social services is contradictory or limited to results from small studies that are unable to accurately predict the long-term effects of new initiatives. The uncertainty of social service knowledge has produced an increased interest in outcome-based research and evidence-based practice, although the use of evaluation research to shape provincial social policy still remains quite limited. On occasion, the weight of research and knowledge about a particular intervention target or strategy becomes a central impetus for new policy development. For example, evidence from multiple studies on the value of childhood development programs has led to the promotion of these programs for children who may be at risk in their early years in many provinces. As well, the adoption of new initiatives is encouraged when evaluation research is able to influence a shift in public opinion, and in these circumstances government is more likely to respond. More attention to the use of evaluation research to shape policy is an important way of connecting policy to practice. While this requires a greater commitment on the part of governments to fund applied research, the growing interest in evidence-based practice may help to encourage this trend.

It is also important to note that all governments do not react in the same fashion to social science information. While government responds to shifts in knowledge or public opinion, there are what may be termed 'early' and 'late movers' on policy initiatives. These differences in responses by governments are shaped by several factors. The most important of these are the availability of resources and whether the evidence from policy or program evaluations is consistent with existing government priorities. If the results from evaluation studies are consistent with a government's general priorities or its ideology, it is more likely that these results will be used to help shape specific policies; conversely, those that contradict a government's general policy direction or its ideological stance are more likely to be ignored.

Box 4.2 Using Research and Evaluation for Policy Development

The adoption of the *Children Act* (1989) in Britain is widely recognized as the culmination of a decade-long process that included systematic consideration of research and evaluation findings documenting the effects of various types of social care arrangements on children and their families. This process resulted in legislation that places an increased emphasis on partnerships with parents, even when children are removed from their homes. For example, guardianship options provide for a continuing role for parents whenever feasible, and there is a great deal of emphasis on family visiting and connections while children are in care. New provisions also place increased emphasis on service options designed to support children in their own homes. In addition, service planning now includes more emphasis on the needs of the child and the outcomes that result from the services provided. New systems have been designed to focus attention on these aspects of the case planning process, and resources have been invested to ensure the implementation of these systems within local authorities throughout Britain.

At a general level, program or policy evaluation involves the systematic collection, analysis, and reporting of information about a program, service, or intervention for use in decision-making. While this identifies evaluation as a technical process, Herman, Morris, and Fitz-Gibbon (1987) note that policy expectations, resources, and other constraints as well as social, organizational, political, and demographic factors significantly affect the implementation of evaluation studies and the utilization of results. These issues blur the lines between tasks within policy and program evaluation in suggesting that both involve activities that are partly social, partly political, and only partly technical. Evaluation in policy-making, then, reflects an action orientation, that is, it is concerned with the adjustment of policy goals, approaches to implementation, or the decision to either extend or terminate a policy.

Program or policy studies make use of methods associated with different approaches to evaluation; Herman, Morris, and Fitz-Gibbon (1987) distinguish between formative and summative approaches. Whereas a formative evaluation examines program or policy processes and is designed to produce information to assist a program in its development, a summative evaluation examines the outcomes, the impact, and the efficiency of a policy.

Formative evaluations, sometimes referred to as process evaluations, are

Box 4.3 Using Policy Research and Evaluation in Policy Analysis

In 1995, the Manitoba Department of Family Services made a policy decision to launch an early intervention program for separating and divorcing parents modelled, in part, on programs first developed in the United States. The three-hour education program, known as *For the Sake of the Children*, provided information on the needs of children experiencing their parents' separation, and it outlined basic strategies to be used in developing a cooperative approach to co-parenting. The program was initially launched as a pilot project with an evaluation component designed to assess implementation and impact, the feasibility of extending the program, and the advisability of making the program mandatory in cases of divorce. The evaluation that was completed provided an assessment of the main effects of this new initiative. The study also identified options, potential consequences, and costs for program extension and expansion. In this case, the evaluation of the program became a key source of information in analyzing the future effects of policy-making in this field. Based on the results from this policy study, the program has been extended throughout the province and has been expanded to six hours in order to incorporate additional information and skill-building activities. (Adapted from McKenzie and Guberman, 1997)

concerned with the components of a policy or program, what services are being provided, and whether the policy or program is reaching those for whom it was intended. Implementation studies involving an assessment of policy processes are particularly relevant to new policies because they attempt to describe and tease out the details of the policy in order to ascertain what is causing certain effects or whether the policy is being implemented as planned. Two major sets of issues are considered: 1) coverage or actual participation in the program by the intended target population; and 2) service delivery (including the entire sequence of activities undertaken to achieve policy objectives). If a policy or program is not operating effectively, an implementation evaluation can help to determine what has gone wrong and what improvements can be made. Often these problems exist in one or more of the following areas: a) a policy approach or design that fails to meet the needs of service users; b) a lack of program acceptance caused by the attitudes of staff members or administrative policies that create barriers to access; c) program management; and d) program costs (Love, 1992).

Summative evaluations concentrate on policy or program outcomes, impacts, and efficiency. An outcome study is concerned with the extent to which a policy meets its objectives, and, where those objectives involve changes for service users, how long those changes last. Efficiency evaluation is concerned with the ratio of benefits to costs; various forms of cost-utility analysis may be performed, including benefit-cost and cost-effectiveness studies. Box 4.4 summarizes how evaluation has been used to assess program outcomes and costs in a particular policy field, and some of the difficulties that can arise. As this example from the family preservation field demonstrates, a narrow focus on efficiency may divert attention from a more comprehensive review of outcomes. This example also illustrates how multiple evaluations of a new policy may highlight differences in the outcomes that may be experienced during implementation. Two important implications are apparent. First, major policy initiatives that are promoted or adopted on the basis of preliminary evaluation findings may fail to live up to expectations. Second, even when research findings are positive, policy analysis requires us to consider a wide range of studies, assess these results critically, and consider their relevance to our particular policy environment.

Box 4.4 Assessing Conflicting Results in Policy Evaluation

The conflicting views supported by research and evaluation in policy development are illustrated by reviewing general developments in the field of family preservation. Early research, associated with the Homebuilders Model (a social support program developed in the State of Washington), demonstrated a significant reduction in the number of children in care and related cost savings through the application of a service model stressing short-term intensive services to families in which children were at risk of out-of-home placement. This focus on efficiency and cost-savings led to legislation that mandated such services in the United States, and there was widespread adoption of family preservation programs. In many states different models of service were developed and implemented. More recent evaluations have raised questions about the methods used in early studies and their results. In some cases, family preservation programs have been linked to situations that led to increased risk for some children. However, those studies have also been criticized on methodological grounds, and the debate between advocates and detractors of family preservation as a solution to the high rate of children in out-of-home care continues, with each side identifying somewhat different outcomes as consequences of this policy choice.

Formative and summative approaches to policy evaluation have been discussed as separate strategies; however, most studies combine these approaches. For example, an evaluation may be concerned with both whether the policy is being implemented as intended, and what the effects of the policy are on service users. However, we stress that the evaluation of new policies requires a special focus on formative issues; that is, the activities and the organizational processes associated with implementation. While both quantitative and qualitative methods are relevant to such studies, the collection of data often involves qualitative interviews with key informants, service user feedback, and a review of documents. Triangulation, which involves collecting data from more than one source, using different data collection methods, or using different investigators, is recommended in such studies.

An evaluation of a family support program in a child welfare agency (Frankel et al., 1996) illustrates a focus on implementation or process issues and the use of triangulation. Because the policy under examination had been in place for approximately three years, attention was also given to documenting some of the policy's early outcomes. One component of the evaluation involved an examination of service users who had received services over the past eighteen months. A file review was completed, but service contracts that had been signed provided incomplete information on both service activities and outcomes. An interview schedule, which identified various types of service activities and outcomes, was then constructed and pre-tested. The members of the service triad (service user, social worker, and family support worker) were then interviewed to obtain information both on services provided and related outcomes. In addition, outcomes were assessed according to criteria such as the number of children admitted to care, days of care, and current status of the situation. Results from these various activities provided a reasonably accurate picture of the services provided by this program, as well as some information on outcomes. When this information was combined with a pre/post study of current service users that applied several standardized child and family well-being measures, it was possible to provide the agency with a good picture of both implementation processes and the early impact of this family support policy.

A primary focus on outcomes may become the purpose of evaluation in mature programs, and in such studies the use of control or comparison groups can provide additional evidence of whether the policy or program is responsible for observed changes in behaviour or outcomes. In recent years, computer-based monitoring systems that incorporate outcome measures have become quite popular, and such systems have the advantage of providing ongoing feedback to program managers and service providers. While these systems are intended to be helpful, certain disadvantages must be recognized. These systems may not be designed to incorporate feedback from service users, and they usually retrieve and record only quantitative information. Thus, these approaches to evaluation may omit the opinions and experiences of service users. In addition, they often fail to promote community and service-user empowerment because institutions, such as government agencies, control both the technology and the information.

The evaluation dilemma posed here is not easy to resolve. Information on needs and resources, program design, activities, effectiveness, and costs are essential requirements for good policy-making. Methods for program and policy monitoring as well as carefully designed impact studies can help to provide this information. But these approaches are not sufficient. We argue that such approaches must be accompanied by more participatory methods if we are to generate the kind of evaluation information needed to design programs and policies that respond most effectively to the differing cultural and social needs of service users.

While participatory methods are not new, there has been a recent renewal of interest in some of these approaches. One of the authors was involved in a community-based research project that featured two rounds of focus group discussions to launch the process of developing standards of child welfare practice for eight First Nations communities (McKenzie, 1997). Books such as *Empowerment Evaluation* (Fetterman, Kaftarian, and Wandersman, 1996) and *Action Research* (Stringer, 1996) outline principles and methods that can be used to promote greater community and service-user control over both the evaluation process and results. Similar issues are raised by Ristock and Pennell (1996), who explore the issue of community research as empowerment within a framework that incorporates both feminist and postmodern perspectives. As well, Health Canada has published a handbook on how stories from service users can be used in health promotion and evaluation (Labonte and Feather, 1996). These approaches to evaluation are valuable because they include the voices of service users. However, to date they have not received sufficient attention by senior policy-makers, including politicians. These individuals often fail to appreciate the results of these studies because the data are regarded as 'soft' or less valid when compared to quantitative information on effectiveness.

To this point we have described policy analysis and evaluation as if all activities were carried out in relation to a single policy. In fact, policy-making often involves the development of several policies embedded within a more general policy direction. This requires the coordinated assessment and development of several policies at different levels, often simultaneously. For example, a new general policy in health care designed to integrate community and institutional-based services is likely to require a new role for hospitals, as well as several new policies that might affect training, utilization, and expenditures within hospitals. For community-based health care services there will also be a number of new policies, such as an increased emphasis on home care that may emerge from this more general policy change. In circumstances such as these, policy analysis and evaluation must be concerned with the actual or anticipated effects of several different policies. Different methods and sources of data as well as different approaches to analysis should be used in more comprehensive policy studies, and multiple policy recommendations that reflect a more coordinated approach to policy development in a particular field of practice is the desired goal. Unfortunately, this more integrated approach to policy evaluation and reform is all too rare in the human services.

An Integrated Model for Policy Analysis

In our discussion of the formulation stage of the policy-making process, we provided an example of how a special lens can be used to link content and process issues in policy analysis. Policy analysis in the human services should consider whether a special lens is required to direct attention to such issues as gender and culture. Although this focus is essential, the analytical process needs to be located within a general framework that enables application to a wide range of policy problems. An integrated model that includes both content and process

group action; thus, it is relevant in assessing the potential strength of interest group influence that might be mobilized around the issue.

In examining an existing policy at the agency or program level, there are some additional questions to consider:

a) What is the basis for policy legitimacy and where does this authority or responsibility lie?
b) Does the desired outcome require system change or system maintenance?
c) What is the level of agreement regarding the policy?
d) What is the nature of linkages between the agency and other relevant systems in the policy environment?

2. Identification of Value Criteria

The second general step in policy analysis is the identification of relevant value criteria. The criteria-based model for policy-making encompasses both general criteria and selective criteria that are specific to the policy issue under consideration. Effectiveness and efficiency are essential criteria, and efficiency assessment may include strategies such as cost, cost-effectiveness, or benefit-cost analysis. Another consideration is adequacy. Adequacy and effectiveness are related concepts, yet it is sometimes important to distinguish between the two. Adequacy can be defined as *the provision of benefits or services to meet the identified need*. Effectiveness, on the other hand, is directly related to the outcome goals and objectives of the policy. Government may develop a work-training program to assist unemployed trainees to re-enter the labour force, sustain employment, and become less dependent on welfare. This goal reflects an effectiveness criterion. However, in assessing the adequacy of the program one may examine the specific elements of the training program to determine their relevancy to the goal of employability in a particular field. As indicated, in examining adequacy more attention is directed to the specific intervention or services that are to be provided.

Two other criteria we include are the policy's impact on rights, statuses, and social justice, and the ability of the policy to promote self-determination among service users.

An important issue is whether or not service users and first-line staff have had opportunities to participate in shaping the policy response under consideration. This participatory element is often omitted from general policy-making models, although, in practice, efforts are sometimes made to elicit some input from these constituencies. Process models of policy analysis are more likely to address questions of public participation, and this is regarded as an important consideration in policy-making and analysis in the human services.

Another important consideration is what Flynn (1992, p. 90) refers to as the SCRAPS test. This test is designed to focus special attention on issues of sexism, classism, racism, ageism, and poverty; the acronym is intended to remind the policy analyst that those who are the victims of such discrimination are likely to receive only 'scraps' without any compensatory attention paid to these issues. During this second step, one can also adopt a special lens that focuses attention on cultural, gender, or other issues. For example, policies that are likely to have a particular impact on women should be assessed by questions emerging from the gender-lens perspective.

The specification of value criteria is included at an early stage in the policy analysis process, although it should be noted that values can also be examined later, particularly in assessing an existing agency policy or in completing an evaluation study of a policy. It is worth repeating that any approach to policy analysis that gives limited attention to values will be incomplete.

Three issues are particularly relevant to the value criteria stage in policy analysis. First, the model of policy analysis outlined here requires the explicit identification of criteria to be used in the assessment process. While criteria are always used in policy analysis they are often not explicitly identified. There is an advantage to being explicit about value criteria because these will have a major effect on the policy decision. The use of explicit criteria serves the interests of transparency and accountability in policy analysis.

Second, value criteria are often used to assess both the existing policy response and alternatives that are generated to respond to the problem. However, they are particularly important in the assessment of alternatives and final selection of the preferred policy choice.

Finally, as noted in Chapter 2 in our discussion of the value criteria model of policy-making, it is also important to recognize that the selection of value criteria is not intended to be an arbitrary exercise that allows analysts to simply impose their particular values on the policy under consideration. Like the conclusions emerging from other types of data, value criteria must be logically defended and justified in order to be accepted as valid. Some value criteria, such as effectiveness and efficiency, are likely to be considered in most policy reviews. Others will be selected based on the issue being considered. Examples of value criteria are illustrated in Table 4.4; however, it is not necessary to use all these criteria in the assessment of any particular policy issue.

We have argued earlier that policy-making in the human services imposes a professional responsibility to address issues pertaining to social justice. In spite of this ethical obligation, it is apparent that differing interpretations of value criteria can arise. However, explicit attention to values will, at least, permit more open dialogue and debate about the normative aspects of the policy issue being considered. While we stipulate this as an obligation in an ethical approach to policy analysis, we are aware of the fact that this is often not done. In fact, new policy proposals often contain language designed to obscure rather than clarify underlying values. For example, the language of community partnerships and decentralization is often used to disguise a government's intent to off-load service responsibility to community groups and organizations. Another job in analyzing public policies, then, is distinguishing between rhetoric and reality!

3. Assessment of Alternatives

The third step in policy analysis involves collecting data on alternatives to be considered in relation to value criteria and the problem analysis and goal selection step. Here one is estimating both the anticipated and unanticipated effects of policy alternatives. Both quantitative and qualitative data collection approaches are relevant, and techniques such as forecasting, social indicator analysis, survey research, and other types of program evaluation strategies may be used.

New policies often emerge without adequate attention to the lessons that can be learned from research studies of various aspects of the policy or similar policies adopted elsewhere. This may be a result of strongly held political or ideological beliefs, which lead to little or no attention being paid to the lessons from research. In these circumstances, policy-makers may omit the policy analysis stage of policy development entirely, or use it narrowly to justify a policy decision that has already been made. For example, many critics felt that the federal government's 1996 reforms to Unemployment Insurance followed a process of analysis, including public consultation, that served primarily to justify a decision that had already been made rather than to identify and consider seriously a range of options for policy reform. In cases such as these, research studies or consultation processes have little integrity and even less influence. Given this scenario, what are the options? One alternative is to encourage external groups to complete an analysis of such policies. These may provide one or more alternative viewpoints on possible effects. Social Planning Councils, the Canadian Council on Social Development, the Canadian Centre for Policy Alternatives, and the National Council of Welfare are but a few of the organizations that carry out such studies. In particular, the National Council of Welfare is well known for its efforts to include an assessment of the impact of government policies on service users.

At a general level, policy tasks at this point may conclude with a clear identification of anticipated consequences. If policies pertain to agency-level issues or require a careful consideration of service delivery questions, this will be insufficient, however. In such cases, an additional concern will be the effects of policy change on organizational functioning. This may require an assessment of the following: the nature of authority, influence, and leadership; patterns of communication; and constraints on policy adoption, including any anticipated resistance to change.

4. Feasibility Assessment

Feasibility assessment is identified here as a fourth step in policy analysis. It is included as a separate step because of its particular relevance to analysis in agency- or program-level policies, and its importance to implementation issues. In assessing feasibility, it is important to consider the relative power of the policy. For example, is legal compliance required or is compliance optional? Resource requirements and their availability are also key considerations.

Two other questions may be important. First, does the policy give rise to newly perceived self-interests that need to be considered? For example, new federal legislation on gun control acted as a mobilizing force for the anti–gun-control lobby. In turn, this required the organization of the Coalition For Gun Control, which played a key role in promoting the adoption of this legislation. Second, is there a logical link between policy options and the original problem as defined, including research or theoretical support showing that the intervention is likely to achieve the intended results? This question entails examining whether new policy options are likely to address the problem, and, if so, to what extent.

5. Recommendations

The final step in policy analysis involves recommendations that may include support for or criticism of a particular strategy and the specification of anticipated or realized effects of particular policy. The strengths and weaknesses of a limited number of policy options may also be summarized at this point, if the intent is to present a range of options to senior policy-makers for final selection. If this approach is taken, selected alternatives should be considered in relation to value criteria and their ability to address the policy problem.

Table 4.4 summarizes the integrated model for policy analysis. Although this model provides only general guidelines for application, it includes elements that encourage connections between the realities of practice and the more general policy questions confronting policy-makers. For example, the identification of key actors and interest groups at the problem-definition step provides information about who is exercising influence at this point in the process. The inclusion of both general and policy-specific value criteria permit the incorporation of elements that may promote increased staff and service user involvement while at the same time answering general questions about effectiveness and efficiency. The addition of a feasibility assessment step directs attention to the implementation stage in the policy process; at this stage, the interests of policy makers and practitioners are most likely to either collide or to coalesce in a new approach to service delivery.

Conclusion

It is important to emphasize the point made in the introduction to the chapter that in most examples of policy-making the stages do not unfold in a linear pattern. Thus information gained in the formulation stage may alter the framing of the problem as established in the initiation stage. Indeed the lessons learned in evaluation may well result in changes in each stage of the process.

In this chapter, we have presented policy analysis as a set of tasks that are integral to all except the execution stage of the policy-making process. In doing so we have distinguished between problem and policy analysis and have described the analysis of existing policies as tasks to be located in the evaluation stage of the process. A general model to be used in completing tasks pertaining to policy analysis has also been presented.

Table 4.4 An Integrated Model for Social Policy Analysis

Step One: Problem Identification and Goal Specification

1. Problem description: nature and scope.
2. Identification of needs and strengths.
3. Causal factors, including assumptions, theories for explanation, and key historical factors.
4. Targets for change and expected outcomes (goals).
5. Key actors and interest groups that shape problem recognition and definition, including their power and influence.

Step Two: Identification of Value Criteria

1. General criteria to be considered:
   a) Effectiveness
   b) Efficiency
   c) Adequacy
   d) Impact on rights, statuses, and social justice
   e) Impact on consumer self-determination
   f) Level of staff and consumer involvement
   g) SCRAPS test or application of a special lens
2. Identify selective criteria specific to the policy under consideration, and provide necessary support for their inclusion.

Step Three: Assessment of Alternatives

1. Identify alternatives to be considered.
2. Collect quantitative and qualitative data on alternatives to be assessed in relation to problem analysis, goal selection, and relevant value criteria.

Step Four: Feasibility Assessment (especially for agency- or program-level policies)

1. Identify the relative power of the policy, e.g., whether or not it requires legal compliance.
2. Identify the resource requirements and availability.
3. Consider whether the policy gives rise to newly perceived self-interests that need to be considered.
4. Examine whether there is a logical link (theoretical or otherwise) between the policy and the problem or goals initially identified.

Step Five: Recommendations

1. Evaluate the policy both in relation to intended goals and in relation to the identified means for goal achievement, and/or specify anticipated or actual effects flowing from a particular policy.
2. If requested, summarize the strengths and weaknesses of optional policy choices in relation to problem analysis and value criteria.

Recommended Reading

1. For a comprehensive review of a number of key issues in Canadian social policy, see J. Rice and M. Prince, *Changing Politics of Canadian Social Policy* (Toronto: University of Toronto Press, 2000).

2. See J. Flynn, *Social Agency Policy*, 2nd edn (Chicago: Nelson-Hall, 1992) for more information on process and content approaches to policy analysis at the organizational or departmental level.

3. Further information on the gender-lens approach to policy analysis can be obtained from Status of Women Canada, *Gender-Based Analysis: A Guide to Policy-Making* (Ottawa: Status of Women Canada, 1996).

4. B. Jansson, *Becoming an Effective Policy Advocate*, 4th edn (Pacific Grove, CA: Brooks/Cole/Thomson Learning, 2003) is recommended for those interested in policy practice and policy advocacy.

5. For further information on problem analysis, needs assessment, and goal-setting in policy-making, see P. Kettner, R. Moroney, and L. Martin, *Designing and Managing Programs: An Effectiveness-Based Approach*, 2nd edn (Thousand Oaks, CA: Sage, 1999). See Chapters 2 to 4 on problem analysis and needs assessment and Chapters 5 to 7 on goal-setting.

Notes

1. In 1994, the federal Minister of Human Resources introduced a Green Paper on social security reforms, and a parliamentary committee held public hearings in major centres across the country. However, groups and individuals wishing to make presentations had to apply in advance to be heard, and government staff and politicians reviewed these applications and selected those who would be allowed to present briefs at these public hearings.

Chapter Five

Implementing Policy

As indicated in the previous chapter, there is a compelling reason for devoting a separate chapter to implementation: it is the stage of the policy process where the connections between policy and practice become virtually inseparable. At the end of what is often a long and laborious process of development, policies eventually result in programs or services provided by practitioners. At the point when practitioners take control they have a variety of options: they can implement the policy as intended by head office, they can improve the policy by ensuring that it complements existing ones and fits with the unique needs of their community, or they can sabotage it by refusing to translate it into day-to-day practice.

In some circumstances before policies leave head office, a great deal of time and attention is given to planning for implementation. Head office staff attempt to anticipate the issues and problems that inevitably will be faced. And of course the more changes required by the new policy, the more complex and larger in size the organization, the more issues and problems will occur. Thus a provincial department of social services that has passed new legislation in child welfare will have to take into account how the changes will affect the judicial system, other departments, and community organizations. As well, field offices across the province will react differently to the introduction of new programs and to the prospect of changing practice.

That said, we recognize that in many instances head office staff have insufficient time to devote to implementation. Initiation and formulation are the most creative and exciting stages in the policy process. Once a new policy has been approved, new opportunities or crises demand the attention of policy-makers. Having experienced the adrenalin rush of policy development, policy-makers may lose interest in what often seems as the tedious work of implementation.

In this chapter, we address both the head- and field-office responsibilities for implementation process giving proportionately more time and attention to the field office. We begin by reviewing the literature and then turn to a consideration of more recent experiences in Canada.

What the Literature Reveals about Implementation

The vast majority of the scholarly literature on implementation is confined to the US and contained within a fairly brief period of time. Its beginnings can be traced to the early 1970s with the publication of *Implementation: How Great Hopes in Washington Are Dashed in Oakland* (Pressman and Wildavsky, 1973). Its demise occurred some 20 years later. The Pressman and Wildavsky book described the implementation of an economic development program funded by the federal government and implemented in Oakland, California. As the subtitle indicates, the story is one of disappointment not because of any wrongdoing or incompetence, but mainly because of the many and largely unanticipated difficulties encountered between the ideas identified in Washington and the realities experienced in Oakland.

A notable contribution of *Implementation* is the concept of 'clearance points'. Like a barge passing through a number of locks where the water has to be raised in order to allow it to continue, policies encounter crucial junctures where opportunities exist to alter direction. The longer the chain from head to field offices, the vaguer the statement of policy objectives, the more clearance points in place, the less likely the policy will be implemented as intended. The authors of *Implementation* argued that in order to improve implementation the number of clearance points should be kept to a minimum, objectives should be stated clearly and precisely, and the head office should take charge of the process. As the research continued, this message came to be known as the top-down approach to implementation.

After considerable experience, researchers using the top-down approach concluded that there are a number of conditions necessary for effective implementation. The conditions are summarized as:

a) clear and consistent objectives;
b) an adequate causal theory;
c) a structured implementation process to ensure compliance by implementing officials;
d) committed and skillful implementors;
e) the support of interest groups; and
f) a stable environment. (Adapted from Sabatier, 1986)

Although theoretically appealing, these conditions are rarely evident in practice. Thus, many years later a review of the literature on the implementation of innovative child welfare programs found that the above conditions had seldom been in place (Cameron et al., 2001). In addition, the top-down approach was severely criticized for its overly optimistic assumption that the implementors would be both skillful and committed. This assumption failed to recognize the realities of the work life of first-line practitioners who in many instances regard new policies as unnecessarily adding to and complicating a crisis-ridden work environment.

A different perspective on implementation emerged with the work of Walter

Williams who was the director of the research and evaluation section of the Office of Economic Opportunity in the United States in the 1960s. During this period, Williams came to realize that many programs introduced by the Office of Economic Opportunity had not been implemented as intended and thus it was difficult, if not impossible, to determine program outcomes.

Together with Richard Elmore and other colleagues at the Institute for Research on Governmental Affairs, University of Washington, Williams focused attention on identifying the complexities inherent within implementation and cautioned that while useful, implementation research 'should not become the new hope for technical ascendance. It should not become the new bandwagon seeking the sure technological fix' (Williams, 1976, p. 292). In his later work Williams came to the view that first-line practitioners in field offices were the most important people in determining whether a policy would be implemented as intended:

> The main message of the implementation perspective is that the central focus of pol-
> icy making should be on the point of service delivery. . . . After the big decisions get
> made at the highest levels, what is done by those who implement and operate pro-
> grams and projects has the critical impact on evolving policy. (Williams, 1980, p. 5)

Elmore carried the case further by arguing that policy-making should be turned on its head. Rather than emanating from the top (i.e., the head office) policy should be made in a 'backwards mapping fashion'. 'The closer one is to the source of the problem, the greater is one's ability to influence it; and the problem solving ability of complex systems depends not on hierarchical control but on maximizing discretion at the point where the problem is most immediate' (Elmore, 1982, p. 21). This perspective came to be known as the bottom-up approach to implementation.

By the 1980s several scholars concluded that neither approach was satisfactory. Two attempts to combine the best of both are briefly noted here. Elmore converted his notion of backward mapping to forward mapping in which he acknowledged that leadership in policy-making usually emanated from politicians and senior bureaucrats. However, these policy-makers neglect field offices at their peril, and meshing the interests and commitment of both those at the top and the bottom of the organization is essential for effective implementation.

Another attempt to synthesize the approaches came from Sabatier:

> In short the synthesis adopts the bottom-uppers unit of analysis—a whole variety of
> public and private actors involved with a policy problem—as well as their concerns
> with understanding the perspectives and strategies of all major categories of actors
> (not simply program proponents). It then combines this starting point with top-
> downers' concern with the manner in which socio-economic conditions and legal
> instruments constrain behaviour. It applies this synthesized perspective to the analy-
> sis of policy change over periods of a decade or more. . . . Finally the synthesis
> adopts the intellectual style or methodological perspective of many top-downers in
> its willingness to utilize fairly abstract constructs. (Sabatier, 1986, p. 38)

Sabatier concluded that the support of an advocacy coalition was a key component for effective implementation; indeed the combination of champions within an organization and influential supporters in the policy environment can go a long way to ensuring that a policy is adopted. But even this combination is not a sufficient guarantee that first-line staff will be committed to implementation.

Another important contribution to understanding the implementation process came from Paul Berman at the Rand Institute. Berman focused attention on the kind of policy being implemented and argued that there is a distinct difference between policies that demand a programmed approach and those requiring adaptation during implementation. Essentially, the argument is that some policies can be laid down and prescribed from head office while others must be adapted to the needs of local communities and different types of service users. The differences between the two approaches are determined by assessing the following factors:

1. scope of the change;
2. soundness of the theory or technology underlying the change;
3. amount of agreement among those affected as to the desirability of the change;
4. degree of control over clearance points;
5. availability of resources; and
6. stability of the environment. (Berman, 1980)

Analyzing the policy using these criteria determines whether it can be implemented in a rather mechanistic, rule-bound fashion or whether a considerable amount of discretion must be left to the implementors. According to Berman, policies that must be implemented in an adaptive fashion are characterized by one or more of the following characteristics: radical and/or extensive change, a tentative or weak theory underlying the change, disagreement regarding objectives of the change by those affected, limited control over clearance points, inadequate or inappropriate resources, and a turbulent environment. In the human services, implementors are primarily practitioners and they are integral to the implementation process; it is their judgment and the use of discretion that has a major impact on implementation outcomes.

By the late 1980s, the interest of the social scientists noted above in the study of implementation had waned considerably. A search of the literature bears out this contention (Peirson, 2002). A total of 90 articles and books on implementation were published in the 70s and 80s, but after 1990 to the present time only 31 could be identified. Williams had warned us not to see implementation as the newest technological fix, but some researchers had pounced on it in the hopes that it would point the way to effective policy-making. Some promising leads were discovered. For example, research revealed what should have been clear all along, namely, that a policy announced is not a policy implemented and that implementation is a neglected but crucial stage of the policy process. The research also pointed to the complexities involved in implementation and the notion of clearance points provided policy-makers with an opportunity to reduce complexity by eliminating some of these junctures. Above all, the bottom-up studies identified the pivotal significance of the field office.

Whether these insights proved to be useful to policy-makers is a moot question. One scholar argued that the research had contributed little in terms of developing 'a coherent, systematic body of knowledge or identifying strategies for effective policy implementation which would be of practical assistance to policy-makers' (Palumbo, 1987, p. 91). A similar view came from Alexander who asserted studies of implementation had lacked 'an integrating framework' and 'if we continue to pursue this multiplicity of approaches without any integrating framework we cannot expect anything but the lack of convergence that has characterized the field to date' (Alexander, 1985, p. 411).

In response to this multiplicity of approaches, Alexander proposed a 'conceptualization of the policy implementation process [that] sees the transformation of intent into action as a continuous interactive process' (Alexander, 1985, p. 412). The *policy-program-implementation-process* consists of the development of a policy in response to a problem, the translation of the policy into specific programs, and the implementation of these programs. One contribution of this conceptualization was the recognition that what happens in each stage affects other stages in a reciprocal fashion. Thus, the experience gained in the implementation stage may result in altering the design of programs and indeed the premises underlying the initial policy stage. Despite its promise, this integrative model did not attract the attention of policy-makers. Alexander notes that he is 'not aware of where/when the model has actually been applied in empirical studies' nor of other efforts to further refine the model (Alexander, 2002).

There are many things that can go wrong in implementation, as illustrated by the example of gun control in Box 5.1. However, some relatively recent studies on the policy process in child welfare in Manitoba and British Columbia reveal that considerable care and attention was given to the implementation stage. We review these examples next to determine if they support the arguments of Palumbo and Alexander.

Implementing Policy in Child Welfare: The Experiences of Two Provinces

McKenzie's (1989) study of the implementation processes in the decentralization of child welfare services in the city of Winnipeg during the 1980s provides some insights into the complexities of the implementation stage in policy-making. In 1982, the Manitoba government made a decision to dissolve the Children's Aid Society of Winnipeg, an agency criticized for its highly centralized and specialized approach to service. Six new, community-based child welfare agencies located in the voluntary sector were established, each governed by board of directors. The policy intent was to establish a more responsive, accessible service system that would include an increased emphasis on early intervention and family support. An implementation-planning phase, which included a central coordinating committee, was established and by April 1985 the six new agencies opened their doors.

Box 5.1 An Implementation Disaster

A conspicuous and highly controversial example of implementation gone awry is the attempt of the federal government to establish a gun registry. The Act requiring owners to register all guns was passed in 1994, but owners were given until 1 January 2003 to complete the registration process and pay the fee. According to the editorial 'Can the Gun Registry be Saved?' in the *Globe and Mail* (4 January 2003, p. A14) only two-thirds of guns have been registered. While some gun-owners objected to the Act on the grounds that it was an unnecessary infringement of their rights, others, including the Canadian Association of Chiefs of Police, have supported the Act on the grounds that it has the potential to reduce crime.

Both critics and supporters have been disappointed if not enraged by the difficulties in implementation that have plagued the Act and have caused the costs to escalate from the 1994 estimate of $2 million to a projected cost in 2004–5 of $860 million. One of the chief difficulties has been the failure to develop and maintain the computer program to record the registrations. A long list of changes in the contracts to outside companies to develop appropriate software has not only been responsible for increasing costs, but has also caused endless frustration for owners trying to register their guns. The editorial concludes, 'The goal is sound. The execution stunk.'

As documented by McKenzie, within two years the number of service-delivery sites had increased from 6 to more than 20, and community advisory committees within a number of agencies had been established. These committees played a prominent role in promoting prevention programs, including resource centres and community development initiatives. There was a dramatic increase in outreach programs even though the nature and scope of these programs varied significantly across agencies. Increased service accessibility arising from this policy change also resulted in an increase in service demand; there was an increase in requests for voluntary services and an increase in child protection referrals. For example, the number of children in care increased by more than 60 per cent, and the number of family service cases almost doubled in the two-year period following decentralization (McKenzie, 1989, p. 153). Although the rate of change also increased in other areas of the province during this time period, Winnipeg's increase was approximately three times that of the rest of the province. While the increased number of children in care was disconcerting to policy-makers, it is a matter of debate as to whether this indicator reflected a positive change in service quality and outcomes. It is of some interest to note that the increase in caseloads experienced in the initial stage reached a plateau and has changed only modestly over the past 15 years. There is much less doubt about the influence of the policy change on outreach, prevention, and the involvement of the community in child and family service issues. All increased significantly, and these results occurred because agencies were given significant autonomy to develop initiatives that reflected local needs and priorities.

Closer analysis of this policy and the approach to implementation gives rise to some interesting observations. First, policy-makers underestimated the extent to which the demand for services would increase, and a subsequent review of workloads resulted in additional funding. Second, the coordination of services within agency boundaries increased with decentralization because staff were more visible and connected to other service providers in their neighbourhoods. However, service coordination across agency boundaries was more problematic. This problem had not been fully anticipated, and community-wide responses to issues such as child abuse were criticized as being inconsistent and somewhat worse under the new decentralized system. Third, the effects of the policy change on first-line staff were somewhat contradictory. Staff experienced higher workloads and relatively high stress levels between 1985 and 1987. At the same time, they had a relatively positive view of the policy change because they were able to participate in shaping service-delivery approaches in their local units. These results tend to provide some support for the position that a synthesis between a more centralized and adaptive approach to implementation is required. A more centralized response is required to affect change in resources, system-wide coordination, and compliance with general standards, although even at this level a commitment to make these adjustments must be present. More responsive and effective services are also encouraged if implementing officials at the local level are given enough autonomy to develop their own approaches to service provision, within general guidelines, including the development of working relationships with other community service providers.

In British Columbia, the *Child, Family and Community Service Act* and the *Child, Youth and Family Advocacy Act* were passed by the provincial legislature in June 1994 but were not proclaimed by the lieutenant-governor until January 1996. The period between passage and proclamation (the date that the Acts became law) was devoted to planning for implementation. The Acts were the consequence of two comprehensive community-consultation processes into child welfare conducted by the Ministry of Social Services in 1991 to 1992. One consultation was devoted to the needs and views on child welfare by the First Nations people of BC and it culminated in the report *Liberating Our Children, Liberating Our Nations* (Report of the Aboriginal Committee, 1992). The opinions of other citizens were expressed in *Making Changes: A Place to Start* (Report of the Community Panel, 1992).

Both community panel reports concluded that child welfare in BC required fundamental reform. The welfare of children should be seen in a societal and community context that recognized that poverty, inadequate housing, and the lack of supports to families severely impacts the ability of parents to care for their children. In addition, the reports criticized the 'social cop' approach to practice that restricted the role of child welfare staff to intrusive investigations.

The process of planning for the development of the new Acts and for their implementation consumed the time and attention of head-office staff for four years. Our attention here is focused on the two-year period between 1994 and 1996, and our sources of information include *Planning for Implementation of B.C.'s Child, Family and Community Service Act* (Durie and Armitage, 1996), and recent interviews with a senior staff member of the ministry who was a key member of the head-office implementation team.

If time, conscious attention to planning, and resources could ensure smooth implementation, the experience in BC exemplifies such a process. A beginning list of the painstaking efforts made during the process follows:

1. appointmenting of a head-office steering committee chaired by an assistant deputy minister and staffed by two staff members in the ministry who had extensive experience in child welfare;
2. forming regional committees to gain the input of first-line professionals; the regional committees were staffed by facilitators seconded from other positions in the region;
3. attending to the concerns of community organizations, sister ministries, the judicial system, and the BC Employees Union, all of which would be affected by the new legislation; and
4. establishing training sessions on a regional basis to acquaint staff with the objectives and provisions of the *Child, Family and Community Service Act* and the *Child, Youth and Family Advocacy Act*.

The primary reason for this careful planning was that these Acts were dedicated to changing the culture of the ministry. The plan sought to change in a very fundamental fashion the day-to-day practice of staff: from adversarial and intrusive to respectful and courteous; from working with individuals on a one-on-one basis to group and community approaches; and from investigation and referral to purposeful planning for change.

Yet, despite this care and attention, the legislation as eventually implemented departed in substantial ways from the vision outlined in *Making Changes: A Place to Start* (Report of the Community Panel, 1992). For example, the section calling for family conferences as a way of making plans for children in a collaborative fashion was not implemented until 2002. What happened?

Without doubt, the most important factor was the formation of a judicial inquiry in 1994 and its subsequent report one year later (Report of the Gove Inquiry into Child Protection, 1995). Given that the ministry had just concluded two substantial reviews of child welfare, that it had followed the recommendations of the reviews and developed two new Acts, and was heavily involved in the process of implementing these Acts, it is perplexing why a minister would decide to launch a judicial inquiry into the middle of this complex and demanding process. The answer is, of course, to be found in politics and the media. A child had been killed by his mother in a small Northern community, and the report by the then superintendent of child welfare into the circumstances of the death was deemed to be too defensive of the performance of staff. Although the minister and the premier at first found the report quite acceptable, it was severely criticized in the legislature and in the press. Bowing to the pressure, the minister sought to deflect attention from the ministry by firing the superintendent and launching an inquiry headed by Judge Thomas Gove.

Had the preliminary and final findings of the inquiry corresponded with those of the community panels, the only effect on the work of the ministry, and in particular on those charged with the responsibility of implementation, would have been the time and energy required to attend hearings and to respond to the many demands from the inquiry for information. But from quite early days it was evident that this was not to be. As noted above, the new Acts promoted a preventive, family support approach to service provision, while the inquiry came to favour a narrow emphasis on protecting children. Hence, conflicting messages began to swirl about the ministry and its objectives—messages that culminated in changes to the *Child, Family and Community Services Act* and in the establishment of a comprehensive, rigorous, and intrusive risk-assessment instrument.

This rather extensive discussion of the Gove Inquiry is important because it points to the salience of the policy environment. Clearly, the turbulent environment disrupted the plans and painstaking efforts of implementors. In an interview, a senior official in the ministry who had been heavily involved in both the development and implementation stages of the legislation identified two revealing criticisms of the process. First, he and other architects of the Act did not realize the extent to which the culture of the 'social cop' approach to practice was embedded in the ministry. First-line staff knew how to investigate, how to interview individuals preferably in their office, and how to refer families needing counselling or other services to community agencies. Although some had experimented successfully with group and community approaches, the majority clung to the practice with which they were familiar. Although, more staff might have been excited by the new approaches called for in the new legislation had not the messages emerging from the Gove Inquiry quickly dashed interest in new approaches. As Smale (1996) has noted, when all about them is changing, when organizational structures are being reconfigured, and when their practice is being scrutinized in the media, practitioners will remain committed to present modes of practice and shy away from ones that are unknown and risky.

The second criticism concerned the environment. In retrospect, the senior official noted that when major changes are involved, when the environment cannot be anticipated or controlled, the most effective strategy may well be to restrict detailed planning in head office, proclaim a new Act or new policy, and deal with difficulties as they arise—in short, to employ an adaptive approach to implementation. Although some planning is required, a lengthy drawn-out process allows resistance to mount and to magnify proposed changes to the point that they seem undesirable. After all, it is human nature to stay with the known, and as the literature on the planning of change has revealed, it will often be resisted unless incentives and rewards are provided to smooth the path of acceptance (see among other sources, Marris, 1986).

The example of the gun registry described earlier in the chapter (see Box 5.1) argues the case for combining programmed and adaptive approaches. In that example, the federal government failed to take into account the reactions of gun-owners and the limitations of computer systems to register the estimated 7.9 million guns in the country. Careful attention to aspects of a programmed approach could have resulted in well-thought-out publicity releases that included the support of the Canadian Association of Chiefs of Police. The complexities involved in registration might have also pointed to more emphasis on an adaptive approach whereby implementation would have occurred on a province-by-province or regional basis in order to ensure that the volume of registrations could be handled, and to allow for adjustments to the system.

Two strategies for smoothing the path of resistance are noted here. First, in situations that require an adaptive approach, the involvement of first-line staff and service users at the outset of the policy process is essential. If they bring their experiences and knowledge to the policy table in the early stages of the process, the likelihood of their cooperation in the implementation stage is substantially increased. We give further attention to the contributions of first-line staff and service users in the following section. A second strategy is to establish the role of 'fixer' (Bardach, 1977). Fixers play precisely the role that the title implies. They anticipate difficulties in the implementation process and they find ways to eliminate or reduce the impact of these barriers. They provide information to allay worries about the new policy, referring to the experience of other jurisdictions in the implementation process and securing new funds or personnel.

The World of the First-Line Practitioner

As noted earlier, for policies in the human services that require an adaptive approach to implementation, practitioners largely determine whether policies will be implemented as intended or whether they will be altered. Our discussion now turns to a review of the capacity and commitment of practitioners to the policy process. In theory, one would assume that because policies affect their work-life and the quality of the services to be provided, practitioners would be keenly committed to the policy process. But such an assumption ignores the fact that first-line practitioners often feel as badly treated by their employing agency as do the users of service. They feel, and in many instances rightly so, underpaid, over-worked, and undervalued by their employers.

Our discussion is based on a number of studies of the work-life of first-line practitioners and begins with the classic book, *Street Level Bureaucracy* (Lipsky, 1980). Although Lipsky's research took place in Boston, Massachusetts, in the late seventies, his observations are as pertinent today in many public service jurisdictions as they were 30 years ago. Lipsky's street level bureaucrats worked in the most difficult of circumstances; they served the poor, those who had committed crimes, and people who were mentally and physically ill. Both the street level bureaucrats and those being served were enmeshed in crises on a daily basis:

> Street level bureaucrats spend their work lives in a corrupted world of service. They
> believe themselves to be doing the best they can under adverse circumstances and

they develop techniques to salvage services within the limits imposed upon them by the structure of their work. At best street level bureaucrats invent benign modes of mass processing that more or less permit them to deal with the public fairly, appropriately and successfully. At worst they give in to favouritism, stereotyping and routinizing. (Lipsky, 1980, p. xiii)

Lipsky argues that from the perspective of service users, practitioners make policy. 'The decisions of street level bureaucrats, the routines they establish and the devices they invent to cope with their uncertainties and work pressures effectively become the public policies they carry out' (Lipsky, 1980, p. xii). Although some service users might have recognized that policies were made by the state legislature and the Boston city council, they interacted daily with practitioners and the decisions that affected them were made by practitioners. In addition, service users were well aware that street level bureaucrats could and did exercise discretion. So practice varied in such matters as whether to grant emergency assistance and whether the assistance would be in cash or by voucher.

Discretion is an important but neglected concept in the human services. Essentially, discretion involves the exercise of judgment in situations where the policy is not clear and where the circumstances of a service user is unique. Some examples illustrate the pervasiveness of discretion in the lives of all citizens: a clerk in the Hudson's Bay Company store decides to answer the phone in the midst of discussing the availability of stock to a customer; a police officer pulls over a motorist and issues a ticket despite the driver's pleas that others had been travelling at far greater speed; a teacher issues a formal warning to a student for misbehaving in class but merely reprimands another for similar behaviour. Discretion is welcomed when it is applied in our favour. It is seen as unfair and capricious when we are singled out for treatment that in our opinion we do not deserve.

Policies represent the intent of organizations to ensure equity, but even the most comprehensive set of policies and attendant procedures cannot cover all situations. Inevitably, practitioners will find it necessary to exercise discretion. On the one hand, a child welfare worker in a rural office visiting a home in response to a complaint of child neglect cannot depend completely on the policy established in legislation and regulations. The policy manuals will be back in the office, the supervisor and other senior officials may not be available for consultation, and the circumstances may be unique and outside the rubric of established policy. On the other hand, a staff member in a social assistance office will be more closely bound by policy, and a supervisor will likely be available for ready consultation. Yet even such tightly regulated situations cannot prescribe what should be done in emergencies.

In the last analysis, discretion represents an exercise in balancing equal treatment for all and giving special attention to the unique circumstances for some. Practitioners want to act in a fair and open fashion. Although they recognize the compelling need for preferential treatment in some situations, they are fully aware that such treatment can be seen as favouritism and in some instances as failing to comply with policy. As noted in the Introduction, in recent years the balance has swung towards policies and procedures that reduce discretion. Instruments such as risk assessment and computerized reporting mechanisms require practitioners to comply with standards developed by head offices, often without input from the local level. Writing two decades ago, Elmore's comments on the connections between implementation and discretion foreshadowed the trend toward standardized approaches to practice:

> The dominant view that discretion is at best a necessary evil and at worst a threat to democratic government pushes implementation analysis toward hierarchically struc-tured models of the process and toward increased reliance on hierarchical control to solve implementation problems. . . . Nowhere in this view is serious thought given to how to capitalize on discretion as a device for improving the reliability and effec-tiveness of policies at the street level. (Elmore, 1982, p. 26)

Lipsky's street level bureaucrats were seen as powerful to service users; how-ever, they viewed themselves as oppressed and as having no capacity to con-tribute to or influence the policy process. Support for Lipsky's findings comes from a study carried out in the Corrections Branch of the Attorney General's Min-istry in British Columbia (Wharf, 1984). The study sought to identify the partici-pation of field-office staff in the policy-making process of the branch. The head office of the branch is located in the provincial capital of Victoria and field offices are scattered across the province. The branch created policy advisory groups that included representation from all ranks—probation officer, district supervisor, regional director, and a policy analyst from head office. This vertical slice arrangement was developed in a deliberate attempt to gain a perspective from each level and to utilize these perspectives in the policy-making process.

Despite this attempt to secure involvement, the consistent message from front-line staff was that 'policy comes from head office to regulate and to control prac-tice' (Wharf, 1984, p. 24). Policy was seen by staff as out of touch with the realities of life in the field, and the constant revisions to policy manuals were viewed with amusement and as the product of head-office staff who had nothing else to do.

The only exception to this view came from the staff of a newly created pro-gram in family court counselling. These counsellors worked out of field offices, but they came together on a regular basis to develop policies. A clear lesson from this study was that if newly recruited and eager practitioners are given the oppor-tunity to participate in the policy-making process, they will do so. Support for this finding also comes from Sabatier's review (1986, p. 27) of successful exam-ples of implementation, which pointed to 'the importance of selecting imple-menting institutions supportive of the new program, and creating new agencies as a specific strategy'. It does appear, then, in organizations where the arteries have hardened or even closed, first-line practitioners will feel oppressed and uninterested in policy and who makes it. However, new and open environments provide opportunities to be creative and to join in the establishment of policies.

Centralization and Decentralization: The Variable of Distance

A final variable in their discussion of implementation relates back to the notion of clearance points but is more explicitly revealed by examining the centralization of authority. Kernaghan and Siegel (1995, p. 55) pose the dilemma in the following way: 'A responsive bureaucracy clearly ought to concentrate on transferring authority down the hierarchy and out in the field; yet the historical claims for a responsible bureaucracy can best be met by retaining authority close to the top where it can be used by the Minister and scrutinized by parliament.' Governments have struggled with this dilemma for decades.

At one point, the cry will be heard that field offices have too little discretion. They cannot adapt programs to meet local needs and cannot take leadership in involving community partners. If these complaints are seen as valid, head offices may reduce their control and enhance the autonomy of field offices. However, when a different set of complaints emerge—that programs are too uneven, that programs available in one office are not provided in other locations—and when issues of incompetence arise, head offices are quick to pull in the reins and develop centralizing measures, including central agencies, restrictive regulations, and close surveillance of performance.

A further complication occurs in countries such as Canada, where governments are responsible for services to communities differing widely in terms of culture, history, and size. Head offices attempt valiantly to develop policies and programs that will be implemented in a consistent fashion across the province, but their efforts are in some ways doomed to fail. Urban neighbourhoods differ considerably from rural and remote communities. Thus, the provision of in-depth counselling services, daycare, and specialized health programs is heavily affected by issues such as diversity, distance, and other factors.

Our discussion of the centralization–decentralization dilemma is illuminated by the findings of a national study of first-line public servants. The researchers interviewed 97 federal and 123 provincial civil servants during a two-year period from 1993 to 1995. The study sought to collect information about the work-lives of civil servants in field offices: what do they do, how, and under what conditions? In particular, the study focused on the relationships and interactions between head- and field-office personnel. The authors claim that the study represents 'the first broadly based study on the function of civil servants and in particular the vast majority of those who work in field offices delivering services to the public'. As they noted, 'Field people felt that head offices believe that field officers do not know what to do or how to do it. This perception existed almost everywhere but varied in intensity by province, department and functional areas' (Carroll and Siegel, 1999, pp. 27, 203).

The study concluded that the greater the geographic distance between head and field offices, the greater the autonomy of field offices. As long as they perform their responsibilities in an appropriate and adequate fashion, as long as no serious complaints of incompetence are heard, as long as troublesome personnel issues do not arise, field offices in remote locations exist in relative isolation from the head office. This finding is similar to that observed in the Corrections Branch study cited earlier. In that study, a probation officer in a small BC office captured the point succinctly: 'We are on the periphery and we like it that way. We just purr along and no one bothers us' (Wharf, 1984, p. 39).

Both positive and negative consequences can accrue from the autonomy afforded by distance. An example of positive consequences comes from a child welfare office in northern BC. Like a pendulum, policy directions from head office in Victoria have swung from a very residual approach to child welfare to an approach focused on early intervention and supporting families and back to the 'social cop' style of work. Regardless of these policy shifts, the Hazelton office has carved out its own mode of practice. In the words of a long-time community resident, '[T]he community makes the office' (Wharf, 2002, p. 51). Captured by this remark is the determination of the child welfare workers in Hazelton to tune their practice to the culture and traditions of the communities they serve. Staff see themselves as members of the community; they are open to the community by listing their phone numbers and by responding to after-hours requests. They involve family members, other professionals, and concerned citizens in determining plans for a particular child. This style of work has enabled the staff to win the respect of the surrounding communities and to be able to call for help when they require it. The success of this approach is indicated by the fact that in the past five years there has been parental consent for all children taken into ministry care. Isolation, however, also affords an opportunity for the development of the condition of 'acute localitis' (Montgomery, 1979), whereby standards and practices that are at variance with those outside the community can occur. Acute localitis allowed the conditions of incest and child abuse to continue over a period of years in the isolated community of Kings County, Nova Scotia (Cruise and Griffiths, 1997).

Clearly, the autonomy afforded by distance provides an opportunity for innovative staff to exercise their creativity. Just as clearly, staff who feel overwhelmed by their responsibilities, who are worried about making independent judgments, who in short are not well prepared and experienced, require the security of a well-supervised central or regional office.

Improving the Implementation Process: Concluding Comments

Since implementation is an integral part of the overall policy process, suggestions for improvement are best left to a discussion of reforming the entire process, and these reforms are discussed in more detail in subsequent chapters. Nevertheless, it is useful to pave the way for these discussions by summarizing some of the main points identified in this chapter.

In our view, the distinction between programmed and adaptive approaches is extremely useful. The implementation of the *Child, Family and Community Service Act* in BC affords a very compelling example of the frustrations encountered when a prolonged programmed planning approach was taken. In that example, earlier implementation and an adaptive approach to implementation might have been more effective. Carroll and Siegel's study of first-line civil servants also reinforces the case for adaptive approaches. Not only does effective implementation rest in the hands of staff in local or field offices, but these individuals are also 'the most important people in government' (Carroll and Siegel, 1999, p. 3). These authors ask, 'Why can't policy and administrative changes originate in field offices? After all if they are going to be implemented in field offices eventually why not allow them to flow from the field offices in the first place?'

The phrasing of these questions reinforces the findings of earlier researchers who argued for closer attention to bottom-up approaches to implementation. The need for more attention to an adaptive or bottom-up model of implementation should not be interpreted to mean that central office is off the hook. In fact, an adaptive approach to implementation requires a commitment from the centre to respond to the local context by introducing policy changes or additional resources if these are required. An adaptive approach to implementation implies that changes are anticipated, and forward-thinking policy-makers will develop a mechanism for monitoring the implementation process and responding with needed changes. The role of a 'fixer' is important to consider, particularly when major policy changes are being introduced. In effect, these views call for inclusive approaches to policy-making. In the next chapter we present a number of these approaches and assess their potential for improving the policy process.

Recommended Reading

1. For critical appraisals of theory and research into implementation, see E. Alexander, 'From Idea to Action: Notes for a Contingency Theory of the Policy Implementation Process', *Administration and Society*, (1985) 16(4), 403–6 and P. Sabatier, 'Top-Down and Bottom-Up Approaches to Implementation Research: A Critical Analysis and Suggested Synthesis', *Journal of Public Policy*, (1986) 1(1), 21–48.

2. For an in-depth analysis of the life of street level bureaucrats, see M. Lipsky, *Street Level Bureaucracy* (New York: Russell Sage Foundation, 1980).

3. For arguments identifying and supporting the case for bottom-up approaches and the importance of local offices, see B. Carroll and D. Siegel, *Service in the Field* (Kingston, ON: McGill-Queen's University Press, 1999) and W. Williams, *The Implementation Perspective* (Berkeley, CA: University of California Press, 1980).

Chapter Six

Inclusive Approaches to Policy-Making

In this chapter we present several examples of inclusive approaches to policy-making: the vertical slice approach, policy communities, community governance, and family group decision-making. These examples are considered within the overall context of citizen participation. The concluding section of the chapter gives attention to the strengths and weaknesses of these approaches.

The Case for Citizen Participation

The literature on citizen participation in social policy is voluminous and our discussion is brief in the extreme. (For some recent sources, see Phillips and Orsini, 2002, and Wharf Higgins, Cossom, and Wharf, 2003.) We simply wish to establish that there has been a long-standing debate in representative democracies about whether citizens should participate in making social policy and if so, how. Is it sufficient to rely on those elected to the various levels of government to make policy? David Zussman, a long-time advisor to the prime minister, and president of an Ottawa think-tank, the Public Policy Forum, answers the question in the affirmative. 'I think a majority of Canadians say to themselves, "Look, I sent you to Ottawa, so do your job and don't keep asking me what the right answer is. Go ahead and do it yourself."' (Zussman, quoted in May 2002, p. A15).We disagree, and our position was stated in Chapter 1 where we argued that such an arrangement results in domination of the policy process and its outcomes by élite members of society.

A long-standing debate on the continuing concentration of power in the office of the prime minister reached crescendo proportions in the latter months of 2002. In the words of the former minister of finance, Paul Martin, 'We have permitted a culture to arise that has been some 30 years in the making, one that can be best summarized by the one question that everyone in Ottawa believes has become the key to getting things done: Who do you know in the PMO (The Prime Minister's Office)?' (quoted in Clark, 2002, p. 1). Mr Martin focused his campaign for the leadership of the Liberal Party on the case for overcoming what has been identified as the 'democratic deficit'.

Some of the reforms that have been suggested in the media and by academics (Phillips and Orsini, 2002) are: electing rather than appointing members to the Senate and vesting some authority with that body; giving more power to back-benchers and allowing them to vote according to their conscience rather than toeing the party line; and referenda. In our view, the first two suggestions make good sense and should be adopted. However, we are most wary of using refer-enda to settle contentious public issues. Such issues require careful study and debate and the members of the public rarely have opportunities for adequate study and reflection. In addition, as a referendum held in BC in 2002 on Aborigi-nal treaty claims clearly showed, the wording of referenda can be slanted in such a way as to virtually assure the outcome desired by the state.

It is, however, curious that these discussions make little or no mention of the kind of models or approaches discussed in this chapter. Our case for these approaches is anchored in the principle of affected interests: 'Everyone who is affected by the decision of a government should have a right to participate in that government' (Dahl, 1970, p. 64). Dahl concedes that the principle lacks speci-ficity and gives rise to some thorny issues. He suggests that the criteria of per-sonal choice, competence, and economy can be helpful in applying the principle. Personal choice refers to the right of individuals to choose to participate or to opt out. Competence suggests that not all individuals can tackle situations requiring advanced skill and knowledge. The criteria of economy means that in issues where a large number of people are affected, some means of representation must be established.

In our view, the principle of affected interests has particular relevance to social policy and to models of policy-making. For example, parents are deeply con-cerned about the health, education, and well-being of their children, and given the opportunity many will participate in policy-making structures that affect their children. Parents have been active participants in the Association for Community Living, school boards, daycare centres, and many other institutions. We hasten to acknowledge that not all citizens have the time or the inclination to participate in matters that affect them. We are also aware that one of the reasons for the lack of participation is that opportunities have traditionally been restricted to meetings held in locations and at times that are inappropriate for many citizens.

The Case for More Inclusive Models
The Vertical Slice Approach

We begin the consideration of more inclusive models that are based on the princi-ple of affected interests with a discussion of a model that is restricted to an orga-nization. Since the publication of *In Search of Excellence* (Peters and Waterman, 1982), many organizational theorists and managers have recognized that a key factor in achieving organizational success lies in valuing employees, treating them with respect, and involving them in decisions that affect them. One executive puts the point in a succinct fashion: 'Happy employees means you are going to have delighted customers which means you are going to have ecstatic shareholders' (Johnson, quoted in Macklem, 2002, p. 27). Yet public sector organizations have not embraced this philosophy. As we argued in Chapter 5, many departments of provincial and federal governments are beset by reductions in the number of jobs through the privatization of functions, by poor morale, and by a lack of support and confidence from their political leaders.

Obviously, this state of affairs cannot be overcome by a single solution. Restoring confidence and morale in the public service requires at a minimum that politicians stop treating government as a problem to be turned over to the private sector and involve civil servants in matters that affect them. One vehicle to secure involvement is to create policy groups within departments. Membership in these groups could consist of a vertical slice of the organization including service users, first-line staff members, district supervisors, and head-office personnel. The policy groups could be assigned responsibility for developing, reviewing, and changing policies in the department whether these pertain to substantive issues or functional matters.

The vertical slice approach allows those being served and first-line staff to learn about budgets and the political aspects of policy-making and at the same time introduces policy-makers to the realities experienced by service users and first-line staff. Rein (1983, p. 142) refers to the knowledge of practitioners as 'hot' in that it is compelling and grounded in people and their troubles. The knowledge of policy-makers is 'cold' since it is removed from immediate and pressing personal crises. Mixing hot and cold knowledge has the potential for shared learning, a concept that also occurs in the following example of shared decision-making.

It will be recalled from the previous chapter that the vertical slice approach enjoyed only limited success in the BC Corrections Branch; obviously, this strategy is not a panacea for organizational reform or for policy-making. In that example, it worked most effectively in a new division of the branch where the task was to create rather than to review and change policy. Perhaps membership in policy groups should be by invitation, thus providing some assurance that only individuals who are interested will participate. A commitment by the chief executive officer to treat suggested changes with respect and to approve recommended changes whenever feasible is essential.

Shared Decision-Making

Our example of shared decision-making is taken from the work of the Commission on Resources and Environment (CORE) established by the BC provincial government in 1992. CORE was given the responsibility of developing land use plans in four regions of the province that had been characterized by intense conflict between the forest industry, local communities, and environmental groups. 'The key challenge was to develop a participation process that would enable strongly opposed and politically influential public interest groups to try to reconcile their differences in a manner that would permit the government to act decisively on many highly controversial land use issues. CORE proposed round table style decision-making (shared decision-making) in which all affected parties would participate in the development of regional land use plans' (Owen, 1998, p. 83). At first glance, it may seem curious to feature an example concerned with environmental issues in a book focused on the human services. We include CORE for two reasons. First, reaching agreement on land use plans has been extremely difficult, marked by hostile relationships and even violence. If land use plans can be developed, there may well be hope for resolving other issues. Second, CORE represents a particularly sophisticated example of shared decision-making and therefore there is much to learn from its experience.

Although government participated in the roundtables, it did so as one participant, not as the ultimate source of authority. It was made clear at the outset that if agreement could be reached by the roundtables, government would approve these decisions. If not, government would use the insights and lessons learned from the roundtables.

Some of the important lessons from the CORE experience make the rather obvious point that resolving contentious policy issues takes time. Many rounds of discussions and negotiations are required to reach agreement by participants who have markedly different agendas and objectives. Second, the process requires skilled facilitators who can bring participants together and ensure that, although disagreements will occur, these need not sabotage the process. Perhaps the most significant lesson is that shared decision-making results in shared learning. All the participants came to the roundtables not only with their own strongly held opinions, but also with equally firm views on the opinions of the other participants. Intense discussions conducted over a period of months allowed both sets of perceptions to change. Participants distinguished between their absolute priorities and other less important matters that could be compromised. Participants also learned where their views of others had been incorrect and were able to alter these. The learning lasted after the termination of the CORE process and was a major legacy of the project.

While consensus was not reached by any of the roundtables, there was a sufficient level of agreement for CORE to develop land use plans for each of the regions, and with modifications, these plans were approved by government. Following submission of the plans, CORE was disbanded. 'It was appropriate that the lead land use planning function be reassumed within government following the developmental phase of CORE. Government works best when it assumes responsibilities directly and delivers services in an unambiguous and accountable way' (Owen, 1998, p. 95). Yet governments do not always work well, and their ability to broker agreements in many aspects of public policy is limited. There may well be a compelling case for the establishment of shared decision-making mechanisms as a regular component of major policy-making initiatives.

Policy Communities

Policy communities are loosely knit groups of individuals interested in and knowledgeable about a particular aspect of public policy. Membership varies depending on the issues. In the human services, membership may include politicians, senior civil servants, and representatives of community agencies. In policy arenas such as banking, the representatives from outside government will be presidents of banks and insurance companies. Policy communities are not usually registered under the *Societies Act* and their activities are conducted in a most informal fashion. At times they may meet on a regular basis and at other times slip into periods of inactivity.

As will be seen as the discussion proceeds, some policy communities have been extremely influential in shaping public policy, yet they typically receive scant attention in the public policy literature. Among the most widely used Canadian policy texts in the past few years are the following: Howlett and Ramesh (1995), Armitage (2003), Brooks (1998), Rice and Prince (2000), and Graham, Swift, and Delaney (2000). Only the Rice and Prince text mentions policy communities. The only book that gives comprehensive treatment to the contribution of policy communities is *Policy Communities and Public Policy in Canada* (Coleman and Skogstad, 1990). A brief review and the conclusions of this book were noted in Chapter 1, but it bears repeating here that the women's movement and the poverty policy community exercised little influence on the policies of the federal government from 1970 to 1990, whereas the banking and forestry communities were extremely influential. Two of the three examples discussed below, the poverty policy community and the financial community, support these findings.

The Poverty Policy Community

This community is of particular interest because it has gone through several stages ranging from an early period where it wielded considerable influence, to the present time where it carries little weight in the Ottawa corridors of power.

The first period occurred during the 1950s when under the auspices of the Public Welfare Division (PWD) of the Canadian Welfare Council (now the Canadian Council on Social Development, CCSD), senior civil servants from the federal and provincial departments of social services and staff of the council met on a regular basis. The original reason for the establishment of the division was to identify and discuss common problems, but under the leadership of several key individuals, it became a vehicle to plan major changes in public assistance programs. As Haddow (1993, p. 25) points out, 'The PWD gave senior public assistance officials an opportunity to reach agreement on policy reforms and to camouflage their activity as the product of a disinterested and prestigious non-governmental organization.' The executive secretary of the division was even more blunt: 'Members of the PWD most of whom are appointed officials, would be placed in an awkward position by having to take responsibility for recommendations which might be considered policy matters and as such more appropriately the responsibility of elected officials.' Their work culminated in the publication of *Social Security for Canada* in 1958 that laid the groundwork for the Canada Assistance Plan enacted by the federal government in 1996.

Wanting to take a more holistic approach to its research and policy-related activities, CCSD dissolved the Public Welfare Division and other divisions in 1969. Even without the structure of the PWD, cordial and supportive relationships between senior staff of the Department of Health and Welfare and the council continued until the mid-1970s. However, in 1976 both the department and the council issued reports recommending reforms in income security. The council attacked the departmental report on several occasions, the latter responded in kind, and the long record of support and cooperation between the two collapsed: 'The Council's capacity to participate in social reform depended on the cogency and originality of its research and policy analysis and on its capacity to serve as a forum for welfare state clients. . . . [But] neither its research results nor its efforts to mobilize program clients gave it access to government decision-making' (Haddow, 1993, p. 181).

The point is important. It argues that in order to influence government polices, it is not sufficient that voluntary agencies produce sound research and timely proposals. Such organizations also require the connections that will ensure their proposals will receive attention. Although a number of policy organizations and think-tanks now exist in Ottawa, and although staff of some of these organizations have good connections with senior civil servants, a policy community of reform-minded civil servants and community representatives does not exist. The scene has shifted dramatically. Instead of a policy community dedicated to improving Canada's welfare state, there is a different, more powerful policy community dedicated to dismantling it. Rather than a social policy community consisting of representatives of agencies like the Canadian Council on Social Development, the Centre for Policy Alternatives, and the Caledon Institute, there is now a financial policy community led by the Canadian Council of Chief Executives. We take up the story of this policy community in a later section of the chapter.

A Disability Policy Community in BC

The story of the efforts of the staff of the provincial government and of community agencies coming together to reform guardianship legislation in BC provides a textbook example of the workings of a policy community. The story reveals both the advantages and some of the inherent difficulties in policy communities where one partner, usually the state, has access to more resources both in terms of funds and people than the community partner.

In addition, the story provides an apt illustration of the concept of the policy window noted in Chapter 2. It will be recalled from this chapter that the policy window opens when problems, politics, and policy solutions, the three key components of the policy process, come into alignment. 'A problem is recognized, a solution is developed and available in the policy community, a political change makes it the right time for policy change and potential constraints are not severe' (Kingdon, 1995, p. 165). With the exception of the policy solution, all the other components were present in the example under discussion. A reform-minded government had just been elected. As well, the relevant community organizations and the newly appointed public trustee were keenly aware of the inadequacies of the existing *Patients Property Act* and committed to developing new legislation.

The initiative for change came from community organizations, and a consortium of five agencies launched a province-wide survey to document problems resulting from the outdated Act. Sometime later, an interministerial committee was formed within the provincial government, and the two groups came together to form a joint working committee. Over a two-year period, 1991 to 1993, this committee worked at a frantic pace: it sought further information from concerned individuals and disability organizations, it prepared a framework document setting out the direction for the new legislation, it provided extensive opportunities for reviews of the document, and it developed new legislation and again sought consultation. In 1993, a new Act was passed in the provincial legislature that 'was heralded by many within both government and community as the best and most innovative legislative framework in North America. The process of its development and passage—the process of community driven legislative reform—is certainly just as unique' (Rutman, 1998, p. 104).

Yet all the provisions of the new legislation were not proclaimed until 2000. What happened to delay final approval for seven years? The essential reason was that the policy window began to close. The resources required to implement the new legislation were deemed too expensive for a government concerned about the estimated costs of implementation, and the attorney general, who had supported the involvement of the disability community and was committed to reforming the legislation, resigned. Political crises, which garnered daily media attention, effectively diverted the government from tending to its substantive policy responsibilities. Finally, the disability community simply ran out of funds and energy.

The lessons from the experience of this policy community are instructive. First, the two partners did not have access to equal funds and staff skilled in research and policy analysis; hence, the partnership was an unequal one. Second, the insistence of the community partners that their participation should not be limited to a few advisors, and that wide-ranging consultation with disability organizations was essential in all phases of the process, appeared to government to slow down the pace of reform. Indeed, some government officials simply did not understand why community partners should be part of drafting legislation. After all, legislation is a state responsibility! Only direct intervention from the attorney general saved the day on this issue.

In spite of these difficulties, assigning policy reform to a policy community has considerable advantages. It encourages the collection of comprehensive information, it secures the cooperation of community agencies that in the last analysis will be responsible for at least some aspects of implementation, and it meets the challenge of doing the people's business in a transparent fashion.

The Financial Policy Community
While the community partners in the disability policy community struggled because of insufficient resources, the same cannot be said with respect to this example of a financial policy community. This community consists of politicians and senior civil servants in the Department of Finance, Treasury Board, and representatives from the Canadian Council of Chief Executives (CCCE).

The CCCE, which changed its name in 2001, was formerly known as the Business Council on National Interests. It was initially formed in 1976 to represent the interests of the financial and business community in Canada. Writing in

1998, Peter Newman noted that the Council has '150 members who control $1.7 trillion in assets, earn annual revenues of $500 billion and have 1.5 million employees'. In some ways, the CCCE could be considered an interest or pressure group committed to pushing the state to adopt policies favoured by the financial community. It is seen here as the business partner of a policy community because of its close contacts and relationships with officials in the federal government. Some examples support this view. Paul Martin was a member of CCCE prior to his entry into politics; when he was minister of finance, Jean Chrétien acknowledged 'that I don't do my budgets without consulting with the Council on Business Interests' (Newman, 1998, p. 157); and the wife of the president of CCCE is an assistant deputy minister in the Department of Finance. Although these and other connections exist between the two partners, perhaps the most significant reason for achieving ready agreement on policy issues is that they share common backgrounds, ideologies, and commitments to a neo-conservative agenda.

The CCCE has been remarkably effective in influencing the policies of the federal level government. The president, Thomas D'Acquino, sums up its achievements in the following quotation: 'If you ask yourself, in which period since 1900 has Canada's business community had the most influence on public policy I would say it was in the last twenty years. Look at what we stand for and look at what all the governments, all the major parties including Reform have done and what they want to do. They have adopted the agendas we've been fighting for in the past two decades' (D'Acquino quoted in Newman, 1998, p. 159). The successful outcomes of this policy community include the dismantling of the National Energy Program, persuading the federal government to give priority to reducing the public debt using as one rationale the high cost of social programs, and becoming the pivotal advocate in the Free Trade Debate, 'spending $200 million in the largest and most powerful lobby effort in Canadian history' (Newman, 1998, p. 156).

Given the commitment of the authors to a philosophy of social democracy, it is difficult to pay tribute to an organization that has done so much to promote a completely opposing ideology, but the strategies employed by the CCCE have been nothing short of brilliant. Rather than waiting for government to enact legislation and policy and then complaining if these measures do not suit the interests of the business community, the CCCE has tried to anticipate the agenda of government and supply government with carefully worked out proposals that, just coincidentally, are those that support and enhance the cause of business. The *strategy of anticipation* works for CCCE because it has excellent sources of information within government and it has enough resources to prepare proposals that meet or exceed the standards of the state.

Community Governance

Community governance brings policy-making and the management of the outcomes of that process to the level of local communities. It is an attractive strategy to both those on the left and on the right of the political spectrum, but this very quality suggests that the concept contains a basic contradiction. Thus, for neo-conservatives, community governance means reducing the size and significance of governments by returning the responsibility for helping individuals and families to churches, neighbourhoods, and charitable organizations. For those who believe in democratic socialism, community governance does not represent an abandonment of state responsibility for the human services, but rather affords the potential of involving more citizens in governance issues. It is a policy direction that has the potential to create small and user-friendly agencies. Although our resolution of this issue will appeal most to those of this political persuasion, we recognize that some on the left favour the centralization of power in the hands of senior policy experts. Our resolution will offend these left-leaning central planners just as thoroughly as it will the neo-conservatives.

We begin by describing what we mean by 'community' and 'governance' and then identify both the advantages and disadvantages of community governance. We note some examples and conclude the discussion by presenting our approach to community governance.

What Do We Mean by 'Community'?

Although 'community' can refer to communities of interest without geographic boundaries, we are concerned here with geography. Thus, 'community' is defined to mean a group of people having common interests and sharing a particular place. But this definition is still imprecise with respect to size since it can refer to neighbourhoods, municipalities, and regions. For our purposes this is not a vexing issue since we argue that the concept of community governance can apply to all these geographic units.

It is important to clarify that our arguments for community governance do not apply to all health and social policies. Some programs such as income security and medicare coverage must be provided at provincial or federal levels. Here, the principle of equity is paramount, and equity demands that all citizens regardless of residence are entitled to the same level of income related to need whether the income is provided through a pension, social assistance, workers' compensation, or employment insurance. We agree with Piven's trenchant criticism of calls to delegate responsibility for income programs to communities: 'The most serious problems in these programs—of inadequate benefits and demeaning treatment of beneficiaries—are surely not likely to be solved by decentralization or community participation. To me such proposals are exasperating for their pig-headed rejection of either history or analysis. No one seems to remember the local and private tyranny that bedeviled relief programs for the poor before they were at least partially nationalized in the 1930s' (Piven, 1993, p. 69).

Leaving aside medicare and social policies pertaining to income security, the issue of which services and programs are most appropriately dealt with at what level is a contentious and slippery one. While it is apparent that the issue cannot be resolved by unambiguous formulas, some clarity can be obtained by examining four principles: affinity; affected interests; accessibility; and a low level of bureaucratization.

The *principle of affinity* suggests that people committed to a religious faith or to cultural traditions have a right to receive services from agencies and practitioners who are also committed to these values. Examples of the principle of affinity include church-sponsored agencies, First Nations agencies, and ethnic agencies. People coming to these agencies know upfront that they will receive counselling and other services consistent with their values and belief systems. 'Affinity is the perception that a provider possesses a unique set of characteristics which are important to the consumer' (Social Planning Council of Metropolitan Toronto, 1976, p. 106).

We have already noted our view that the *principle of affected interests* (Dahl, 1970) should play a prominent part in determining who plans and governs human services. This principle has been prominent in the development of programs and agencies by groups with a particular interest or cause. Some examples include Associations for Community Living, transition houses, women's centres, and antipoverty organizations. And in order for the principle of affected interests to work, the remaining two principles come into play.

The third principle is that of *accessibility*. In his contributions to the Seebohm report on the reorganization of health and social services in the United Kingdom, Roy Parker captured the essence of accessibility by the phrase 'pram-pushing distance' (Report of the Committee on Local Authority and Allied Services, 1968). Such services include daycare; meeting places for children, youth, parents, and seniors; and neighbourhood-organizing activities. Although the principle of accessibility must be operationalized differently in urban and rural areas, the experience of neighbourhood houses and community schools is that accessibility—both in terms of location and a welcoming, user-friendly philosophy of service—is a determining factor in the use of services. One of the few empirical studies of the effects of decentralization in child welfare demonstrated that accessibility was directly associated with service utilization: 'To summarize, service demand as reflected by caseload increases in child abuse, family service, and children in care increased at a much higher rate in Winnipeg following the transition to decentralized, community-based services than elsewhere in the province. These data along with the evidence of increased activity in prevention and early intervention demonstrate that regionalization led to significant increases in the utilization of child and family services' (McKenzie, 1991, p. 61).

Finally, the *principle of a low level of bureaucratization* calls for a flat rather than a hierarchical structure in organizations. Flat structures provide a hospitable environment for the human services by reducing the number of managerial positions and by providing the potential for a high degree of collaboration between the executive and first-line staff.

These principles provide guidance rather than precise direction and require an adaptive approach to implementation. Taken together they make a convincing argument that governance should be suited to the geographic area and the people to be served. Thus, neighbourhood houses should be governed by residents of the neighbourhood since services are available only to these residents. However, services such as mental health and child welfare, which affect a large number of people, may need to be organized on a regional basis and governed by an elected board that is representative of the citizens in the area.

What Do We Mean by 'Governance'?

A number of attempts have been made to clarify the meaning of 'governance' at a community level. Basic to the concept is the delegation of authority and responsibility from senior levels of government that have traditionally been responsible for health and social services. One author distinguishes among political, geographic, and administrative decentralization (Rein, 1972). Geographic decentralization consists of the establishment of local offices without any transfer of power. Political decentralization delegates policy-making authority to the local unit, while administrative decentralization is more restrictive and grants autonomy only with respect to specified tasks.

A more elaborate and better-known framework is the ladder of citizen participation referred to in Chapter 4 (Arnstein, 1969). Arnstein developed the framework in an attempt to clarify the levels of engagement of citizens in the Model Cities programs in the United States in the 1960s. While the ladder refers to citizens rather than communities, the basic intent of the framework—to distinguish between differing levels of control—applies just as clearly to communities as to citizens. It will be clear as the discussion proceeds that our view of community governance involves the top three rungs of the ladder: citizen control, delegated power, and partnership arrangements.

Before proceeding to the discussion of advantages and disadvantages of community governance, we note that neither of the frameworks identified above speak to practice, and in our view a community work approach to practice is an essential component of community governance. The discussion of the work of the Hazelton office in Chapter 5 captures the essence of community work, but it is appropriate at this juncture to describe the approach in a more explicit fashion.

A community work approach to practice contains the following characteristics. The people being served:

1. become partners in developing and managing programs that affect them;
2. become partners in identifying and then taking action to change harmful and negative conditions that are present in their neighbourhood; and
3. have reserved seats at policy-making tables to ensure that not just the professionals and other experienced volunteers participate.

A community work approach to practice is the antithesis of the current and strongly held view in which, in the guise of attempting to coordinate services and ensure accountability, people being served are cast as 'cases' and professionals as 'case managers'. This 'solution' has arisen because many individuals are buffeted by problems such as poverty, inadequate housing, unemployment, unsafe neighbourhoods, and difficulties in marital and parent/child relationships. But unlike the interconnectedness of these issues, programs have been developed on a specialized basis and are offered by agencies with specific functions. Since these agencies are often located in different areas, people must traipse from one area to another, and not infrequently they receive different responses to questions and conflicting advice and opinions.

This scenario is described in detail in the first volume of the Gove Inquiry into Child Protection in British Columbia (Report of the Gove Inquiry into Child Protection in British Columbia, 1995). This inquiry made 116 recommendations, and pertinent to this discussion are the following recommendations: that services should be integrated, provided in a common location, and governed by regional boards of elected citizens; and that a system of case management be developed and implemented. The inquiry concluded that case management is required to ensure that clients do not fall between the cracks of programs and providers.

In our view, the recommendation calling for service integration and community governance was sound and progressive, but it was ignored by the NDP government in power at the time. Of interest is the fact that the Liberal government, elected in 2001, has acted on the recommendation, and regional authorities are to be in place in 2003. While the Minister of Child and Family Development has a deep commitment to the notion of community capacity building, it is clear that the decision to create these authorities was motivated in large part by an overriding concern to reduce government spending. The funds to be made available to the new authorities will be substantially reduced from amounts previously allocated to the ministry. This example of community governance represents a clear case of off-loading responsibilities previously assumed by the state to citizens working as volunteers in church, state, or charitable organizations.

Community governance should not provide an excuse to off-load resources. Being close to and aware of community needs and resources, community governance has the potential to come to grips with the multi-agency problem described in the Gove Inquiry. It might reduce the number of agencies and thereby the number of service providers involved with any one family; it might organize common sites of operation, and, as a radical innovation, install citizens as the managers or co-managers in the planning and implementation of the services that affect them. In brief, it can lead to more effective services; it may, in time, also result in more efficient services.

The Advantages of Community Governance

The case for community governance is summed up in three propositions:

1. People respect more those laws on which they have been consulted.
2. People identify strongly with programs they have helped plan.
3. People perform better in projects they have assisted in setting up. (Bregha, n.d., p. 3)

Simply put, community governance provides more space for more people to participate, to develop a constituency for the human services, and to increase the sense of participants' self-worth. The advantages have been identified in greater detail by many authors (see, among others, Pateman, 1970; Clague et al., 1984; Cassidy, 1991). They can be enumerated as follows:

1. Community organizations are connected to local customs and traditions. They

are intimately aware of the history of issues and of what has been done in the past to resolve these issues.

2. Action on community issues is likely to be faster if the decisions are made at a local level rather than at senior levels of government.

3. Community governance provides an opportunity for people to learn about the process of governing; thus, it serves as a training ground for engagement in other political arenas.

4. Community governance affords an opportunity for social learning, for individuals to become knowledgeable about social issues and the complex interplay between personal troubles and public issues.

5. Community governance contains the potential for building a constituency for the services being governed. Thus, a constituency for education has been built through citizens participating on regional school boards and parent advisory committees.

All the above advantages occur because community-governance structures are small and accessible. It is easier for citizens to be involved in, to have contact with, and to influence small governing units as opposed to regional and provincial governments. The experience of the Greater London Council, which experimented with various kinds of both functional and geographic structures, was that 'the smaller the unit, the more effective was its attack on hierarchy, fragmentation of services and the deskilling of professional talents' (Murray, 1993, p. 61).

However, the advantages of small governing structures are countered by the claims that they are costly and inefficient. We discuss these claims next.

The Disadvantages of Community Governance

Earlier we referred to one significant disadvantage of community governance—the condition of 'acute localitis' (Montgomery, 1979). Acute localitis refers to the potential for communities to become closed and intolerant of diverging patterns of behaviour. Although the rural community of old is often romanticized today as a place of support and mutual affection, we often forget that these were also often places of intolerance and even cruelty. As a consequence, many individuals fled to the anonymity of cities, where their views and behaviour were accepted or at least tolerated.

A second disadvantage noted above is that community governance affords an opportunity for neo-conservative governments to reduce costs. Critics of community governance and, indeed, of most forms of participatory democracy often claim that these structures waste time and energy. They argue that they represent yet another layer of government in our already complicated government system. The development of a New Directions policy for health care in British Columbia provides an instructive example of the potency of this argument. This policy was established by an NDP government following a Royal Commission initiated by the previous government. The commission recommended that funding and the delivery of health services be placed under regional control 'closer to home'. New Directions proposed implementing this reform by establishing regional and community health boards composed of elected citizens. From the outset the policy was hailed by the advocates of community governance as innovative and imaginative. It was also severely criticized by opponents on the grounds that it would create an expensive and bureaucratic form of governance. Attempts to implement New Directions consumed the better part of three years and, in the end, the critics won. The initiative was discarded as too 'expensive and bureaucratic'!

Similar arguments were made in 1991 when community-based child and family service agencies in the city of Winnipeg were disbanded and organized under one administrative authority. However, despite predictions of cost savings, there was no evidence that a return to a more centralized structure with a reduced level of community control realized this goal. In fact, costs continued to escalate.

Examples of Community Governance

Several examples of community governance come to mind. Voluntary agencies have traditionally been governed by their communities, whether these are geographic or interest communities. Agencies such as transition houses, child sexual abuse centres, Children's Aid Societies, Associations for Community Living, the United Way, and Social Planning Councils are governed by boards of directors. Since the elections of these boards are generally confined to members of the society legally responsible for the agency, and since many members come from the middle- and upper-income classes, charges of élitism are not uncommon. Indeed, some of these agencies have become closed to all but the members of the society and their friends.

Other examples include regional school boards and community health centres. While elections to these agencies can be contested by any citizen, the charge of élitism is still relevant. As we noted earlier, the ability to participate successfully in the electoral process depends on the availability of financial resources and influence, and this tilts the scale heavily in favour of middle- and upper-income earners.

In a very real sense, particularly in small communities, municipal governments can be considered examples of community governance. Voter turnout for municipal elections is lower than for provincial and federal elections, perhaps reflecting a commonly held view that the most important decisions are made by the senior levels of government. Nevertheless, these elections are often hotly contested affairs, and the controversial issues of policing, housing, recreation, and zoning that confront municipal councils involve difficult policy decisions. And while arguments for the amalgamation of contiguous municipalities and school boards are frequently heard, they are resistant to these initiatives because of the loss of local autonomy. In the last analysis, people prefer school divisions or municipal governments that are local, more accessible, and consist of people who are widely known in the community.

The Effectiveness of Community Governance

The effectiveness of community governance is difficult to establish. The first question is, effective compared to what? Other levels of government? Business corporations? What are the indices of effectiveness? While the effectiveness of the ministries of provincial and federal governments are occasionally evaluated, we rarely venture into the daunting task of an evaluation of an entire government.

As noted earlier, voluntary agencies, such as those financially supported by the United Way, represent a form of community governance. These agencies occasionally experience management difficulties stemming from conflicts between members of the board, or between staff and board members; however, the structure of local governance has generally remained in place. This long-standing record is a remarkable testimony to the salience of the principles of affinity, affected interests, and a low level of bureaucratization. Other successful examples of community governance come from the establishment of Health and Human Resource Centres in British Columbia (Clague et al., 1984), from the regionalization of child welfare services in Manitoba (McKenzie, 1991), and from Shragge's (1990) review of alternative service organizations in Montreal. Unfortunately, some of these structures have been discarded by governments ambivalent about community empowerment. Nevertheless, Shragge's conclusions provide an apt summary of the case for community governance:

> The community-based option has shown itself to be responsible and innovative, creating new approaches and service delivery at a level that can respond directly to a range of community needs and problems. One critique of the post-war welfare State centres on its bureaucratic structure, overreliance on professionals, and the fact that planning and control of services are remote from the local community. Clearly, alternative service organizations are able to address these problems even with their chronic underfunding. (Shragge, 1990)

Finally, some insights into effectiveness can be gleaned from the studies of well-performing organizations. Building on the work of Peters and Waterman (1982) and a study by the auditor general (1988), Brodtrick (1991) developed a set of criteria that exemplify well-performing organizations in the public sector. These criteria are:

1. An emphasis on people. People are challenged and developed; they are given power to act and to use their judgement.
2. Participative leadership. Leadership is not authoritarian but participative whenever possible.
3. Innovative work styles. Staff reflect on their performance and seek to solve problems creatively.
4. Strong client orientation. These organizations focus strongly on their clients and derive their satisfaction from serving the client rather than the bureaucracy.
5. A mindset that seeks optimum performance. People hold values that drive them to seek improvement in their organization's performance. (Brodtrick, 1991, pp. 18–19)

There are many similarities between the characteristics of well-performing organizations and the type of community governance we have in mind. The common characteristics include inclusiveness, valuing individuals, flat rather than steep organizational arrangements, and small in scale and size.

Towards a Resolution

In our view, community governance is the model of choice for many, although not all, programs. Indeed, a very short program ladder consisting of only three rungs can be identified. The first rung consists of those programs that are purely local and, here, community governance or control should be the rule. The second rung refers to delegated power whereby legislative and resource responsibility is retained at the federal or provincial levels but operating responsibilities are delegated to communities. Child welfare and health services fall on this second rung. The third rung is concerned with programs in which the principle of equity is of fundamental importance. This requires a partnership arrangement between community and senior levels of government. Examples of these programs include social assistance, employment insurance, and pensions for the elderly. Here, community groups and organizations can make an important contribution by evaluating the outcomes of these programs and communicating the results to senior levels of government. Although these organizations will not be primarily responsible for setting policy or delivering services, they provide essential information about the contents of these policies and the nature of the services that should be provided.

As we have noted throughout this book, the effectiveness of policy is ultimately determined by the capacity of the local service delivery unit and the relationships that prevail among staff members and those being served. Unfortunately, efforts to reform the human services usually concentrate on changing structures and rarely on redistributing power from politicians and bureaucrats to service providers and users.

In the last analysis, the resolution of the issue depends on whether one favours the centralization or the dispersal of power. Centralists point to the advantages to be gained from governing structures that enable decisions to be made quickly, with a minimum expenditure of time and energy. They view the work of committees—especially meetings that are long and inconclusive—as a waste of time.

For their part, the proponents of the dispersal of power base their arguments in part on the axiom of Lord Acton—power corrupts and absolute power corrupts absolutely! From this perspective, power-sharing reduces the chances of a few people governing in their own interests and contributes to the development of a more informed and more responsible citizenry. The concern about wasted time and energy is countered by the response that participation is cost-effective because it avoids mistakes in implementation that frequently occur when those who must implement a policy have had no part in its development.

The dilemma is summed up by the observation that 'the real debate is not about cost savings; it is about the nature of local territorially-based communities and about their potential for democratic self-governance within the complex political and economic environment in which we find ourselves' (Sancton, 1997,

p. 30). In our view, community governance of the human services represents an essential addition to the limited range of opportunities for citizens to contribute to democratic self-governance. As we have emphasized throughout this book, the representative system of governance is open only to those with the financial resources, the time, and the self-confidence to participate. We have emphasized, too, that the priorities of those individuals who make policy in the human services are vastly different from those who receive the services. Community governance would pave the way for some improvements in an otherwise severely restricted form of democracy.

Family Group Conferences

Family group conferences represent an example of an inclusive approach that pertains primarily to practice. Pioneered in New Zealand in the 1970s, family group conferences are an attempt to resolve differences in the fields of child welfare and juvenile justice. Family group conferences have been described as a success in New Zealand (Maxwell and Morris, 1995), and there have been a number of pilot projects in Canada. Results from the Newfoundland Project (Burford and Pennell, 1995) indicate that family group conferences can secure the cooperation of families and that families have much to contribute.

Like the CORE process, family group conferences bring all the affected individuals together to make joint plans. Thus, in child welfare where a complaint of child neglect or abuse has been received and verified, parents, children, members of the extended family, professionals like teachers and nurses with a knowledge of and interest in the children come together to work out a plan that will ensure the safety and well-being of the child. Again like CORE, a facilitator is responsible for organizing the conference, for obtaining relevant background information, and for ensuring that discussions proceed in a courteous and respectful fashion. If agreement cannot be reached, the child welfare worker has the responsibility to refer the matter to family court.

It is difficult to imagine an approach to practice that fits with the social work value of self-determination and the objective of the profession to empower those being served more completely than family group conferences. Yet the approach has not been embraced by most child welfare agencies in the country, primarily because these agencies are in a constant state of crisis and have little or no capacity to welcome innovations. In addition, social and other human service workers are most comfortable with an individualistic approach to practice. They are accustomed to seeing clients on an individual basis and most often in their agency offices. Most are decidedly uncomfortable with group work approaches and particularly those that transfer some power to groups.

By involving those being served and according them a place in decision-making, the family group conference represents an inclusive approach to practice. In addition the approach contains the potential of practice influencing policy. The experience accumulated through conferences can be used to inform policy, and the confidence gained by those being served and by first-line staff in these conferences may well enable them to participate more effectively in the policy-making process.

The Pros and Cons of Inclusive Approaches: Concluding Comments

It is apparent, as emphasized in our discussion, that we favour the establishment of inclusive approaches. The vertical slice approach to policy formation within an organization and the family group conference model are relatively easy to implement. Community governance brings policy-making and management of human service to the local level. To ensure that service users and first-line staff can participate, seats at the policy table can be reserved for members of these groups. The establishment of policy communities in fields of practice such as child welfare would extend the range of available information and expertise to include service users and practitioners.

In our view, the concept of shared learning is perhaps the most important contribution of inclusive approaches. Although we introduced this concept in the discussion of shared decision-making, it can and does occur in the other approaches. Shared learning breaks down misconceptions that often stand in the way of reaching agreement, it brings in the perspectives of the first-line practitioners and of service users, and in so doing enriches the information at the policy table.

Two disadvantages of inclusive approaches have been noted. First, they involve more people in the policy process and in turn this can extend the time needed to reach a decision. Second, decentralization and community governance can provide an opportunity for neo-conservative governments to reduce resources for the human services. But the primary problem facing the introduction of inclusive approaches is that they require those holding power to transfer some of that power to those who do not. Surrendering power does not come easily and for many, including senior bureaucrats, it represents an option they will not willingly accept. Yet transferring power is essential in implementing inclusive approaches and we return to this complex issue in the final chapter.

Recommended Reading

1. For an entertaining and illuminating account of the influence exercised by the élites in Canadian society, see P. Newman, *The Titans: How the New Canadian Establishment Seized Power* (Toronto: Penguin, 1998).

2. For a historical review of the poverty policy community, see R. Haddow, 'The Poverty Policy Community in Canada's Liberal Welfare State', in W. Coleman and G. Skogstad, eds, *Policy Communities and Public Policy in Canada* (Toronto: Copp Clark, 1993).

3. For a review of citizen participation in policy-making, see S. Phillips and M. Orsini, *Mapping the Links: Citizen Involvement in Policy Processes* (Ottawa: Canadian Policy Research Networks, 2002).

Chapter Seven

Policy-Making in Aboriginal Child and Family Services

The purpose of this chapter is to explore briefly some of the trends in policy-making in child and family services both within Aboriginal communities and in the interactions that occur between Aboriginal organizations and government. There is a wide range of publications on Aboriginal issues, and a growing number of these reflect the voices of Aboriginal people. The Aboriginal voice is not directly represented in this chapter. As non-Aboriginal people, we acknowledge the inherent limitations of providing an 'outsider' perspective on Aboriginal policy-making, and we do so cautiously and with a great deal of respect. However, one of the authors has had extensive experience in working with Aboriginal people, particularly in the area of Aboriginal child and family services, and it would be a serious omission in a book on Canadian social policy to fail to highlight some of the important policy-making developments occurring in the Aboriginal context.

The Policy-Making Context

The oppression of Aboriginal people has been well documented (see, e.g., Report of the Royal Commission on Aboriginal Peoples (RCAP), 1996; Assembly of First Nations, 2000). Indeed, it has been noted that Canada has been ranked at or near the top by the United Nations as the best place to live in the world, yet First Nations people living on reserves are ranked 63rd on a human development index (Fleras and Elliott, 1999). Health problems are more common among Aboriginal people, and despite major improvements, infant mortality rates are still twice as high in First Nations communities than in Canada as a whole. Suicide rates among the Aboriginal population average two to seven times that of the population for all of Canada, and chronic diseases such as diabetes and heart disease are increasing (Federal, Provincial and Territorial Advisory Committee on Population Health, 1999). The incarceration rates of Aboriginal people are five to six times the national average, Aboriginal children are overrepresented among those in the care of the child welfare system, and Aboriginal women are among the most severely disadvantaged in Canada (RCAP, 1996).

These circumstances are important to recognize; however, they do not tell the whole story. First, these data vary a great deal among groups and communities. Second, descriptive information on social conditions is inadequate without a discussion of causality. Finally, such information neglects the strengths and resiliency of Aboriginal people, and these are essential to any discussion of policy-making in the Aboriginal context.

The prevalence of health and social problems in many Aboriginal communities is closely related to the history of Aboriginal-white relations in North America. The legacy of colonization is reflected in government policies that deliberately undermined the viability of Aboriginal communities, divesting them of their land, culture, and tribal authority (Frideres, 1998). The treaties, which created reserves to deal with the 'Indian problem', and the *Indian Act* were instrumental in this process. But the residential school system and, after the 1960s, the mainstream child welfare system, also played key roles, not only in the assimilation of Aboriginal people, but also in undermining Aboriginal communities and culture. In residential schools, which were operated primarily by Catholic and Protestant churches with government support, Aboriginal traditions including one's language were banned (Miller, 1996).

In a Manitoba study conducted in 1994, 43 former residents of residential schools were interviewed (Manitoba Joint Committee on Residential Schools, 1994). Respondents related stories of excessive discipline and abuse, ridicule, and demeaning punishment. Almost half the respondents related experiences of sexual abuse. Three additional traumas were identified as having lasting effects on adult adjustment and parenting. One was the lack of love in most relationships with caregivers and teachers. Second was the denial of cultural expression, such as language, and the ridicule heaped on Aboriginal traditions, including spiritual beliefs. Third was the loss of a family experience, including the opportunity for positive bonding with parents, which was identified as having a continuing impact on adjustment and intergenerational parenting practices. As described by one respondent: '[I]t robbed me of my family life because I don't think I learned how to love—my whole childhood was stolen from me.' For many, the loss of a family experience was the most traumatic experience of the schools.

While the residential school system was an obvious instrument of colonialism, McKenzie and Hudson (1985) have demonstrated how the child welfare system, beginning with the 'sixties scoop' (Johnston, 1983) acted in similar ways by separating Aboriginal children from the families, communities, and culture.

Although the impact of the residential school system and conventional child welfare practices, prominent during the 1960s and 1970s, are essential aspects of understanding Aboriginal reality, not all problems can be fully explained by these developments. Other structural causes such as systematic racism, poverty, and inadequate opportunities are also important.

Problem analysis and needs assessment, as documented in Chapter 4, is an essential step in the policy-making process yet it needs to be matched with an understanding of strengths and resilience. Many individuals who attended residential schools not only survived but also emerged to play leadership roles within the Aboriginal community. At the collective level, cultural traditions and practices, including the role of the extended family have become key elements in the renewal of Aboriginal communities and their way of life.

Much has changed in Aboriginal services, both in relation to practice and policy in the past two decades. New agencies have been established to provide a variety of child and family-focused interventions, often using traditional frameworks such as the medicine wheel or circle as methods of organizing interventions (Graveline, 1998). Healing in an Aboriginal context is closely linked to spirituality, beginning with the individual and building outward to include family, community, and society (Assembly of First Nations, 2000; Connors and Maidman, 2001). For example, a successful community model of healing from child sexual abuse using the circle and concepts based on the medicine wheel has been established in Manitoba on the Hollow Water First Nation (Aboriginal Corrections Policy Unit, 1997). Within an Aboriginal worldview, healing and wellness are based on a commitment to holism, which can be defined as achieving harmony and balance among the physical, mental, spiritual, and emotional components of one's being. Holism is also connected to the development of a positive Aboriginal identity, and the focus on identity and its relationship to cultural expression has recently received increased attention in the literature on social work practice (Hart, 2002; McKenzie and Morrissette, 2003).

Local governance in the human services has transformed policy-making in many Aboriginal communities. In First Nations, local control of many health and education services are common, and the majority of these communities now have locally controlled child and family service agencies providing child welfare services under agreements that require federal funding and compliance with provincial legislation and standards. Aboriginal agencies have also developed in the urban context to provide early childhood education, interventions related to family violence, and a variety of youth and family related services. For example, Native Family Services of Toronto now has more than 150 employees and provides a range of culturally appropriate child- and family-related services in Canada's largest city.

Some of the services that have developed have been quite innovative. On the Kahnawake First Nation near Montreal, a highly successful model of community social services based on the principles of integration and wraparound services has been developed. An effective model of community-controlled child welfare services has been established by the Cowichan tribes in BC (Brown, Haddock, and Kovach, 2002). A wide range of community-based prevention services have been developed by West Region Child and Family Services in Manitoba and on the Blood First Nation in southern Alberta. Another example is the development of a custom adoption program by the Yellowhead Tribal Family Services Agency in Alberta.

There have also been some important developments at the national and provincial levels. In Saskatchewan, the Federation of Saskatchewan Indian Nations has developed its own child welfare legislation. Although this legislation does not have legal authority, it is frequently referenced as guidance in agreements that are established with First Nations in that province. Aboriginal political organizations at both the national and provincial levels have exerted considerable influence on social policy, primarily through a social advocacy stance; as well, specialized social policy organizations have been established. In child and family services, the First Nations Child and Family Caring Society of Canada has received funding from the Voluntary Sector Initiative, and now has an Ottawa-based office to coordinate selected policy initiatives across the country. In Ontario, there is an Association of Native Child and Family Services Agencies with a small staff complement to coordinate and promote effective policy-making in First Nations child and family services. These organizations, which perform roles often identified with both policy communities and advocacy groups, have the potential of influencing ongoing policy development in child and family services. Unfortunately, the two organizations noted above have very limited resources, and of course, this restricts their capacity.

There are many descriptive accounts of the evolution of social policy affecting Aboriginal people over the past decades; however, there is a noticeable absence of material to describe either the policy-making processes or preferred models of policy-making within the Aboriginal context. What follows is a summary of three different examples of policy-making in the field of Aboriginal child and family services. One example is drawn from the federal policy-making arena, a second comes from the provincial level, and the third reflects an organizational approach.

Shared Decision-Making at the Federal Level

In Chapter 6, shared decision-making was discussed as a model of inclusive policy-making. Such a model is important in policy-making where interactions are required between communities and government or where groups with power and authority are required to establish mutually acceptable policies and programs. However, the authenticity of shared decision-making processes is often difficult to establish, except through experience. Indeed, these processes are often described as collaborative or as partnerships even though many fail to live up to this potential. Partnership and collaboration, like shared decision-making, requires a commitment to shared power in shaping policy solutions; in addition, it requires policy actions that emerge from shared understanding or the joint decisions that have been made.

The Joint National Policy Review process is examined as an example of shared decision making. This process—a collaborative effort between the Assembly of First Nations, represented by First Nations child and family services agency directors, and the Department of Indian Affairs and Northern Development (DIAND)—was initiated to address problems in funding and related service development in First Nations child and family services.

Funding formulas and the level of funding are central to policy-making in child welfare because they play a key role in defining both the nature and scope of services that can be provided. The level of funding is closely tied to service quality, and the funding formula is an important determinant of the nature of services that will be provided. For example, if funding is provided primarily for protection services related to investigation, risk assessment, and out of home placement costs, this restricts the ability of an agency to provide early intervention and family support services.

Funding for First Nations child and family services was rationalized in a new funding formula established by DIAND that became effective in 1991. This formula, known simply as Directive 20-1, provides for operational grants to agencies based on the child population served by the agency and several other factors, including an allowance for remoteness. It also indicates that funding for child maintenance (i.e., the cost of maintaining children placed in alternative care) is to be reimbursed based on actual costs allowed by the relevant provincial authority. This formula, established as a top-down directive with little input from First Nations service providers, has been criticized for some time. Among other inadequacies, the formula used to establish the basic allocation for an agency has not been adjusted for changes in the cost of living since 1995.

In the mid-1990s, new First Nations child and family service agencies were beginning to develop in Saskatchewan. These First Nations controlled agencies, funded by DIAND, provided child and family services on reserves subject to provincial child welfare legislation. Concerns were raised in the province about funding issues with a request that DIAND address these; however, First Nations child and family service agencies in other provinces objected to a regional approach to issues that were, in fact, national in scope. Following meetings with DIAND officials in Ottawa, an agreement was struck to conduct a national policy review into First Nations child and family services in 1998. It took approximately one year to negotiate terms of reference for a process that would include equal representation from DIAND and First Nations child and family service agencies operating under the umbrella of the Assembly of First Nations. Each DIAND region (New Brunswick and Nova Scotia make up one region and other regions are equivalent to provincial boundaries) appointed one DIAND representative and one First Nations child and family service director to a Joint Steering Committee. A Project Management Team and a Policy Review Group, each adhering to the equal representation principle between DIAND and First Nations, were established (McDonald et al., 2000).

The first task was to hire research consultants to complete policy reviews on four thematic areas: agency governance, legislation and standards, communication issues, and funding issues. Funding issues, including the approach to funding service delivery and child maintenance, were central issues. The research projects were initiated in December 1999 and completed in May 2000. Project reports were then combined in a final report (McDonald et al., 2000) with a series of recommendations. Recommendations included the need to revise funding formulas to provide for a wider range of early intervention services, address inadequate elements in the current formula for supporting agency operations, and develop culturally appropriate service standards. An action plan for ratifying the report of the Joint National Policy Review and implementing recommendations through an ongoing partnership model was outlined.

The implementation phase included the development of a joint national committee to coordinate implementation activities at the national level and the establishment of regional tables, again based on the principle of partnership. Regional tables were established because of the recognition that it was also important to engage with representatives of provincial governments and that regional variations created issues that needed to be resolved at that level.

After the completion of the Joint National Policy Review, a separate study on the use of block funding in child maintenance was commissioned (McKenzie, 2002a). This review was designed to lead to a Cabinet submission for authority to establish flexible funding agreements for the child maintenance component (i.e., costs for foster, group, and institutional care) of an agency's child welfare budget. Agencies that entered into these agreements would receive a block grant that could be used for early intervention and family support programming if savings in the money spent on out-of-home care were realized.

Results from this experience in shared decision-making at the federal level have been mixed. The process initially generated goodwill and a shared understanding of issues that has helped senior policy-makers in DIAND in their efforts to promote policies on behalf of First Nations agencies. As well, special submissions for the 2003–4 budget were made for increased funding for family support services in First Nations communities and for authority to establish flexible funding arrangements for First Nations' agencies. While the flexible funding proposal was approved, new funding for family support services was not included, and this has led to considerable frustration on the part of those who have invested in the process. First Nations participants at the policy tables have not been involved in meetings beyond the divisional level in DIAND. Thus, the development of final proposals and the presentation of these proposals to central bodies such as Cabinet and Treasury Board have been handled by senior departmental staff. Delays have also been a factor. For example, ratification of the report of the Joint National Policy Review by the minister of Indian Affairs was delayed by several months and this has meant that implementation is far behind schedule. And while there has been support for both the process and many of the recommendations within the Social Policy Division of DIAND, resistance has been encountered at other levels, including Cabinet and Treasury Board. Some of this resistance reflects a concern about cost implications, but there is also little appreciation for the partnership approach to policy-making and the need to expedite the excessive bureaucratic procedures that too often impede rather than enable new policy initiatives at the governmental level.

Creating a Policy Community at the Provincial Level

The second example described in this chapter is a provincial initiative launched in Manitoba to restructure child welfare services in the province, whereby new Aboriginal authorities would assume responsibility for the provision of child and family services to most, if not all, Aboriginal service users throughout the province. This initiative is known as the Aboriginal Justice Inquiry Child Welfare Initiative because the recommendation on which the policy was based first appeared in the Report of the Aboriginal Justice Inquiry released in 1991 (Hamilton and Sinclair).

This model reflects aspects of shared decision-making in that policy-makers from Aboriginal organizations and government became involved in negotiations that led to new proposals on how child welfare services would be transferred to new Aboriginal authorities. However, because both Aboriginal and government partners shared a strong commitment to a common policy outcome at the outset, that is, the transfer of jurisdiction to Aboriginal authorities, this example is more reflective of a policy community. Participants worked together in developing ways to make this policy goals a reality, and although differences have emerged, these have been related to operational and implementation issues rather than the essential purposes and intent of the new policy.

In 1999, the NDP government initiated a process that is designed to transfer responsibility for the provision of child welfare services for all Aboriginal people in the province to new Aboriginal Child and Family Service authorities. Unlike the devolution process in BC described in Chapter 6, this initiative was not designed as a cost-saving venture but as a method to support Aboriginal jurisdiction over child welfare services. As noted, the policy change reflected a recommendation originally made in an inquiry into Aboriginal justice in the province, and it was consistent with requests from both the Manitoba Metis Federation and First Nations groups in the province for greater control, particularly over services provided to Aboriginal people living off-reserve.

In Manitoba, First Nations controlled child and family service agencies have been providing a full range of child welfare services on reserves since the mid-1980s under a tripartite arrangement that includes provincial legislation and standards and federal funding. However, approximately one-half of First Nations people in the province live off-reserve, and these families and children generally receive services from non-Aboriginal agencies. In addition, Metis people have no separate child welfare agency designed to respond to their particular needs and aspirations. Aboriginal children make up the majority of children-in-care population in the province; for example, in 2001 it was estimated that Aboriginal children made up about 21 per cent of Manitoba's population under the age of 15, yet they accounted for 78 per cent of the children in care (Manitoba Family Services and Housing as cited in Joint Management Committee, 2001). The policy change contemplated, then, was designed to provide Aboriginal people with greater control over the provision of child welfare services to Aboriginal families and children and enable more community-based, culturally appropriate models of service delivery.

An inclusive policy-making process that involved the provincial government and Aboriginal political organizations in the province was established, based partly on the new NDP government's commitment to a more collaborative approach and Aboriginal demands for greater control over both the process and outcomes of policy-making in child welfare. Three Aboriginal partners were identified: the Manitoba Metis Federation (MMF), the Assembly of Manitoba Chiefs (AMC) representing Southern First Nations, and Manitoba Keewatinowi Okimakanak (MKO) representing Northern First Nations.

The first step involved negotiations between the province and Aboriginal organizations. This led to the signing of three separate Memorandums of Understanding (MOUs) between the province and each Aboriginal group. Subsequently, all four parties signed a Service Protocol Agreement that identified a framework and principles for the planning process. Each stakeholder group (the two First Nations groups were defined as one stakeholder group in determining committee memberships) had an equal number of representatives on the various policy-making structures, a decision that put government members in the minority. The structure included an Executive Committee, a Joint Management Committee, an Implementation Committee, and working groups.

The Joint Management Committee is generally responsible for the initiative and it reports to the Executive Committee, which includes two provincial ministers and representatives from the three Aboriginal partners. The more detailed policy-making activities occurred at the Implementation Committee level that was responsible for coordinating the planning process, developing the initial conceptual plan, and establishing detailed implementation guidelines. This committee also received reports from seven working groups, set up to review and make recommendations on topics such as legislative change, financing, and service delivery models.

Policy-making discussions at the committee level produced some interesting policy debates. For example, the minister had outlined three key principles for the new initiative. The reforms were to be cost-neutral, new services would be provided under a delegated authority model (i.e., services would adhere to provincial legislation and standards, as amended), and service users would have a choice about which authority to access for services: The General Authority (non-Aboriginal), Metis, First Nations North, or First Nations South. Although the principle of delegated authority has been accepted, modifications have been made to the other two principles because of Aboriginal objections. For example, the province has provided significant transitional funding and the choice of which authority provides services has been somewhat restricted. The right to choose a service provider was a particularly contentious issue. Given the dominant society's historical pattern of assimilating Aboriginal people, it was argued that the new Aboriginal authorities should not be denied the right to reclaim their members by becoming the service providers of first resort. Those opposing this viewpoint asserted the rights of service users to self-determination as a guiding principle. Under the present arrangement, the service user still has some level of personal choice; however, the first priority will be to refer users to the service provider that best matches their cultural background.

Four different child and family service authorities have been established under new legislation that entrenches the right of Aboriginal people to receive services from agencies established under a governance structure composed of persons directly appointed by the political body that represents their people. Each authority has a province-wide mandate and can provide services to families and children from its cultural group anywhere in the province. However, each authority will not have service delivery units in all parts of the province, and contractual arrangements with the primary service provider in a community will occur in circumstances where the designated authority does not have an office in the area.

For example, in all likelihood a Metis family living on reserve will receive service from the First Nations agency providing service on that reserve. Joint intake procedures have been developed to provide emergency services and to identify the Authority of Record for the child and family (i.e., the authority from which they would normally receive service based on their cultural affiliation). If an agency representing their Authority of Record exists in the area, they would normally be referred to this agency for continuing services. There is an assumption that members of First Nations, persons identifying as Metis, and non-Aboriginal persons, will want to be served by service providers mandated by their respective authorities. Aboriginal families and children currently receiving services from non-Aboriginal agencies will be transferred to new First Nations and Metis service providers along with related resources—a procedure that will lead to a dramatic downsizing of non-Aboriginal child and family service agencies in the province.

The new policy initiative developed through this partnership model was in the process of being implemented at the time of this writing, and outcomes cannot be accurately predicted given the magnitude of the change process that is involved. However, some preliminary observations, particularly in relation to the policy-making process, can be made. First, there has been a significant level of collaboration between government and Aboriginal participants, including a determination to circumvent bureaucratic imperatives that interfered with the general policy intent. A problem-solving approach based on respect and goodwill has characterized the process, and this has enabled the development of a model that may facilitate the provision of more culturally appropriate child welfare services in the province. For example, the drafting of the *Child and Family Services Authorities Act* was done in close consultation with the Implementation Committee. This Committee developed detailed specifications of what should be in new legislation and then government personnel drafted the legislation. Draft legislation was then returned to the Committee for comments and suggestions for revision prior to debate in the legislature and government was responsive to most of these suggestions. Government has also been responsive on other issues, including funding for training and the transitional costs pertaining to the development of new authorities and Aboriginal agencies.

Second, despite the collaborative approach taken by government with representatives from Aboriginal groups in the province, there was a failure to consult with and inform other important constituencies, particularly in the formative stages of the policy process. Although there was a general public consultation process in the fall of 2001 after the development of the conceptual plan, this process was quite limited. For example, only 12 town hall meetings, as they were known, and 15 focus groups were held throughout the province. In addition, the province made little effort to involve non-Aboriginal agencies or staff in the process. This failure has contributed to feelings of low morale among current child welfare staff and may lead to resistance in the policy implementation phase. Although some of these reactions are normal in any major policy change that may affect future job security, among other things, much of this could have been avoided. Indeed, most child welfare staff were supportive of the general policy goal even if they were concerned about implementation issues and processes. And as noted in Chapter 5, the involvement of existing staff is essential in ensuring service quality and continuity in the implementation phase.

Finally, there are some shortcomings to the policy-making process itself. The initial goal was focused primarily on a change in jurisdiction where service users in child welfare would receive services from authorities based on their cultural affiliation. Of secondary importance was a shift in the service paradigm to a more family support, resource-oriented approach to child welfare. Although this issue was not neglected entirely, it is anticipated that new agencies, established as a result of a change in jurisdiction, will create their own model of service. For example, they might reduce expenditures on high cost methods of out-of-home care and re-invest these savings in more community-based services. This may occur, but there has been no detailed attention to approaches that might shift the provision of child welfare services from a model that focuses almost exclusively on 'search and rescue' to one that includes a major emphasis on early intervention and family support. Nor has there been any government commitment to new expenditures to 'jump-start' such a paradigm shift.

Community Governance and Child Welfare

In this example, we explore the outcomes emerging from an inclusive approach to policy development undertaken by a First Nations child and family services agency operating under a community governance structure.

West Region Child and Family Services has provided a full range of child welfare services to nine First Nations communities in Manitoba since 1985. It is recognized as an agency that exhibits best practices in child and family services, and in 1998 it received the Peter T. Drucker Award for Canadian Non-Profit Innovation for its work in early intervention and family support and the use of the medicine wheel as an organizing framework for these services.

The agency has made innovative use of flexible funding for child maintenance since 1992 when it negotiated the first block funding agreement in First Nations child welfare with DIAND. This agreement capped the amount of money received for child maintenance (i.e., foster, group, and institutional care costs) based on the previous year's actuals and a projected cost increase for the upcoming operating year. However, the agency was permitted to use any money not required for out-of-home care costs to develop alternative programs focusing on early intervention and family support. By developing lower-cost alternative care options for children, such as a therapeutic foster care program, the agency was able to provide good-quality, culturally appropriate care for children requiring placement while reducing some of its costs on expensive residential care in places like Winnipeg. In turn, these savings have helped to establish a wide range of early intervention and family support programs. In 1999–2000, almost one-third of the agency's child maintenance allocation was being spent on alternative programs while the agency continued to provide high service to those children requiring out-of-home placement (McKenzie, 2002a).

Of particular importance to the continued success of this agency has been its adoption of an inclusive approach to policy-making that includes staff, community members, and service users (McKenzie, 2002b). The agency uses a community-based planning approach at both a regional and local level to receive feedback on existing services and to develop new initiatives. For example, regional operational workshops, involving all staff and a wide range of representatives from each community, are held every two years. A similar exercise occurs at the local level; each community-based service team organizes a community-planning workshop on child and family services annually or every two years. Not only are these helpful in realizing the goal of community accountability, but they also serve as a means for setting priorities, community education, and recruiting community volunteers.

The organizational structure of the agency also facilitates community involvement. Each local community has a community-based service team, and these staff work in collaboration with a Child and Family Services Committee. This committee of local volunteers plays an active role in providing advice and assistance on both child protection and prevention matters.

The focus on a collaborative process to community building also characterizes some of the work with service user groups. One illustrative example was the Vision Seekers Program, a partnership program designed to develop life skills and educational upgrading for youth. Working in partnership with other funders, the agency hired community facilitators to undertake a circle consultation process with youth and other community members to develop the program.

A collaborative working style is characteristic of the agency's internal operations and staff play an important ongoing role through their participation in service team meetings and the management team. In addition, they are engaged in special initiatives such as the planning and management of community prevention initiatives (see Box 7.1).

Conclusion

Aboriginal people, more than any other group in Canadian society, have had policies 'done to them'. Only in the past 25 years has that begun to change. Yet uncertainties persist because of problems in funding and the inconsistent approach of governments in establishing a policy framework that will promote both local autonomy and service quality. In addition, there are contradictions within some Aboriginal organizations and communities where top-down hierarchical models of policy-making prevail.

We first consider the contradictions that exist within some Aboriginal communities and organizations. It is often argued that the more hierarchical models of power and control that exist in some Aboriginal organizations reflect patterns learned through the legacy of colonization. Although this may be true, the reality often leaves many involved in the human services (both service providers and service users) with unmet needs and feelings of disempowerment. Under these circumstances, local control is an imperfect solution. Although we recognize this problem, it is equally clear that substituting government authority for local control is unlikely to resolve these difficulties. First, the state has a poor record of

Box 7.1 Community Governance in Action: An Example of Inclusive Policy-Making

Faced with a dilemma of how to plan and deliver community-based prevention programs to nine First Nations communities, West Region Child and Family Services developed a collaborative approach to planning, implementing, and evaluating the variety of community-based initiatives that could be financially supported through a fund set up for this purpose. Although the amount of funding is significant, there is never enough to fund all programs that can be sponsored to support at-risk children and families. Thus there was a need to establish priorities among a variety of proposed new initiatives, and to institute a process for doing this that could be used for each annual budget cycle. The first step was to design a method that would enable good decisions, involve key people in the process, and be regarded as fair by participating staff and communities. This involved the participation of community-based prevention staff, along with senior staff, in setting criteria for the selection of projects, and a protocol for proposal development and accountability. On an annual basis in each community, local staff now undertake a planning process to design and prioritize program initiatives, in collaboration with their local child and family service committee. These are then formally submitted to the agency's selection committee comprised of selected senior staff and one prevention worker from each community. Following an agency decision on the amount of money to be allocated to community prevention programs, the selection committee then meets to make decisions on which programs will receive funding, and the amount of funding to be allocated. As the budget is significant, each community receives approval for several initiatives. Responsibility is then transferred to the local prevention workers and child and family services committees to complete the detailed planning and implementation stages for each approved project. Local staff and committees are also responsible for submitting a report to account for expenditures and provide evaluative feedback after each community project has been completed.

protecting the rights and aspirations of Aboriginal people, and second, changes that are likely to be both responsive to community and long-lasting must come from within. This is not to suggest the government has no role. It has a responsibility to ensure the essential rights of citizens no matter where they live and facilitate processes consistent with the basic tenets of democracy and community capacity-building. Standards and accountability mechanisms for services delegated to community-based organizations are necessary, and these can enhance the provision of high-quality services.

We turn now to an examination of the role of government and Aboriginal organizations in the making of Aboriginal social policies.

Some of the seeds of change were sown in the 1970s, but it was the next two decades that saw more dramatic changes in the development of Aboriginal social policy. The impetus for many of these changes resulted from two parallel processes. On the one hand, Aboriginal organizations became an effective social movement in making the case for a number of changes consistent with the goal of self-government. Although some disruptive tactics, including various kinds of blockades, reflected levels of discontent, the strategy also included advocacy and negotiation efforts that were persuasive with government. As well, there was a growing number of reports and studies that documented both the high level of need and the failure of past government policies. This culminated with the appointment of the Royal Commission on Aboriginal Peoples (RCAP) in 1991. Canada's most expensive commission released its final report in November 1996 along with 440 recommendations. The information from this report and others, coupled with a general level of public support for changes, have helped to build support for the devolution of at least some level control over Aboriginal policy-making to Aboriginal organizations and communities.

Three examples of inclusive models of policy-making were summarized in this chapter, and some tentative conclusions can be drawn from these experiences. The shared decision-making approach at the federal level has had a limited impact on policy outcomes to date, and it has been a very time-consuming process. This may reflect, in part, the complexity of policy-making processes at the federal government level. Without a genuine commitment on the part of government to modify the bureaucratic procedures that often get in the way of collaborative approaches to policy-making, shared decision-making can raise expectations that may not be realized. However, the collaborative model related to the Joint National Policy Review is continuing and some significant policy changes may yet materialize. It will be important to examine the results from this experience as the process unfolds.

The policy community approach in the Aboriginal Justice Inquiry Child Welfare Initiative appears to have been successful in establishing the framework for a policy change that will have major implications for the provision of child welfare services to Aboriginal people in Manitoba. Control over all child welfare services in the province will be transferred to Aboriginal authorities, and new legislation provides a framework for the development of culturally appropriate services. While the realization of intended policy outcomes will be dependent on the success of the implementation phase, there has been a strong commitment among the key stakeholders to break new ground in building a collaborative approach to policy-making. If there is an ongoing commitment to an adaptive approach to implementation, the potential benefits of this policy change will be increased.

The community approach to policy development established by West Region Child and Family Services provides an exemplar of what can be accomplished when an inclusive model is embraced as a comprehensive approach to policy-making at the community level. However, the success of this model is also dependent on other factors, and two of the most important of these are effective leadership and skilled and committed staff.

Recommended Reading

1. For a more detailed discussion of social work practice with Aboriginal Canadians, see B. McKenzie and V. Morrissette, 'Social Work Practice with Canadians of Aboriginal Background: Guidelines for Respectful Social Work', in A. Al-Krenawi and J.R. Graham, eds, *Multicultural Social Work in Canada* (Toronto: Oxford University Press, 2003), pp. 251–82.

2. For a detailed review of the Hollow Water model for dealing with sexual abuse, see Aboriginal Corrections Policy Unit, *The Four Circles of Hollow Water* (Ottawa: Supply and Services Canada, 1997).

3. For more information on healing in Aboriginal communities, see E. Connors and F. Maidman, 'A Circle of Healing: Family Wellness in Aboriginal Communities', in I. Prilleltensky, G. Nelson, and L. Pierson, eds, *Promoting Family Wellness and Preventing Child Maltreatment* (Toronto: University of Toronto Press, 2001), pp. 349–416.

This chapter reviews the contributions of feminist thinking to policy-making. If I were writing this chapter a decade ago, I would take a very different tack than I will today. Much has changed in the past 10 years, including the vibrancy and currency of the women's movement. Further, issues of concern to feminists have been swept off the policy table in the rush to clean house of social programs and enhance the role of private interests in what used to be public responsibilities. There has been a sea change in expectations concerning the role of government and the rights of citizens to demand action to redress inequities. Even in academia, there is cold comfort. Some scholars claim that the women's agenda of the past 30 years has been largely accomplished now that women are occupying some of the key roles in academic administration and gaining proportional representation in many disciplines. These researchers ignore the fact that they are confusing gains for all women with the progress of those who are more privileged.[1] Some fields, including social work, that were formerly sympathetic have turned attention to thinking that subsumes feminist perspectives under broader theorizing about oppression, and race in particular. Feminism seems out of fashion in many quarters.

In this chapter, I take issue with these scholarly assertions and argue that more than ever it is crucial to include feminist perspectives in relation to social problems and policy responses. I examine some of the foundations of feminist thinking and its importance to current issues, and I then look at two gender lenses prepared by the Status of Women Canada and by the BC government that offer frameworks for including feminist thinking in policy-making.

Feminist Thinking

Feminist thinking is very consistent with the aims of this book, connecting policy to practice, since it emphasizes the importance of connecting the experiences of those on the ground with both policy and practice. It identifies an agenda for policy-makers based on issues that are often buried, because the voice of women is not frequently heard in policy-making circles. Yet, since most of the clients and workers in the human services are women, their perspectives are crucial to include in this process.

The following example illustrates the dimensions and importance of feminist thinking. A few years ago, I was involved in a research project examining policy alternatives to address the issue of women and substance use during pregnancy (Rutman et al., 1999). During the project, a team of Aboriginal researchers met with rural Aboriginal women to discuss whether women should be restrained or incarcerated if they continued to use substances during pregnancy. Initially, the women in the group agreed with the idea, citing their own experiences within their families and voicing concerns about future generations of their people. However, as they considered the question, they thought about how such a policy would actually play out in their lives. Which women would be restrained? Mostly Aboriginal women, they predicted, even though more non-Aboriginal women use substances during pregnancy. Why? Because Aboriginal women are more visible to those in the helping and policing professions, because they have fewer resources to resist and challenge policies, because they frequently live in rural areas where treatment facilities are nonexistent, and because they are generally disregarded were some reasons cited. The women reflected on the inordinate numbers of Aboriginal peoples in federal and provincial jails as a similar consequence of applying policies without regard to differing circumstances.

They also suggested that resources used for incarceration would continue to funnel funds away from helpful programs and that the policy would continue the stereotyping of Aboriginal people. Within and amongst their own communities, they concluded that the policy would further separate communities and residents already disadvantaged by historical, geographical, and economic realities. They gave examples of hardships that some women and their families would suffer.

Although they resisted an incarceration policy, they proposed solutions of their own. These included such ideas as reinstating the practice of traditional home visitors, usually senior women in the community, reforming health care funding policies so that funds could be distributed to women's organizations concerned with health and social issues, and dismantling the Band Council structures created under the *Indian Act*. To them, Band Councils reflect the colonizing aims of government policies and undermine the hereditary organization of communities, creating élites within the community and disenfranchising many women. The women were also careful to underscore that their suggestions might work for their Tribal Council and communities but may not suit others.

Schroedel and Peretz (1994), reflecting on the same issue in the United States where several states have enacted policies permitting the incarceration of women using substances during pregnancy, raise another question. Why has the focus of media and research turned relentlessly on women's behaviour during pregnancy and not on other toxic hazards in the environment or to the effects of alcohol and drug use by men that can damage sperm and lead to violent behaviour towards pregnant women?

There is no overt conspiracy among lawyers, medical professionals and journalists to define fetal abuse in a manner that blames the woman while ignoring the man's role. Instead there is simply a pre-disposition to view the world through analytical lenses that replicate and reinforce the existing gender biases. (Schroedel and Peretz, 1994, p. 355)

This discussion by Aboriginal women and American scholars illustrates several central planks of feminist theorizing, which in itself contains many different and sometimes opposing strands. Although it is impossible to provide a thorough review of feminist thinking and its variations and controversies, a few essentials require mention.

The principle that equal outcomes will not occur by treating everyone the same is fundamental to feminist thinking. That Canadian women do not have the same economic advantages as Canadian men at the beginning of the twenty-first century, although they have the same access to public education where they perform at least as well as their male counterparts, is clear evidence of this fact. Most institutions and policies have been designed and are controlled by middle-aged men, not by any conspiracy but by tradition and by the ongoing advantaging process within these patriarchal structures that maintain this tradition. How that advantaging process works is often unrecognized because it is so familiar, so accepted, and so normalized. One component of this process is the creation of knowledge: Whose way of perceiving the world becomes accepted knowledge and whose ways are ignored? For instance, the idea of reforming Band structures imposed on Aboriginal nations has not gained the same currency as incarcerating women who use substances during pregnancy. Feminist thinking seeks to disrupt that sense of normalcy.

Creating space for different ways of knowing is one way to challenge the status quo. From the experiences of women in daily life come the questions: How does this process affect me and how is it perpetuated? Why are things the way they are? This examination frequently reveals the interconnection between dichotomies—the economic and the social, the private and the public, the emotional and the rational— that frame our 'usual' thinking. Disrupting the old adage that women are too emotional to think rationally has been particularly important in enhancing women's contributions to policy-making. Feminists have revealed that feelings held by men and women play a significant role in the shaping of policies. They have further demonstrated that highly emotional experiences can nonetheless motivate action and inspire innovations. The work of Mothers Against Drunk Drivers (MADD) is a good illustration of this. Formed by a few women who lost children in automobile accidents, the group has a strong record in gaining acceptance for their policy suggestions.

Further, as women understand their own experience of oppression and advantage, they develop an understanding of the experiences of others who suffer disadvantage. The Aboriginal women who spoke about being marginalized connected this to the behaviour of some men in their communities; in turn, they related this to the patriarchal systems imposed on the men by white government policies. Feminist thinking exposes injustice in many quarters, working from the individual injustices experienced by women. And it benefits from other theories of oppression, such as those developed by Aboriginal peoples and others regarding colonization. It enriches these theories, exposing how gender interacts with other socially constructed disadvantages. Feminism is most misunderstood on this particular issue because there is a common misconception that it reveals the oppression of women only. The strength of feminism lies in its grounding in the everyday experiences of half the population and the movement beyond that to uncover how systems work to perpetuate inequities for many.

This process of uncovering injustices reveals clearly that while all women are negatively affected by patriarchal values and systems, some women and some groups of both men and women are more harmed than others. Although those who feel the pain of oppression most severely are those most disadvantaged by race, class, gender, ability, sexual orientation, and other socially constructed categories of privilege, individual identities can change in different circumstances. In one group, for example, individuals can be privileged on some occasions and severely penalized in others. As Yeatman (1993) notes: '[T]he realization that western women can be, at one and the same time, both the victims and beneficiaries of globalization, has forced western mainstream feminism to lose its innocence' (p. 228).

This same message is echoed by Brodie (1995, p. 79): '[feminism] has lost the moral high ground that comes with the depiction of all women everywhere as victims of patriarchy.' Perhaps one of the most important advances in feminist thinking is the concept that because of the differences amongst women it is important to break down such overarching concepts as feminist, oppression, patriarchy, organizing, and the state. Within each of these concepts are many competing definitions and different experiences that enrich thinking.

Embedded in the notion of movement between privilege and disadvantage is another key plank of feminist thinking: Women are not only victims of oppression but also actors within oppressive systems who can maintain and disrupt them. Creating different ways of knowing is one way of disrupting. Demonstrating other ways of making decisions and taking actions besides those generally accepted as proper and professional is another. The latter section of this chapter examines the contributions of feminist perspectives to thinking and behaving differently in policy-making processes.

The Women's Movement in the Current Context

Earlier, I commented that the women's movement seems to be flagging at the turn of this century compared to its stature and energy of previous decades. Has feminist thinking and action simply 'had its day' or is it finding new expressions to deal with tough new realities?

Margaret Little (1999) makes an argument for the necessity of feminist thinking to address the economic and ideological propositions of neo-conservatism, yet she underscores the difficulty facing women, particularly poor women, as they try to make such a challenge. She observes that the changes to income-assistance programs, including reduced benefits and workfare, are premised on the notion of the gender-neutral worker who, except for training and life skills, will be able to find employment. The home work of women, including child and elder care, is ignored in this construction and illustrates how treating everyone equally leads to unequal outcomes. At the same time, welfare-policing policies that include 'snitch lines' and administrative surveillance have the impact of casting income recipients, particularly women, as morally suspect. Searching out whether women are co-habitating with partners has been a thrust of these programs. Because women are more likely to be poor than men, they bear the brunt of these policies that both reduce their incomes and the moral authority for them to protest these reductions. This latter point is key. Although it has always been difficult to mount public sympathy for those on income assistance, in the past mothers were deemed to be somewhat more 'worthy'. No longer. And mobilizing action on their behalf is made more difficult, even though the need for that action is greater now.

Another force constricting women's space for mounting protest has emerged from alliances and choices that feminist groups have made to combat the impact of neo-conservatism. For instance, Wendy McKeen (1999) provides a detailed account of how the feminist agenda on women and poverty shifted from the quest to obtain independent benefits for women, regardless of their family affiliations, to a strategy to improve the lot of women by improving the condition of the poor overall. The seeds for this shift emerged over the last two decades, as feminists tried to enhance the 'deservedness' of poor women by focusing on the single mother. Thus it was a short journey from the focus on the single mother to an emphasis on child poverty, and feminist groups joined with other social justice organizations in Campaign 2000 in an effort to eliminate child poverty by the year 2000.

One response by the federal government, the National Child Benefit (NCB) and the National Child Benefit Supplement (NCBS), introduced in 1998 to address child poverty, has received mixed reviews. Chapter 9 takes up the story of these programs, but it is pertinent to note here that some provinces have chosen to deduct the NCBS from welfare payments with the result that some families on income assistance, mostly female-headed families, have received little if any increase in benefits to date (Swift and Birmingham, 2000).[2] Abrupt cut-off lines making irrational divisions between families with almost the same incomes, the selective nature of the program leaving out many families and insufficient funding overall making little dint in poverty, are other concerns (Durst, 1999; McKeen, 2001). Most particularly for this discussion, it has obscured the fact that most of the people who are poor are women with dependent children.

Brodie (1995) provides a comprehensive analysis of the challenges facing feminist organizations in Canada and elsewhere, such as the diminishing of welfare state provisions and the loss of confidence in the state to ameliorate inequities through direct programs; the casting of feminist organizations as special interest groups, opposed to the needs and desires of 'ordinary' Canadians; the acceptance of economic independence as a badge of citizenship in spite of the demands of home; the rise of part-time non-unionized jobs; and the faith in the capacity of the private sector, both the home and business, to address social needs. She emphasizes that all these forces have reduced the opportunities and space for feminist voices. Those protesting the restructured state appear to be out of step with the times, hanging on to the old 'nanny state' with no new visions to inform governments. Not surprisingly, many feminist activists have turned away from opposing state actions to protest global economies and systems that are wreaking havoc with deeply held understandings about citizenship, environment, and social responsibility. Naomi Klein's *No Logo* (2001) is a good example of feminist analysis about the connections between social and economic well-being. Feminist groups, such as the National Action Committee on the Status of Women, have connections with women's organizations throughout the globe and use these to challenge basic tenets of globalization. Yet, abandoning the protest against the dismantling of human services within a country such as Canada is tantamount to admitting that neo-conservatives have a point.

How to act with vision and purpose in these circumstances is indeed a challenge, particularly since funds for such organizing have been reduced as part of government cutbacks. Brodie (1995) suggests that a fundamental strategy is to challenge the orthodoxy of the neo-conservative claims at every opportunity and in terms that both underscores their contradictions to Canadian traditions and values and links them to violations of national and international human rights agreements. Roy Romanow, reporting in his Commission on the Future of Health Care in Canada (2002), illustrates this approach, but it is too early to determine its effectiveness. He dismantles arguments about the cost effectiveness of private health care systems and instead calls on Canadians to reaffirm their commitment to national health standards and delivery. Neo-conservatives were quick to denounce the report as 'living in the past' and the work of an avowed socialist.

A further approach, disguising feminist agendas in the gender-neutral manifestos of others, has proven a highly compromising and ineffective strategy to advance women's concerns. It is better to be clear about the feminist agenda and join with others whose concerns are sympathetic to women's issues and share energy and strategies with them. The strategy of 'seizing the moment' is also one that has proved effective for women and others with little power in policy-making processes. For instance, a particular scandal or tragedy may open public debate and provide opportunities for action where none existed before.

Another long-standing strategy has been to introduce feminist thinking and structures within government and to deploy feminists in a wide range of state positions where they can, through daily actions within government and connections with community feminist groups, seek to change the culture of policy-making (Rankin and Vickers, 2001). The work of these 'femocrats' has been very important in several areas, including policies dealing with violence against women and education and training for women.

> Our research concludes that, particularly in an era marked by globalization and decentralization, 'bothering with government' is still pivotal to the achievement of equality and justice for all women. We encourage feminist organizations to engage in an ongoing evaluation of the political opportunity structures they face and call for renewed debate on how feminists can work most effectively with policy makers. Finally, we argue that women's policy machinery can be an important partner with feminists in public policy debates, but new channels of communication between state feminism and women's movements are required. (Rankin and Vickers, 2001, p. 36)

The development of gender lenses that infuse all policies with gender concerns from the outset is one outcome of the work of 'femocrats' and is the subject of the next section of this chapter. These lenses attempt to open new channels of communication amongst policy-makers and women both within and outside government.

What Does Feminist Thinking Offer to Policy-Making?

Feminists can seek to influence large-scale government policies, as well as more local ones. The gender lens discussed in Chapter 4 is one tool for introducing feminist thinking into policy/practice, although its actual use in practice is very uneven. In Chapter 4 the gender lens developed by the BC Ministry of Women's Equality (1994) was introduced, but a gender-sensitive model for policy analysis has also been developed by Status of Women Canada (1996). The lenses are written for those in policy-making positions to ensure that whatever policies are under consideration—be they the introduction of rapid transit, a change to the forest practices code, or the introduction of zero tolerance for family violence—consider the impact on women and men:

> It makes it possible for policy to be undertaken with an appreciation of gender differences, of the nature of relationships between women and men and of their different social realities, life expectations and economic circumstances. Gender-based analysis challenges the assumption that everyone is affected by policies, programs and legislation in the same way regardless of gender, a notion often referred to as 'gender-neutral policy'. (Status of Women Canada, 1996, p. 1.2)

Both gender lenses under consideration (federal and provincial) in this section of the chapter unfold according to the stages of policy/practice development that are discussed throughout this book. While they propose approaches for infusing feminist thinking into policy-making, they could also apply to professional practice. The similarities between the policy-making process and the problem-solving process used by many professionals, including social workers, has been long evident (Wharf and Callahan, 1984).

The BC lens makes the case for feminist thinking in policy through the introduction of 10 principles, many of which are discussed earlier in the chapter. The principles are:

- Every government policy has a human impact.
- Policies affect men and women differently.
- Women are not a homogeneous group.
- Policies must attempt to create equal outcomes for men and women.
- Equal outcomes will not result from treating everyone the same.
- Equal outcomes benefit everyone.
- Policy-makers bring their own biases to the job.
- The best policies are those where consultation has played a considerable role.

- Special measures are required so that those disadvantaged can make their views known.
- Consultation is ongoing and not a one-off business.

At each stage of the policy-making process, the lenses provide a series of questions that emerge from these principles and that policy-makers should address (see Chapter 4). In the discussion that follows, a few key points illustrate the principles in action at each stage.

1. Identifying the Issues

At the first stage of policy-making, problem identification, the gender lens requires policy-makers to consider the issue from the perspective of women in particular and include the views of women and men from disadvantaged economic, social, and cultural groups. Of course, the principal strategy for understanding issues in this way is to listen to women and provide opportunities for them to make their views known. Listening to and beginning with the client's definition of the problem or issue has long been a hallmark of social work practice.

Although this advice seems logical, the reality of taking it is more complex. In recent years, funding for women's groups and research has fallen markedly. Thus, consulting on a consistent basis is made more difficult and requires additional resources. How women define the issue will not in all likelihood fit with government agendas and preconceived notions about how problems should be solved.

Yet, as the lenses make clear, every issue has a gender component. For instance, developing policies on highways may seem gender-neutral until consideration is given to such things as the effects of highway location on affordable housing, public transportation, and the location of schools and community resources. Consider the following example. Young people leaving care argue for bridging policies to help them establish themselves as independent adults before financial and social support is withdrawn—the kind of support that parents continue to give to their 'launching' children well into their twenties (National Youth in Care Network, 1998; Strega, 2000). A gender analysis of this issue, however, reveals that young women in care may define 'launching' differently because some of them already have children of their own.

2. Defining Goals and Outcomes

Gender lenses urge policy-makers to understand again how naming specific goals and outcomes could affect men and women differently and, in particular, how outcomes could be achieved equally for men and women by creative thinking. It suggests that policy-makers should deconstruct such gender-neutral terms as farmers, workers, dependants, clients, and taxpayers, and consider the differences that gender creates within these groups. For instance, the BC lens provides an example of a policy goal of increasing the numbers of 'young people' entering the sciences, targeting five hundred additional youth each year. Without examining the issues preventing women from choosing scientific pursuits, the policy will continue to favour young men. Setting targets for female enrolment with outreach programs to interest them can redress these imbalances.

3. Defining Information Needs and Conducting Research

Here the gender lenses emphasize how policy-makers' values and preconceptions can get in the way of knowing what is necessary to develop equitable policies. To address this barrier, they recommend such approaches as obtaining information 'on the ground' from women's organizations and from creative, informal resources, comparing their own values with those of others and with research findings, and designing creative research methods to ensure that the views of men and women will be known.

There are several research groups in Canada that focus on feminist research issues and methods, although funding for these is modest when compared with all funding provided for research. The Status of Women Canada research program, the Canadian Research Institute for the Advancement of Women, the Freda Centre for Research on Violence Against Women and Children, and the National Action Committee on the Status of Women are a few. Other research resources are contained within universities.[3] Feminist research, however, faces many challenges. Research methods are frequently nontraditional and fight to gain credibility with generally accepted ways of creating knowledge. The scope of feminist research is broad: investigating new issues and challenging the research findings of others. For instance, the Fraser Institute, a right-wing think-tank, has many resources to commit to research that discredits the value of social programs while women's groups scramble for dollars to challenge these findings.

4. Developing, Analyzing, and Choosing Options

The gender lenses stress the importance of evaluating options for their implications for men and women and for taking a longer-term outlook on the evaluation, particularly in how options that require resources now might be cost effective over the long term.

The case of Kimberly Rogers, the woman under house arrest for welfare fraud, illustrates how failing to evaluate options related to their implications for women and men can have devastating consequences. On 25 April 2001, Kimberly Rogers was convicted of defrauding Ontario Works because she was receiving benefits and also had a student loan. She was sentenced to 6 months of general house arrest and 18 months of probation with no right to receive further benefits for 3 months (a lifetime ban has since been implemented for others who commit the same offence). She lost her drug prescription coverage, and although she had no other income was required to make restitution of about $14,000. At the time, she was 5 months' pregnant. A law firm launched a Charter Challenge, and her benefits were reinstated pending the outcome of the challenge to be decided in September 2001. She committed suicide in August of that year during a heat wave in Sudbury.

The public debate was intense. The policy of a lifetime ban on benefits and house arrest has been the focus of the debate. How such a policy affects men and women differently has received less attention.[4] Clearly, policy-makers who chose the option of a lifetime ban on those who contravene welfare regulations did so without consideration of the differential impact on women and men. As women are most likely to be the ones who care for children, their loss of benefits will affect their children (the regulations cut off the mother but continue payments for her children reducing family income overall). Further, women with children are more likely to remain longer on income benefits than their male counterparts, making it more likely that they will run afoul of regulations. Even if they find work after being banned from income support, women still earn significantly less than their male counterparts and have to cope with inadequate and expensive child care provisions. The possibility that the lifetime ban contravenes the Charter of Rights and Freedoms seems possible, although the Charter Challenge was dropped with the death of Ms Rogers. Section 15(1) of the Charter states:

> Every individual is equal before and under the law and has the right to the equal protection and equal benefit of the law without discrimination and, in particular, without discrimination based on race, national or ethnic origin, colour, religion, sex, age or mental or physical disability.

It would be possible to argue that women do not have equality before this law as it penalizes them more severely. This policy option clearly requires review because of the inequality it creates.

5. Communicating Decisions about Policy and Programs

Communications should acknowledge those who have participated in policy decisions and the gender implications of the policy. The importance of framing messages and matching media to audience is emphasized in feminist lenses. It is recommended that community-based media, such as newsletters, bulletins, and pamphlets, be distributed to particular income, cultural, and gender groups. Of course, Internet is a valuable resource for communicating policy decisions.

Making the connection between how policy-makers communicate with their public about policy and programs and how professionals similarly communicate with their clients about case decisions is important. Case decisions often reflect policy realities, and the communication of policy may come, one by one, in case-work relationships. Much of my research has focused on how 'clients', all women, perceive their interactions with workers (Callahan, Hooper, and Wharf, 1998; Callahan et al., 2003). A strong theme in this work is the gaps of communication that exist between workers and women: withholding important information, providing information in technical language, providing too much information particularly when women are in crisis, and relying on verbal rather than written information are some of the issues that policy-makers and professionals need to address.

6. Evaluating Outcomes and the Process

The gender lenses are silent on implementation and contain few remarks on evaluation. This is unfortunate because it is here that many policies flounder and others are transformed remarkably from their original intent. Feminists, like others, are recognizing that implementation is key to ensuring policies are more than window dressing. However, inadequate funding, poor preparation, and the lack of ongoing commitments continue to plague policies.

Ellen Pence and Melanie Shepard (1999) along with the Praxis International organization in Duluth, Minnesota, have developed an interesting approach that combines monitoring implementation and evaluation. The organization works on addressing violence against women, particularly in the home. The authors observed that although new and progressive policies against violence in the home had been implemented, they often took very different expressions in actual practice and sometimes made matters worse. So they became interested in evaluating the work of police, the courts, and social workers. In particular, the authors noted that the work of one organization often contradicted the work of another.

An outcome of these observations was the development of the safety audit. Based on the research methods of Dorothy Smith (1987), the safety audit begins with an examination of what happens on the ground: How do police officers decide what should be done when they receive a call involving a domestic dispute? What are the tools that they use to make that decision? What forms do they fill out? Who do they call, and what happens then? By examining the decision-making processes and the attendant work that accompanies these decisions, the safety auditors trace what happens in the case and whether the outcomes actually led to improved safety in the home. They can identify points in the process where other options could occur and they can raise questions about the data used to make decisions. The safety audit pays attention to interorganizational relationships (or their absence) and is a useful tool for government organizations and community groups to evaluate how policies work in practice. The safety audit is similar to the process of tracking individual circumstances and outcomes that is used on a regular basis by social workers and others in practice.

Paying attention to the gender-lens approach to policy-making can enrich the process in several ways. It demands wide and ongoing consultation with those most affected by the policy and suggests creative ways for that consultation to occur. It encourages relationships between those on the 'inside' and those in community. It challenges policy-makers to understand their own values and perspectives and how these may influence the policies that they develop. Most importantly, it reinforces an understanding of how seemingly fair and equal policies contribute to the ongoing marginalization of many citizens.

Conclusion

Oscar Wilde once said that the trouble with socialism was 'that it took up too many Sundays'. Some feel that one of the troubles with feminism is similar: it takes too much time and demands too much effort. This chapter has focused on the contributions of feminist thinking to the policy-making process, while the particular issues that feminist groups want addressed such as violence against women, poverty, working conditions, or sexual assault have been placed in the background. The importance of these issues must not be forgotten, yet this chapter like the book focusses on policy-making processes.

Throughout the chapter, I have tried to indicate the value of using feminist thinking in policy-making to enrich it. And there have been successes. When I began to participate in feminist groups in the 1960s, the world was a very different place for women. There were few women in any of the well-paid professions such as law and medicine; divorcing women had no claim to the matrimonial property; First Nations women lost their status if they married nonstatus men; sexual assault was often blamed on women; and most young women did not expect to have a career and marriage at the same time. Dramatic changes have occurred since then and feminist groups can take credit for many of these, working outside and within policy-making structures.

What has changed less are these policy-making structures and processes. They still creak along founded on beliefs about who the experts are and what the proper processes for making decisions are. Some have argued persuasively that the changes to policy-making that have occurred have been primarily negative ones. As managerial thinking about human services as commodities and professionals as suppliers has gained ground, decision-making has become even further removed from the realities of those on the first line and those who are the clients.

Feminist thinking presents a challenge to these processes. It argues for more time, broad consultation, and different expertise. It doesn't fit well with governments in a hurry and governments under attack: thus the title of this chapter—chalk and cheese—an expression that means 'worlds apart' (Schur, 1987). How to open up these processes while recognizing the realities of the hurly-burly of policy-making is the ongoing challenge. I have presented some suggestions that include policy-making lenses. Remaking formal organizations along collaborative lines, using some of the thinking of Aboriginal peoples and social movements, is a further suggestion. Changing professional practice so it mirrors the changes that are aspired to in policy-making is yet another.

If I were to identify the most important contributions of feminist thinking to policy-making, it would be the feminist practice of building relationships across differences—a process grounded in feminist challenges to dichotomous thinking. For instance, as Pence and Shepard illustrate, demanding government attention to the issue is only one part of addressing violence against women. Feminist action groups must build relationships with other social movements and with sympathetic professionals, and encourage them to put the issues on their agendas. They must also forge connections with those inside bureaucracies such as hospitals, police, and governments who may be able to do something specific about the problem. Relationship-building is essential so that large, sometimes recalcitrant organizations can move in different directions. It requires the development of tolerance and respect amongst people with very different views of the world and the relinquishment of a self-righteous stance by groups within and outside the 'system'. These relationships must be genuine if they are to succeed. All this is well known by human service practitioners and others who have learned the importance and skills of relationship-building as the cornerstone of practice.

Helping to put a problem on the agenda of others is indeed important but having solutions to those problems is another essential contribution of feminist thinking: women are agents of change as well as victims of oppression. Transition houses are a clear example of the success of this strategy. Women simply opened up safe houses, initially squatting in abandoned buildings and gradually gaining community and government support for their efforts (Pizzey, 1977). By working out solutions, even those that are small and short-lived, groups with little contact can sit down face-to-face and dispel myths about one another. Relationship-building occurs. Other solutions may be sought. Again, social workers and other human service workers know the value of promoting small steps in the process of change, of celebrating them, and using them for more relationship-building.

Changing the policy-making processes to include the women who are affected by the issues is common sense. And without such changes, the process of addressing inequalities may simply reinforce them, an outcome of no small irony.

Recommended Reading

1. See S. Bear with the Tobique Women's Group, 'You Can't Change the *Indian Act*', in J. D. Wine and J.L. Ristock, eds, *Women and Social Change: Feminist Activism in Canada* (Toronto: James Lorimer and Company, 1991) for an excellent example of Aboriginal women organizing to affect change in the *Indian Act*.

2. J. Brodie, *Politics on the Margins: Restructuring and the Canadian Women's Movement* (Halifax: Fernwood Publishing, 1995) provides a thorough examination of the challenges facing the Canadian women's movement in light of globalization.

3. L. Briskin and M. Eliasson, eds, *Women's Organizing and Public Policy in Canada and Sweden* (Kingston, ON: McGill-Queen's University Press, 1999) provides a rare opportunity to compare the efforts of Canadian and Swedish women and their organizational strategies.

Notes

1. The elevation of women to decision-making positions within postsecondary institutions without altering the values and structures governing those decision-making processes has resulted in few changes in the overall functioning and agendas of such institutions. In fact, some of the women achieving these positions have done so precisely because they fit in well with traditional organizational expectations.

2. New Brunswick and Newfoundland have been exceptions, and by January 2004 the clawback will be eliminated in Manitoba. Prince Edward Island and Quebec reduce welfare rates by a portion of the supplements, allowing some to flow through to recipients. The agreement between the federal government and the provinces stipulates that provinces that reduce social assistance expenditures because of the National Child Benefit are supposed to re-invest these funds in programs to benefit children and families.

3. The Ontario Institute for the Study of Education and York University are two such locations.

4. An exception was the National Association of Women and the Law that formed a coalition with the Canadian Association of Elizabeth Fry Societies, the Legal Education and Action Fund, and the National Anti-Poverty Organization, to serve as interveners at the inquest with the aim of identifying the effects of federal and provincial government policies on poor women.

Chapter Nine

When Inclusive Approaches Are Not Enough

This chapter considers ways of influencing policy when traditional approaches have failed to produce desired outcomes and when inclusive models have not been put into place. It is, of course, entirely possible that inclusive approaches may have been attempted and found wanting, but at least in these approaches, both those being served and practitioners have had an opportunity to contribute their wisdom. The groups and individuals addressed in the chapter are think-tanks, social movements, advocacy groups, and whistle-blowers. We begin with a discussion of the context that faces those who attempt to influence policy, a discussion that has been foreshadowed in many of the previous chapters.

Throughout the previous chapters we have emphasized that social policies represent the concrete expression of the ideology of the government in power. Thus neo-conservative ideologies in the provinces of Ontario, Alberta, and British Columbia have resulted in reducing the size and scope of social policies and in transferring many programs to the private sector. By contrast, the forms of social democratic governments in Quebec, Manitoba, and Saskatchewan have made some efforts to maintain and expand social programs, although the scope of any innovations has remained relatively modest. In any context, the more resolute the ideology and the more secure the party in power, the more difficult it is for outside groups to influence policy. Indeed, in seeking to do so, such groups confront head-on the bedrock values of the party in power.

We have also emphasized that policies are set by the prime minister or premier and by their cabinets. Rank and file legislators often have little or no influence in establishing policy. Cabinets are composed of politicians who are the most committed to the party ideology and hence a 'cabinet with a cause' is a formidable vehicle for change. Such a cabinet is unlikely to be dissuaded from its agenda even by carefully assembled evidence—unless, of course, the evidence fits with its agenda. In a review of Daniel Ellsberg's book *Secrets: A Memoir of Vietnam and the Pentagon Papers*, Nicholas Lemann (2002, p. 99) concludes by saying, 'It is not what we know, but what we believe in that makes all the difference.' Cabinets with a cause believe, and believe fervently, in the rightness of their cause.

We have only to look at the actions of governments in Ontario and Alberta in the fields of social assistance, daycare, and education to find evidence of these strongly held convictions. Nor are cabinets with a cause easily deterred from their commitments by demonstrations and marches. Such protests are quickly dismissed as the actions of radicals and special interest groups that do not reflect public opinion. Indeed, the current climate in Canada facing groups wanting to change policies they deem to be unfair and inadequate is most inhospitable.

Think-Tanks

The label 'think-tanks' applies to organizations established for the purpose of doing research on public issues. The largest and best known on the international scene are located in the United States and include the Brookings and Hoover Institutes and the Rand Corporation. In Canada there are more than one hundred think-tanks, ranging from the Conference Board of Canada with a budget in excess of $200 million and a staff of two hundred to the Caledon Institute of Social Policy with its three staff members and a budget of $1 million (Lindquist, 1998; Abelson, 2002).

Although all think-tanks are committed to research, some place their research in an ideological frame and use the findings to advance this ideology. For example, the Fraser Institute clearly states its frame of reference in its letterhead and publications noting that it has been committed to 'offering market solutions to public policy problems since 1974' (personal communication). Regardless of the problem being studied, the Fraser Institute seeks to find remedies that will emphasize the contribution of the private market sector and at the same time will reduce the size and scope of government. By contrast, the research inquiries of the Centre for Policy Alternatives will most likely lead to solutions in the form of expanded public policies with a focus on social justice.

Think-tanks seek to influence government in a number of ways. They bring the results of their research studies to the attention of senior officials in government and try to convince these officials of the validity of their research and the importance of their proposals. In addition, many think-tanks take on a responsibility for public education. Staff members of the Fraser Institute and the C.D. Howe Institute contribute newspaper columns on a regular basis and several groups participate in public forums and conferences.

Whether these efforts are successful is difficult to determine. One review seeking to answer the question 'Do think-tanks matter?' concluded, 'Depending on the specific policy issue that is under consideration and the particular stage of the policy-making process that one is focusing on, scholars may walk away with the impression that think-tanks are either extremely influential or entirely irrelevant. Both impressions would be right.' Despite this overall conclusion, Abelson singles out some think-tanks that in his view have influenced policy: 'Indeed by focusing on Ken Battle's contributions to the development of social welfare policy in Canada, one might conclude and justifiably so, that the president of the Caledon Institute has had a profound impact on shaping public policy. A similar conclusion might be reached in examining the contribution of the C.D. Howe

Institute to the free trade debate and to the future of the Canada Pension Plan' (Abelson, 2002, p. 161).

Returning to the Lemann observation that it is not what we know but what we believe in that matters, it seems reasonable to argue that conservative governments will favour the research and the findings of conservative think-tanks. By the same token, social democratic governments will look to think-tanks that espouse their convictions.

Finally, we note that in their day-to-day work some think-tanks resemble policy communities: 'Although Maxwell (President of the Canadian Policy Research Networks, CPRN) does not downplay the importance of media exposure, she maintains that think-tanks exercise the most influence working with key stakeholders behind the scene, not by discussing policy issues with reporters. Maxwell believes that part of CPRN's role is to bring together senior bureaucrats, academics and representatives from the private and not-for-profit sector in closed door meetings to discuss social and economic policy issues' (Abelson, 2002, p. 68)

And like the example of the Canadian Council of Chief Executives discussed in Chapter 6, think-tanks such as the Canadian Policy Research Networks and the Caledon Institute on Social Policy use their contacts in government and their accumulated knowledge of the workings of government to anticipate issues on the government's agenda and to offer proposals to address these issues. Again, the notions of the policy window and the convergence of interest are persuasive in suggesting why some proposals from think-tanks are accepted and others die on the vine.

Social Movements and Policy Advocacy Groups

Social movements and advocacy groups have been a prominent part of the social policy scene in Canada for many years. Chapters 7 and 8 noted some of the roles played by First Nations' and women's groups. In this section we focus on the Independent Living (IL) movement in the disability community as an example of a social movement and Campaign 2000 as an example of an advocacy group.

The Independent Living Movement

In Chapter 6 we considered the disability community in BC as a partner in a policy community dedicated to changing guardianship legislation. But parts of the disability community have also acted as a social movement in significantly influencing the policies of the state with respect to conditions for persons with disabilities. This is particularly evident in the disability community's efforts to promote the independent living paradigm as an approach to service delivery.

We define social movements as broadly based groups of people who share a common characteristic that unites them, at least in a loose-knit fashion, in collective action for social change. The history of social movements since the last half of the twentieth century includes feminist organizations, the civil rights movement, and welfare rights coalitions, to name a few. One of the seminal texts on social movements is Piven and Cloward's (1977) text on poor people's movements in the United States. Fagan and Lee (1997, pp. 151–3) discuss some of the characteristics of social movements and the extent to which the disability movement can be classified as a social movement:

1. *Social movements embrace alternative forms of political action.* Disabled people have done this through self-organization and control by disabled people of the organizations representing their interests.
2. *Social movements advance a critical evaluation of the values and structures of dominant society.* The disability movement has done this by highlighting the denial of citizenship rights arising from practices and policies that define disabled people as dependent and in need of care based on a medical model of rehabilitation.
3. *Social movements promote collective action to achieve goals in both a national and international context.* A disability movement based on the independent living philosophy has developed in many countries and has international links through cross-national cooperative endeavours and organizations such as Disabled People's International.

In brief, the disability movement has taken direct action to challenge both the failings of the state and the public view of the disabled, and in so doing it has built a sense of solidarity among the disabled people for social and economic reform. It is useful to take a closer look at the disability movement as a social movement, with a particular focus on Canada, and our analysis pays particular attention to the Independent Living movement.

The Canadian Independent Living movement can be traced to its American precursor, which was formalized by the establishment of the Center for Independent Living in Berkeley, California, in 1972 (Shapiro, 1994, pp. 51–3). The development of this centre followed initiatives for reform that began at the University of California where physically disabled students, known then as the 'Rolling Quads', developed a Physically Disabled Students' Program (PDSP) aimed at promoting independent living. Among other things, the PDSP set up its own wheelchair workshop, developed an independent housing venture, and established an advocacy program to assist both disabled students and non-students to challenge the medical model with self-help and group organizing. Three service principles central to the independent living philosophy at Berkeley came to be recognized as beginning cornerstones to the independent living philosophy: consumer control, flexibility, and services that are responsive to the recipients' needs.

In a review of the Canadian Independent Living movement, Valentine (1994) associates the rise of the movement in Western Canada with the values of consumer control and self-help in the early 1970s. Provincial organizations were formed in Saskatchewan, Manitoba, and Alberta, and the momentum of these organizations and a national conference in Toronto in 1973 led to the formation of the Coalition of Provincial Organizations of the Handicapped (COPOH) in 1976 (now known as the Council of Canadians with Disabilities). COPOH, as a national consumer organization, focused its energy on human rights legislation, revision of building codes, establishment of public transportation services for persons with disabilities, and efforts to improve employment through job creation and policy change.

There was a rapid growth of the consumer movement at the local, provincial, and national levels, and in June 1980, COPOH held its third national conference in Vancouver. At this conference, Canadian consumers were introduced to an alternative view of rehabilitation—the independent living paradigm, a model consistent with the growing grassroots interest in consumer control and self-determination. This paradigm, posed as an alternative to the medical model reflected in rehabilitation programs of the day, stressed the problems created by the dependency arising out of the medical model and solutions based on peer counselling, advocacy, self-help, consumer control, and the removal of barriers to independent living. This mantra quickly became the guiding philosophy of the emerging Independent Living movement in Canada.

Henry Enns, a social work graduate from the University of Manitoba who became physically disabled as a teenager because of arthritis, became a strong advocate of the movement. His leadership and the assistance of the Mennonite Central Committee, which funded an early feasibility assessment, led to the establishment of Canada's first Independent Living Centre (ILC) in Waterloo, Ontario, in 1982 with funds provided by the Secretary of State. The United Nations also declared 1981 as the International Year of Disabled Persons, and this helped to focus national attention on disability issues. For example, the federal government funded several national projects and appointed a Special Committee on the Disabled and the Handicapped. This committee published a series of reports entitled *Obstacles* and several recommendations provided further support and impetus to the independent living movement.

Nyp (2002), who reviews the history of the ILC of Waterloo Region, documents the growth of this consumer-based self-help organization over 20 years from a fledgling organization operating out of a Sunday School room in a Mennonite church to a major consumer-based service organization with a budget of nearly $5 million and more than three hundred staff. Operating four supportive housing units and a variety of other programs, including peer support and information and referral, the agency has become a model of a consumer-based organization that has successfully combined service with individual advocacy and self-help.

There are now 25 independent living resource centres across Canada, and a national coordinating body known as the Canadian Association of Independent Living Centres (CAILC). Independent living centres emphasize consumer control, cross-disability issues, community-based approaches and the full integration and participation of disabled people in Canadian society. Disabled people make up the majority of staff and board positions in these organizations, and their influence on disability issues with governments at all levels has been significant. With government assistance improved accessibility, supportive housing units, new legislation, public transportation for the disabled, and direct support and advocacy services have been established. The movement is also active on an international front. For example, the Canadian Centre on Disability Studies, based in Winnipeg, has projects to promote independent living in Russia and Ukraine.

There are some differences between the IL movement in the United States and Canada. The American IL movement concentrates on service delivery and collective advocacy equally and has been directly responsible for the *Americans with Disabilities Act*. In Canada, the collective advocacy role has been carried more directly by the Council of Canadians with Disabilities (the successor to COPOH), although the CAILC works closely with its counterpart on these initiatives. Both organizations reflect an independent living philosophy and thus are considered as parts of the movement in Canada.

It is important to consider some of the reasons for the relative success of the IL movement. First, disability issues are perhaps less partisan in a political sense than many other social policy issues, partly because disabled people are likely to be seen as more deserving than some other groups. Thus government support, although never a guarantee for consumer-based initiatives, is somewhat more likely. Second, the IL movement benefited from growing national and international awareness of the need to address disability issues in a more responsive and respectful fashion. Finally, the movement quickly became a very effective lobby group. There is no doubt that this can be attributed to effective leadership that was able to establish a broad base of support for a consumer-initiated approach to policy development.

The IL movement has also influenced the development of community-based responses within the professional rehabilitation field, and this response has become known as Community Based Rehabilitation (CBR). CBR is led by professionals and focuses on developing partnerships between rehabilitation professionals and communities—families and persons with disabilities—to deliver a more effective range of services to disabled people. CBR focuses on translating clinical knowledge into self-help skills so disabled people can take more ownership of their own health. There are tensions between the two groups partly because CBR is led by professionals rather than by consumers, but there are similarities in the focus on personal empowerment and self-help.

There are also shortcomings within the IL movement that must be recognized. IL, as a consumer movement, is sometimes criticized for failing to represent the broad spectrum of disabled people (Lysack and Kaufert, 1994). For example, despite the commitment to cross-disability issues, the movement has often focused more directly on challenges experienced by those who are physically disabled. As well, the IL movement has remained largely an urban-based movement and its influence in rural and Aboriginal communities has been less profound. Despite these limitations, the accomplishments of the IL movement stand as a tribute to the vision of those who have been involved with this consumer-based movement.

Campaign 2000

According to three individuals who were involved in the beginning days of Campaign 2000, '[s]ince 1991—through research, advocacy, political lobbying, media events, partnerships with a major retail business and public education activities—Campaign 2000 has focused public attention on the more than 1.4 million poor children in Canada, one of the wealthiest countries in the world' (Popham, Hay, and Hughes, 1997, p. 248). The impetus for Campaign 2000 came from a resolution in the House of Commons approved by members of all political parties to end child poverty by the year 2000. In a committed attempt to ensure that the government would live up to this promise, a number of social policy and advocacy organizations such as the Canadian Council on Social Development, the National Anti-Poverty Organization, and the Toronto-based Child Poverty Action Group developed a national action plan. A cornerstone of this plan was that pressure could best be brought to bear by a network of local and provincial organizations dedicated to the elimination of poverty. The founding organizations sponsored a number of meetings across the country attended by members of anti-poverty groups, academics, and staff of human service organizations. At a national meeting and only after prolonged discussion and negotiations, the following goals for Campaign 2000 were approved:

- To raise and protect the basic living standards of all families in all regions of the country so that no Canadian child would ever live in poverty.
- To improve the life chances of all children so they can fulfil their potential and nurture their talent, and become responsible and contributing members of society.
- To ensure the availability of secure, adequate, affordable, and suitable housing as an inherent right for all children in Canada.
- To create, build, and strengthen family supports and community-based resources in order to empower families so they can provide the best possible care for their children. (Campaign 2000 as quoted in Popham, Hays, and Hughes, 1997, p. 254)

The network of Campaign 2000 consists of 87 national, provincial, and community organizations. The anchoring base for the network consists of a national coordinator and one support-staff person who from the very beginning have been housed in the Family Service Association of Toronto. Funding for the staff and the activities of Campaign 2000 come from a wide variety of sources including the Laidlaw Foundation and the Children's Aid Society of Toronto Foundation.

The principal strategy employed by Campaign 2000 has been to prepare an annual report card that displays changes in the number of children living in poverty by province since the House of Commons resolution. The report card highlights the consequences of child poverty and proposes strategies to eliminate or at least reduce poverty among children. The national report cards are released on November 24, the anniversary of the all-party resolution, and have received considerable publicity. Campaign 2000 is now so well known that the national coordinator has been invited to comment on the federal budget and its consequences for child poverty, both on TV and in national newspapers.

We believe that Campaign 2000's work has been influential in ensuring that child and family poverty remain an important public priority in Canada. Most recently we were encouraged to read the commitment in the Speech from the Throne. The government will put into place a long-term investment plan to allow poor families to break out of the welfare trap so that children born into poverty do not carry the consequences of that poverty throughout their lives. It will again significantly increase the National Child Benefit for poor families. (Campaign 2000, 2002)

Campaign 2000 is not without its critics. Not surprisingly, neo-conservative politicians scoff at the annual report card. Thus the former premier of Ontario, Mike Harris, contemptuously dismissed the 1999 report card saying, 'The report is hogwash. It's based on false data' (Campbell, 1999, p. A3). The accusation of false data is based on the use of Statistics Canada low-income cut-offs, which are commonly used by social policy organizations (the exception is the Fraser Institute) as the measure of poverty in Canada. And some biting critiques have come from feminist scholars. For example, McGrath claims that

> [t]he child-centred advocacy strategies used by advocacy groups such as the Child Poverty Action Group have inadvertently supported the position of business interest groups that seek to reduce the role of government in social programs. . . . The neoliberal ideology promoted by the private sector seeks to privatize the responsibility of children with the state intervening only when the children are deemed at risk. (McGrath, 1997, p. 186)

We acknowledge that the concerns of feminists such as McGrath have some merit. Pursued in a very narrow vein, a focus on child poverty can obscure state responsibility for a broad range of social issues. However, we recognize that the focus on child poverty was selected in order to downplay the negative image placed on 'welfare mums' by the press and the public. In addition we note that, as exemplified in its statement of goals and in its report cards, Campaign 2000 has been careful to note that the poverty of children cannot be separated from the poverty of families in which they live.

A Policy Debate

In an attempt to identify the strategies and the outcomes used by social policy reform groups, we wrote to a number of national organizations and posed this question: 'In attempting to influence the policies of the state, what works?' The organizations contacted were as follows: Campaign 2000, the Canadian Council on Social Development, the Caledon Institute, the Council of Canadians, the Centre for Policy Alternatives, the National Anti-Poverty Organization, the National Council of Welfare, and the Fraser Institute. Responses were received from the Caledon Institute, the National Council of Welfare, and Campaign 2000. We include a discussion of their responses later, particularly in relation to the National Child Tax Benefit.

In communication with us, the former and present directors of the National Council of Welfare and the national coordinator of Campaign 2002 were extremely critical of the federal government's commitment to progressive social policies. Steve Kerstetter, the former director of the National Council of Welfare put the point bluntly: 'Almost nothing works when the government in power is dedicated to paying down the debt, to reducing taxes and in general ignoring the poor' (personal communication). However, these respondents, along with the president of the Caledon Institute, lauded the introduction and subsequent enhancement of the National Child Benefit. The federal component of this program is an income-support benefit paid out to low-income tax filers, based on the number of their dependent children and on their taxable family income. The National Child Benefit is the umbrella name for the payments made by the federal government and investments made by provincial and territorial governments in children's programs. The federal payment, a result of changes introduced in 1998, is known as the Canada Child Tax Benefit (CCTB). It is the basic benefit paid out to low- and middle-income families based on family income. The National Child Benefit Supplement (NCBS) is the monthly payment made to low-income families only. A number of provinces claw back this amount or a portion of it from the welfare poor.

Although they supported the National Child Benefit, respondents, with the exception of the president of the Caledon Institute, disapproved of the clawback provision that allows provinces the option of recovering the amount of the National Child Benefit Supplement paid to those receiving social assistance. If provinces claw back these funds, they are supposed to reinvest these funds in children's programs. The responses of the director of the National Council of Welfare and of the president of the Caledon Institute with respect to that issue are reproduced here in some detail because they provide a rare insight into the policy debates that can occur between social policy groups dedicated to reforming social security benefits (see Boxes 9.1 and 9.2).

Box 9.1 The Position of the Caledon Institute on the National Child Benefit

Probably no area of Canadian social policy has seen more change than child benefits, referred to here as income payments in the form of cash and/or income tax reductions on behalf of children. Through the politics and policy development process of 'relentless incrementalism', a long series of changes to federal child benefits between the late 1970s and early 1990s eventually created a rationally designed child benefit geared to family income. Although not as generous as social advocates would want, it offered a sound platform that could be raised in the future.

There is more to the story though, in that benefits paid to people on welfare created a double benefit because people received two income-support payments for their children—one from the federal government and one from the provincial government. However, the working poor, perhaps with no more disposable income than someone on welfare, received federal benefits only. This two-tiered child benefit unwittingly contributed to what Caledon dubbed the 'welfare wall' and created a disincentive to work. If families left welfare for the workplace, they lost thousands of dollars of child benefits in cash and in kind (for example, supplementary health care) at the very time that they saw their (typically) low wages reduced by income and payroll taxes and stretched by the cost of employment-related expenses such as clothing, transportation, and child care.

Reforms to the federal-provincial/territorial National Child Benefit (NCB) were negotiated in 1997 to resolve this structural flaw. The federal government redesigned its Child Tax Benefit into a Canada Child Tax Benefit. This component of the NCB is paid out by the federal government to families based on their income and the number of dependent children, and the federal government has been phasing-in substantial increases in payments to low-income families (the program also provides benefits to non-poor families with the amount diminishing as incomes increase). In 2000, Ottawa restored full indexation (automatic increases based on increases to the cost of living) thus allowing the benefit to keep pace with cost-of-living increases. The second part of the NCB is the provincial/territorial component. For their part, many provinces and territories have been able to reduce their welfare-delivered child benefits to correspond with the federal benefits that are paid, as long as they reinvest such savings in other programs for low-income families (for example, early childhood education, child care, income-tested child benefits, and earnings supplements). The major objectives of the new National Child Benefit are to promote market attachment by ensuring that families are better off working and to prevent and reduce the depth of poverty. The Canada Child Tax Benefit (including both the basic benefit and National Child Benefit Supplement) paid a maximum of $2,444 for one child in 2002–3 and this was increased to $2,632 in July 2003.

Although most social policy advocacy groups criticized the National Child Benefit mainly for not providing a real cash increase to families on welfare, the initiative is widely viewed as the most promising advance in Canadian social policy since the coming of medicare. The NCB is a rare reform because it involves not just Ottawa and the provinces and territories working together—a rare sight indeed in these years of uncooperative federalism—but it also requires these two levels of government to implement reforms that depend on the other. As well, the reform was accomplished quickly through a pragmatic political agreement, not through a lengthy process of new legislation.

The criticism of the clawback misses the whole point of the NCB, which is to get child benefits out of welfare and replace them with equal, portable child benefits for all low-income families. Because benefits are inclusive in that they are available to all families subject to income levels, they avoid the stigma of welfare. Those who oppose the clawback argue in effect that we should continue with the unfair, irrational system the NCB was created to fix. They are effectively saying that welfare families should continue to receive double the amount of child benefits as working-poor families, which in turn means that there will continue to be a welfare wall in which families that leave welfare for work suffer a large loss of benefits for their kids just as they are trying to get established in the workforce. There is also a broader issue. Caledon believes that Canada should abolish welfare and replace it with better income supports and services. The NCB is a big step forward in that difficult but necessary reform. (Adapted from correspondence received from Battle, 2003; reproduced with permission)

Box 9.2 The Position of the National Council of Welfare on the National Child Benefit

Benefit
Our most recent and major success I would say is our work in raising the flag on the clawback of the National Child Benefit (NCB). . . . The Council endorsed the good intentions of the federal government and the massive infusion of money in the new program. The Council was also extremely critical of the process of negotiating the deal with the provinces and territories, especially the part of the deal that allowed the provinces to claw back part of the new money from the poorest of the poor, those families with children that are forced to rely on welfare.

The Council feels very strongly that the clawback was bad social policy. Although we believe in creating incentives to work, we do not believe that the way to create those incentives is by reducing the already inadequate incomes of families on welfare. It seemed particularly futile to begin a program of family policy with such a strong 'stick' approach (as in carrots and stick) in the absence of the carrots, such as educational supports and a labour market and child care system that would permit all low-income parents on welfare to respond to this disincentive to welfare by getting jobs—especially jobs that pay enough to take a family off welfare.

The failure of all levels of government to raise—or even attempt to raise—welfare incomes for families with young children was especially shocking in an era when overwhelming evidence of the significance of early child development and the impact of poverty on child health was emerging.

We made several proposals for programs that would support low-income families—the 'working poor' that the NCB was supposed to help—while also supporting welfare poor families. The major recommendation we made was the creation of a system of high-quality, affordable child care. Child care is the most important of programs that would make it possible for parents of young children to return to school or work and to increase their chances of raising their children out of poverty.

Currently only Newfoundland and New Brunswick have resisted the temptation to take any of the National Child Tax Benefit. Prince Edward Island and Quebec now only take a part of the benefit, and Manitoba will eliminate the clawback by January 2004.

We never said that the whole child tax benefit was bad policy. . . . We suggest that the Canada Child Tax Benefit (CCTB) needs to be developed in the context of a more integrated family policy. That policy needs as its core a system of good, affordable child care. Along with increases in the base benefit of the CCTB, low-income families will be better off. (Adapted from correspondence received from Roulston, 2003; reproduced with permission)

We do not intend to comment in detail on the positions expressed in Boxes 9.1 and 9.2, and suggest that students may want to do further research on the two positions and debate this issue further. However, it is interesting to explore one point raised by the Caledon Institute in more detail. The president of the Caledon Institute notes the following: 'The National Child Benefit is one of the rare reforms in the history of Canadian public policy that sold itself to governments of all political stripes and hues by virtue of the logic of its substantive policy rationale—which is to break down the welfare wall that stands in the way of families moving from welfare to work, to provide secure, fully indexed, portable and non-stigmatizing benefits that treats all low-income families equally and includes them in a social program that serves virtually all families, poor and non-poor alike, and to help reduce the depth of poverty' (Battle, 2003). However, the different responses of provincial governments seem to reflect some conflicting viewpoints. Two provinces do not reduce welfare benefits at all (Manitoba will be a third by January 2004), others claw back only some of the National Child Benefit Supplement, and still others claw back the full amount. For some provinces, it appears that the ability to claw back these funds has allowed them to determine their own priorities and to develop programs with greater political payoffs than providing 'additional money to people on welfare'. As well, we suspect that for some neo-conservative governments, an increase in welfare benefits runs counter to their ideology. For them, a punitive approach to welfare recipients is seen as consistent with promoting workforce attachment. An important question to consider in examining this issue is whether one can advance policy options that will provide improved benefits and services for those on welfare while retaining cash and in-kind incentives related to employment and labour force attachment.

Whistle-Blowing

The final strategy for criticizing policies that are seen as harmful is *blowing the whistle*. Although the use of the masculine pronoun is inappropriate in the following quotation since some of the most prominent whistle-blowers are women, the quote sums up the essence of the act of whistle-blowing: 'The message of the whistle-blower is seen as a breach of loyalty. Though he is neither coach nor referee, the whistle-blower blows the whistle on his own team' (Bok, 1984, p. 215). Although employees are often required to take an Oath of Office that forbids them to divulge information learned on the job (and certainly this is the case in government ministries or departments), those who blow the whistle are so convinced that the activities of their organization are harmful, they have no option but to disregard the Oath of Office. And as will be evident in the following discussion, if an employee disregards the Oath of Office it can lead to ridicule, and even dismissal.

The person who first gave prominence to the act of whistle-blowing is Daniel Ellsberg. Convinced that the president of the United States and his Cabinet colleagues were not receiving sufficient and accurate information about the progress of the war in Vietnam, Ellsberg released 'the Pentagon Papers' to the *New York Times* in 1971. The papers consisted of a 7000-word history of the Vietnam War and were published in the *New York Times* and other newspapers (see Ellesberg 2002). Once identified as the source of the information, Ellsberg resigned, and was charged with breaching confidentiality. Although he was eventually found not guilty, his career as a promising policy analyst with government and the Rand Corporation came to an abrupt end. Indeed, the ramifications of his actions were such that a former head of the Rand Corporation who remained a close friend of Ellsberg also lost his job.

Loss of employment is a common consequence of high-profile whistle-blowing. Jeffrey Wigand blew the whistle on the Brown Williamson Tobacco company because, contrary to its public pronouncements, the company was deliberately increasing the amount of nicotine contained in cigarettes, and he was fired. Wigand's story is told in a most compelling fashion in the movie *The Insider*. An equally engrossing film, *Silkwood*, reveals the whistle-blowing activities of Karen Silkwood. She became convinced of the health hazards involved in handling plutonium fuel rods in her place of employment. Both films provide some telling insights about the courage of whistle-blowers and the consequences of their actions. Wigand was fired, his pension and medical benefits were terminated, and he was harassed by Brown Williamson to such an extent that his mental health deteriorated and his marriage collapsed. However, Wigand subsequently overcame these difficulties and became an internationally known advocate for the antismoking cause. Tragically, Karen Silkwood was killed in a traffic collision that the movie suggests was far from an accident.

Ellsberg gave whistle-blowing a public profile some 30 years ago; however, there are a number of recent examples that highlight both the importance of and the ramifications from breaching confidentiality and loyalty to an organization. A Canadian example is that of Dr Nancy Oliveri, a medical researcher with the Hospital for Sick Children in Toronto and an adjunct member of the Faculty of Medicine at the University of Toronto. Oliveri became concerned about the potentially harmful effects of a drug she had played a pivotal role in developing. Despite the terms of a contract that allowed only the drug company, Apotex, to factors and that allows for the incorporation of more specialized considerations within the value-criteria stage is discussed next. This proposed model is accompanied by the following qualifications. First, policy analysis, like policy-making, is not a linear process, and related tasks must be approached with adequate recognition of this fact. Second, the tasks in policy analysis are affected by the scope of the problem or issue being considered. For example, estimating the policy effects from major changes in legislation is a more complex undertaking than an analysis of program options for adolescent sex offenders in a particular community. Nevertheless, the general process is similar. Third, supplementary questions or considerations should be incorporated whenever necessary, but this is particularly true when assessing small-scale policies at the organizational level. The proposed model has five steps: 1) problem identification and goal specification; 2) selection of value criteria; 3) assessment of alternatives; 4) feasibility assessment; and 5) recommendations. As this outline indicates, the model can be applied to both the problem analysis and policy analysis tasks in the policy-making process.

1. Problem Identification and Goal Specification

Policy analysis begins with an examination of the problem or need, and several key questions are important to consider:

a) What is the nature of the problem?
b) Who are the people experiencing the problem, and what are their characteristics?
c) How does the problem affect individuals, the community, and society?
d) What are the barriers to services at this time for the particular group of people most affected by the problem?
e) Who recognizes that the problem exists?
f) What are the causes of the problem, including relevant theoretical considerations and historical factors?
g) Are there ethnic, gender, and class considerations in identifying the problem?
h) What previous strategies have been tried and what has been their level of success?

There is some overlap between these questions and results that might be obtained from a needs assessment study. However, information on needs is used to begin to identify solutions or possible responses to a problem. In addition, a comparative study of needs may help to support the development of a policy response to the problem. As noted earlier, a needs assessment should be accompanied by the development of an inventory of strengths and resources, particularly when any new policy is directed at a community or special group. It is particularly important to identify those likely to be affected by the policy change, how service users are expected to respond to the new policy, and the desired outcome. Relevant actors and interest groups—and the extent of their power and influence—should also be identified at this stage. A related consideration is the salience of the issue. *Issue salience* refers to the ability of the issue to give rise to

tively unknown. The experiences of two Canadian social workers who blew the whistle are described below. The first is Bridget Moran, who was a social worker in the BC Ministry of Social Services in the 1950s and 1960s. Moran decided to blow the whistle on her ministry after years of attempting to change policies through the regular channels had failed.

Bridget Moran commenced her career in social work in Prince George, BC, in 1954. She describes her responsibilities in the following words:

> Starting in Prince George, my region extended sixty miles across dirt roads to Vanderhoof. West of Vanderhoof I travelled fifty miles and more to the settlements of Fort Fraser, Fraser Lake, Endako, and beyond. I drove south from those settlements over logging roads to reach a number of homes. North from Vanderhoof I covered the forty miles to Fort St. James again on dirt roads. . . . In that huge wooded territory which I reckoned to be about the size of Holland, I was responsible for the elderly, the poor, people of all ages with mental and social problems and the infirm. My area included one Indian residential school and five reservations, every one of them a text book study in poverty, disease and despair. (Moran, 2001, p. 29)

At that time Prince George, like other Northern communities, was desperately short of resources to aid families and children. Not only were the social workers of the ministry overwhelmed by the size of the districts they had to cover and the enormity of the problems they encountered, but they were also in many ways the only source of assistance. Prince George lacked all the resources typically found in communities today: mental health services, transition houses for abused women, group homes for children, and neighbourhood houses for families. Unfortunately, the persistent efforts of Moran and her colleagues to gain additional staff met with little success. Faced with this lack of response, Moran decided to go outside the usual channels and to bring the situation facing her and the families she served to the attention of the Social Credit premier of the province as well as the public. In December 1963 Moran wrote to Premier Bennett, with copies to newspapers in Prince George, Vancouver, and Victoria, and to the leaders of the Conservative, Liberal, and New Democratic parties. Moran concluded her long and detailed letter with the following words:

> Every day here and across the province social workers are called upon to deal with seriously disturbed children. We have no psychiatrist, no specially trained foster parents, no receiving or detention homes to aid us. We place children in homes that have never been properly investigated, we ignore serious neglect cases because we have no available homes. Inadequate? Yes. Dangerous? Yes. . . . The group for whom I am begging help will continue to cost money, more and more money. So it becomes, does it not, a question not of whether we will spend money but of how that money will be spent? (Moran, 2001, p. 70)

Although Moran never received a reply from the premier, the letters to the opposition parties occasioned a veritable spate of questions in the legislature and newspapers gave extensive coverage to Moran's concerns. Within weeks she became a *cause célèbre* in BC and gained considerable support from colleagues, from faculty members in the School of Social Work at the University of British Columbia, and indeed from the public. And initially at least it seemed as if the accusation of inadequate resources had produced the desired effect. Additional staff were promised for the Prince George Social Services office and there was a commitment to establish a mental health office. However, both promises faded quickly. And the predictable response of organizations confronting whistle-blowers occurred again in Moran's case. She was accused of exaggerating the problems. The member of the legislature for Prince George and the minister of finance dismissed her claims by saying 'she was only a part time social worker who became overwhelmed by her job' (Moran, 2001, p. 87). Finally, Moran was suspended from her position. Although the same suspension was lifted for colleagues who had supported her, it remained in effect for Moran.

A recent example suggests that some support for whistle-blowers may be available through the Canadian *Charter of Rights and Freedoms*. In 1998 Jason Gibson, a social worker employed by the Alberta Department of Family and Social Services, wrote a letter to a member of the Opposition expressing his concerns about the planned redesign of services to children and families in the province. He sent copies to his own MLA, the minister, and the regional board responsible for social services. As a consequence, Gibson was reprimanded. He filed a grievance that was dismissed and the case was then reviewed by the Alberta Court of Queen's Bench. The court delivered a mixed decision, and both the government and Gibson appealed to the Alberta Court of Appeal. In its judgment, the Appeal Court agreed with Gibson. It cited the Canadian *Chapter of Rights and Freedoms* in finding that the reprimand of the social worker violated his right to freedom of expression. The Appeal Court also cited the Supreme Court of Canada in concluding that an employee's duty of loyalty needs to be balanced with the right of free expression, including the ability to criticize government, provided it is framed with restraint. In this instance, the concerns expressed related directly to the ability of social workers to effectively protect children from harm and the social worker's criticism had no adverse effect on his ability to perform his duties (Lancaster House, 2002).

We wonder whether first-line practitioners are aware of the Charter protections of freedom of expression and this decision, which appears to offer protection for whistle-blowers provided that they 'frame their concerns with restraint'. Would more whistle-blowing occur if this information were widely available?

While the resource situation has improved in all communities across the country since Moran's days, there remains a continuing mismatch between the extent and severity of social problems and the resources available to respond to these problems. And there have been numerous efforts by social workers to bring attention to the gap between problems and resources as shown in the following excerpt:

> Prince Edward Island social workers consider child and family services in crisis. Saskatchewan social workers staged a provincial day of protest. There are calls for

reform in the Alberta child welfare system. Yellowknife social workers have filed a grievance case citing dangerous conditions because of high caseloads. Newfoundland/Labrador echoes workload concerns. Nova Scotia is concerned about training and service coordination issues. (Hart, 2001, p. 17)

With Gibson as a prominent exception, the recent calls for changes in child welfare do not rely on whistle-blowing by an individual. Rather, they take the form of group protests where a local office stages a day of protest, a union files a grievance on behalf of child welfare staff, or a provincial association of social workers registers its concerns with the minister and senior staff of the provincial ministries.

Conclusion

Given a largely bleak picture for influencing social policy in federal and provincial governments, what strategies work? The national coordinator for Campaign 2000 noted that finding support from groups and associations that would not automatically be classed as 'soulmates' was invaluable in keeping the subject of child poverty alive in the media and on the agenda of governments. Thus Campaign 2000 seeks allies from churches and labour unions. The work of the Caledon Institute illustrates the usefulness of the concept of the policy window where a policy specialist in cooperation with like-minded individuals in the Department of Finance (a policy community) proposed a solution with supporting rationale directed at reducing the size and severity of a problem (child poverty). And since the initiative for the NCB came from Battle, this example illustrates that social policy groups can put the strategy of 'anticipation', noted earlier in our discussion of policy communities, to effective use.

Based on the foregoing discussion, three strategies seem to have merit. The strategy of anticipation, where clear proposals are made on emerging issues, has been used successfully by both the Canadian Council of Chief Executives and the Caledon Institute. Another example that has yet to be placed in the success category comes from the work of one of the authors. Given the expressed commitment of the BC government to community capacity-building, a group of retired social workers sought to take advantage of this commitment by arguing the case for increased resources for neighbourhood houses. Their brief presented evidence that neighbourhood houses are in a pivotal position to develop capacity in communities (Wharf et al., 2003). Although the brief received a sympathetic response from the minister for child and family development and his senior staff, no additional funds have yet been provided for neighbourhood houses.

The strategy of anticipation requires the capacity to discern future policy directions, and to develop reports that manage to combine the values and interests of both the advocacy group and government. Although this strategy may be effective on some occasions, there will be many issues where the values of the two are diametrically opposed. In these circumstances, this strategy is unworkable.

The work of the National Council of Welfare and Campaign 2000 reflects a second strategy. The reports of these organizations have reminded politicians and the general public that much remains to be done in building an effective social security system. Although governments have not necessarily adopted their recommendations, these organizations have helped to keep issues, such as poverty and homelessness, on the policy agenda. These efforts have achieved some success as indicated in a national poll conducted just prior to the 2003 federal budget. In that poll, public support for social spending was relatively high and child poverty was second in order of priority after health care as the preferred choice for new investment (McCarthy, 2003, pp. A1, A4).

The third strategy is that of whistle-blowing. Whistle-blowing is a courageous act that needs to be carefully assessed. It becomes justifiable when all possible efforts to resolve issues through established channels have failed and when the issue should not be ignored. Whistle-blowers will also offend some staff in their organization who may choose to ignore the issue or simply disagree that the issue is serious enough to risk disciplinary action. Certainly, some whistle-blowers have brought unsafe or unsatisfactory conditions to the attention of the public and these have led to changes. But even with the protection afforded by the *Charter of Rights and Freedoms*, whistle-blowing will be seen within an organization as a disloyal act. Although it is clearly an option to be considered, whenever possible, the whistle-blowing should be done by groups rather than individuals.

Recommended Reading

1. For an intriguing account of her experience as a whistle-blower, see B. Moran, *A Little Rebellion* (Vancouver: Arsenal Pulp Press, 2001).

2. For an insightful review not only of Ellsberg's book but also of the contribution of such information to policy-making, see N. Lemann, 'Paper Tiger: Daniel Ellsberg's War', in *The New Yorker*, 4 November 2002.

3. For an early account of the work of Campaign 2000, see R. Popham, D. Hay, and C. Hughes, 'Campaign 2000 to End Child Poverty: Building and Sustaining a Movement', in B. Wharf and M. Clague, eds, *Community Organizing: Canadian Experiences* (Toronto: Oxford University Press, 1997), pp. 248–72.

Conclusion

The intent of this concluding chapter is to reinforce the argument made throughout the book on the importance of inclusive approaches to policy-making. The argument is strengthened by references to the literature on policy-practice, and we pay particular attention to the work of Donald Schon and Martin Rein (1994), who have made distinguished contributions to the study of policy-making.

In addition, we refer to the connections between our objectives and the argument made by a number of scholars who take the position that injustice and inequities in income and wealth characterize Canadian society (Carniol, 2000; Mullally, 1997, 2002). These scholars urge social work practitioners to engage in efforts to transform society, that is, to change the grand issues of social policy in order to achieve social justice for all Canadians.

Towards Inclusiveness in Policy and Practice

Although neglected and often ignored at present, inclusive approaches have the potential to improve policy-making and policy outcomes. We have argued that attention to the principle of inclusiveness in the human services is the single most important reform needed in policy-making because processes that exclude the knowledge of those who receive services and those of practitioners will usually be incomplete and inappropriate. Service users experience the reality of living in poverty and in unsafe neighbourhoods, a reality unknown and foreign to those who have traditionally made policy.

We acknowledge that adding more people makes for an often time-consuming, frustrating, and messy policy process. Nevertheless, in our view 'participation is cost effective through cost avoidance' (Thayer, n.d., p. 19). To repeat once again, taking time to hear opinions voiced during the policy-making process can avoid the delays and difficulties that often occur in implementation.

Although our arguments have been based on experiences in the human services, some supporting evidence comes from the federal Department of Fisheries and Oceans. At one time a highly respected agency, the department 'has taken a dramatic tumble from grace, lurching from crisis to crisis, while salmon runs plummeted and fishers lost their jobs by the thousands' (Hume, 1996, p. B1). A number of reasons have been suggested for the department's decline; however, the most persuasive is the change in management structure: from a decentralized structure that was local and that listened to the views of fishers to a highly centralized and remote agency located in Ottawa.

Strategies to Influence Policy

We have presented a number of strategies to influence policy, and these can be divided into two sets. The first are internal to an organization and distinguished by inclusivity. They consist of the vertical slice process, community governance, policy communities, and the practice approach of family conferences. All these extend the usual level of participation in policy-making and in practice. Since all will at times encounter differences and sometimes outright conflict, the method of choice in dealing with disputes is shared decision-making. The discussion in Chapters 7 and 8 support both the principle of inclusivity and shared decision-making. As Callahan notes, 'If I were to identify the most important contributions of feminist thinking in policy-making I would focus on the feminist practice of building relationships across differences' (Chapter 8).

The second set of strategies represents the efforts of advocacy groups, social movements, think-tanks, and whistle-blowers that attempt to influence policy from outside. We have noted that well-researched briefs and reports from these groups are often not usually sufficient to bring about the desired changes. In keeping with Lemann's (2002) observation that 'it is not what we know but what we believe in that makes all the difference' (p. 99), governments most often listen to the views that conform to their own. However, a strategy of anticipating the policy agenda and responding positively to this can be effective, particularly if it is used by a policy community with membership from government and research groups or think-tanks.

A New Kind of Professional?

We turn now to consider whether the principle of inclusiveness requires a new kind of human service professional. Our vision of the professional is one who surrenders the desire to control while acknowledging that there are some limits imposed by legislation, by budgets, or, increasingly, by time. These professionals welcome the contributions of those being served and work hard to establish relationships characterized by partnership, although they recognize that at times they may have to assume the role of the senior partner.

We struggled to find a role model for the kind of professional we have in mind. In an earlier draft of the chapter we suggested the profession of architecture as a model, on the grounds that at least some architects take seriously the role of consultant in their work with clients. Architects are knowledgeable about construction, about stress factors, and about the pros and cons of various kinds of building materials. But they do not know the specific tastes of their clients with respect to the size of the proposed house, the configuration of rooms, and the personal preference for building materials and interior design. The best results occur when the knowledge and experience of both architect and client are harmonized. However, in reflecting on this suggested role model, we took account of Murray's observation that 'architects design houses for council tenants according to space standards that they have never had to experience themselves' (Murray, 1993, p. 60).

In fact, it becomes clear that the closest approximation to our desired model lies within the profession of social work, particularly in the heritage charted by community organization. We recognize that there are examples of community organizers who have aspired to the role of expert, whether as social planners or community therapists. Certainly one can find support for these roles in the literature of community organization. Kahn's (1969) early work in social planning as well as the expert agent of community change described by Lippitt, Watson, and Westley (1958) come to mind. But such works are in the minority: the bulk of the literature in community organization and the majority of practitioners in the field exemplify the respectful, 'consumer-centred' professional. Achieving partnerships among those involved in the human services will not be easy, particularly since some who receive service may not choose a partnership model or may have few supports to assist them. But these difficulties should not destroy the potential for building partnership wherever possible. The kind of professional we have in mind, then, is characterized by the following attributes:

1. listens and incorporates into practice the experience of those being served;
2. respects those being served and treats them as citizens;
3. provides relevant information and research;
4. analyzes information and the pros and cons of various alternatives to resolving issues;
5. communicates in plain language both in speaking and in writing;
6. prepares draft reports for discussion and summary reports at closure;
7. organizes meetings at times and locations convenient to all;
8. chairs meetings when appropriate;
9. ensures that all affected have the chance to participate and to provide leadership; and
10. has thorough knowledge of the community and of the issues facing those with whom she or he works.

Professionals do have unique and specific knowledge and skills. They know other professionals; they are aware (or should be) of power and how it is unequally distributed in Canadian society; they are cognizant of insights based on research and studies of change in other jurisdictions; and they are knowledgeable about their domain of practice, whether in the sphere of policy or direct practice. Thus, policy professionals know about the policy-making process, the preferences of the government in power, and the context of the budget and resources available, and this information must be communicated in a respectful fashion to those being served.

An intriguing example of role reversal in partnerships occurred in a social action group in Toronto called the Just Society Movement. This movement was made up mainly of poor people, and the involvement of professionals was allowed only on terms laid down by the activists. Care was taken to sort out the relationship to ensure that professionals did not dominate the organization. A condition for participation by professionals was 'a personal commitment to action and change as a base from which one could then contribute personal skills, insight and knowledge' (Buchbinder, 1979, p. 147). Most importantly, the relationship between the two could not be a 'professional' relationship based on the exercise of 'power over' by the professional.

Our view of this distinct role for professionals in the human services is similar to the conceptualization of the policy-practice role in social work, a role that has received attention in recent years. The policy-practice role is described in the following terms:

> Policy-practice in social work is an approach in which social policy and direct social work practice are combined. It is practised by front-line social workers or supervisors in either public or private settings. Requisite to policy-practice behaviour is the requirement that direct service practitioners, including supervisors, understand and analyze the effects of extant social policy on clients and participate in the modification of social policy that is harmful to clients. These behaviours are operationalized at several levels: the personal, the organizational and the legislative. (Wyers, 1991, p. 246)

Some social work educators have argued that the policy-practice role is so important that it should be recognized as a distinct and new role in social work (Jansson, 1994). Although Jansson (2003) expands his concept of policy-practice in his latest book to place more of an emphasis on policy advocacy and the strategies to be employed in this role, these functions are still often seen as separate from the role performed by the majority of practitioners in the human services. Although we agree with the importance attached to these functions, creating a new, specialized role is not necessarily the answer. In our view, these responsibilities are part and parcel of the role of all first-line practitioners and policy professionals. Creating a new role opens up the possibility of letting both practitioners and policy-makers off the hook from their responsibilities to develop inclusive policy-making structures and processes.

A Different Form of Inclusivity

A different form of inclusiveness in policy-making is presented in the work of Schon and Rein. These scholars have written extensively on the notion of framing and reframing policies. It is impossible to do justice here to the authors' often abstract but intriguing account of resolving policy controversies in their 1994 publication, *Frame Reflection: Toward a Resolution of Intractable Policy Controversies*. However, their primary contention echoes the argument noted throughout this book—that policies are framed by the ideologies and experiences of those who participate in the policy-making process. Since these ideologies often conflict, especially in the most vexing policy matters, resolution is always difficult and often unsatisfactory. Schon and Rein suggest that tackling these dilemmas requires that all the people involved in the process reflect on their own and others' constructions of the problem at hand. The similarity between frame reflection and shared decision-making and shared learning is readily apparent.

Frame reflection requires 'a triadic relationship of research, policy and practice' (Schon and Rein, 1994, p. 197). The triad is necessary because policy-makers are simply too busy and too removed from practice to engage in reflection;

researchers lack sufficient knowledge of the realities of the policy-practice connections; and practitioners, while knowledgeable, lack influence and power.

Schon and Rein (1994) sum up the requirements for frame reflection in the following way:

- ability to contribute to the creation and maintenance of a climate of mutual trust among policy inquirers;
- ability to put yourself in the other party's shoes—to discover where they are coming from—in personal and institutional terms, including especially the action frames that shape their interests;
- possession of double vision—the ability to act from a frame while cultivating the awareness of alternative frames;
- appreciation of the necessarily political character of policy design without the cynicism that often attaches to such an appreciation; and
- skill of inventing new policy modifications and practices with an eye to resolving frame conflicts. (Schon and Rein, 1994, p. 207)

There are differences between *Frame Reflection* and this book. One example is that *Frame Reflection* includes researchers/academics as members of the triad because researchers are often in a position to both reflect on framing issues as well as analyze and evaluate outcomes. However, we believe that the inclusion of service users is also crucial, and in our view the triad should be a quartet.

Social Work and Social Transformation

As noted earlier, several prominent academics have argued that social workers should focus on transformative efforts that will bring about social justice for all Canadians and not just a privileged few. Thus Mullaly (2002, p. 205) states, 'Anti-oppressive social workers will, for the most part, work within the dimension of structural or social transformation. All attempts should be made to link everyday practice at whatever level at which one is working to the goal of social transformation.' The dimensions of social work practice identified by David Gil, who also argues the case for connecting the resolution of immediate problems to reform and transformation, provide a useful framework for this discussion. We recognize that these dimensions may not fit with all human service professions but they can be adapted as required.

- *Amelioration:* alleviating suffering by providing material goods.
- *Control:* controlling, regulating, and monitoring the behaviour of certain individual and groups.
- *Adaptation:* assisting individuals to adjust to the existing social order.
- *Reform:* working to bring about changes that will benefit individuals but will not in any substantial fashion alter existing policies and structures.
- *Structural transformation:* working with social movements and other groups to overcome the fundamental causes of oppression and injustice. (Adapted from Gil, 1998, pp. 68–85)

We have a great deal of sympathy with the position of these authors and agree that a number of strategies are available to human service workers who are committed to structural change. One is to engage in the political process. Social workers have run for political office, some have been elected, and some have occupied key positions, including the premier of a province (David Barrett in BC), and leaders of a political party (Audrey McLaughlin and Alexa McDonough of the New Democratic Party). Many others have worked diligently in political campaigns.

A second option is to join with social movements such as the feminist, First Nations, gay and lesbian, and disability movements in their efforts to bring about change and to urge that these movements find common rather than separate grounds for their change efforts. Again some social workers have followed this path.

A third strategy is to support the work of social research/advocacy organizations such as the Canadian Council on Social Development, the Centre for Policy Alternatives, the Caledon Institute, and the Council of Canadians that focuses on problems such as globalization and the unequal distribution of income and wealth in Canada. At the community level some social planning councils and antipoverty groups have a long record of sound research and campaigns against homelessness and poverty.

Although we applaud social and other human service workers who have pursued the above strategies or have been able to suit their day-to-day work in such a way that it supports transformative efforts, the number of individuals that take up these causes remains in the minority. As we have emphasized, neo-conservative policies have turned human service organizations into agencies of inspection and practitioners into agents of control. They spend most of their time dealing with crises and have neither the time nor the energy to engage in work that addresses structural transformation.

Given this bleak picture, is there any reason to suggest that social workers and other human service workers will be able to change practice and their workplaces? Can they alter the approaches of amelioration, control, and adaptation to such an extent that these become positive functions rather than controlling and inspecting the lives of service users? Our discussion takes the form of questions rather than assertions grounded in experience. However, our position is that if human service workers cannot change practice and their workplaces, there is not much hope for success in altering societal structures.

As a beginning step, could the task of amelioration be reframed from one that provides material goods only after intrusive investigations conducted in a mean-spirited fashion to one that sees the meeting of need as a right and an entitlement? Could the task of adaptation take the form of structural empathy (Carniol, 1995) whereby counselling directed at assisting service users to cope with current realities is accompanied by information about structural matters such as the responsibility of the market economy and of employers for unemployment? Could the task of control adopt a partnership approach where service users play a significant role in making plans that affect their lives? For example, risk assessment procedures could be conducted in a more democratic fashion with practitioners and services users sharing their knowledge about how to develop plans for the care of children who may be or become 'at risk'.

All these questions might be answered in the affirmative if community work approaches were adopted and placed in the mainstream of practice. Community work was outlined as an aspect of community governance in Chapter 6, but it might be useful to note the salient characteristics here. It is an approach that views those being served as residents of a community who, while requiring some services, can also contribute to the life of the community. It incorporates much of the concept of the caring community argued by McKnight (1995) but does not devalue or deny the assistance practitioners can provide (Wharf, 2002). Indeed, the cost of the current approaches to practice may well push policy-makers to view community social work as a preferred approach.

These questions could also be answered in the affirmative if practitioners developed alliances between themselves and those they serve. Developing such alliances clearly represents a radical notion given the stresses faced by human service workers. However, practitioners and those they serve are becoming increasingly dissatisfied with policy and practice as these are currently organized. Practitioners are frustrated in their efforts to provide useful and relevant assistance, and, for their part, service users bitterly resent the treatment they often receive at the hands of overworked and overwhelmed practitioners. The discontent provides an opportunity for constructive action.

The unique contribution of these alliances would be to change practice because policy reforms often leave practice untouched. The alliances might focus initial attention on identifying the ingredients of effective practice and might insist that those being served have the responsibility to contribute both to the definition of the issues facing them and to the resolution of these issues. As McKnight (1995, p. 48) observes: 'There is no greater power than the right to define the question. When the capacity to define the problem becomes a professional prerogative, citizens no longer exist. The prerogative removes the citizen as problem definer, much less problem solver.'

Practitioner–service user alliances have a vital contribution to make. They might begin in a very informal way at the local level, for example, through meetings in neighbourhood homes or at sympathetic community organizations. Indeed, progressive regional managers in provincial departments of social services and executive directors of Children's Aid Societies might provide modest resources like access to computers to support the work of these alliances.

Another version of these alliances might take the form of service user organizations aided by a few key professionals. Certainly, many examples of groups such as the Association for Community Living have made important contributions to legislation, policy, and practice. Such groups have prospered in large part because they include a wide spectrum of citizens ranging from working-class people to civic and business leaders. Groups made up solely of recipients of social assistance have enjoyed far less success in changing policies although the National Anti-Poverty Organization and some provincial and local counterparts have been tireless advocates of more adequate benefits for those who require social assistance.

Participation in groups enables members to recognize that their situation is not unique nor solely of their own making. Groups can also take action both on matters affecting them and on larger community issues. For example, in the Empowering Women Project identified in the Introduction, a group of single-parent women took action against the former husband of one of the members. Although forbidden by a court order to visit his ex-spouse, the man frequently parked his truck outside her house in an obvious and successful attempt to harass her and the children. The group informed the man in writing that they were aware of his behaviour, that they would monitor his parking, and that they would notify the police of their surveillance. The harassment stopped.

This group also developed a cooperative garden and food exchange that stretched their budgets. Cooperative arrangements concerning daycare, clothing, and food offer direct benefits and also have an invigorating and empowering effect on participants by providing opportunities to create and contribute. Cooperative efforts go a long way to prevent citizens from becoming 'clients' primarily dependent on others.

One conspicuously successful example is Women for Economic Security (WES) in Chicago. Funded by the Woods Charitable Foundation (WCF), it has established seven chapters and enrolled 350 members from some of the poorest neighbourhoods in Chicago. O'Donnell summarizes the contributions of WES:

> Including clients in the policy-making process seems to have been an essential step in the development of programs that can yield service user-agency cooperation. In the years of Woods Charitable Foundation's investment in participatory welfare policy-making, benefit increases were secured despite the state's severe fiscal problems, a policy dramatically limiting the 'sanctioning' of welfare recipients (cutting off benefits for apparent failure to comply with rules) was secured, and a workfare program was dramatically redirected from forcing participants into job search programs to encouraging volunteer participation in education programs. (O'Donnell, 1993, p. 634)

In closing, it is our view that participation in any or all of the above change efforts would allow human service workers to confront the ordinary issues of social policy, and in so doing, improve policy and practice. Whether these steps would lead to effective engagement with the grand issues is a moot question. But if an alliance of practitioners, service users, and academics succeed in improving policies, reforming practice, and in bringing shared decision-making into workplaces, they will have brought about significant changes. In so doing, they may gain the confidence to join with others in challenging those societal structures that create and maintain oppression in Canadian society.

Recommended Reading

1. For a sophisticated analysis of the policy-making process and the education of policy analysts/researchers, see D. Schon and M. Rein, *Frame Reflection: Toward the Resolution of Intractable Policy Controversies* (New York: Basic Books, 1994).

2. For arguments in favour of structural transformation, see the following: B. Carniol, *Case Critical*, 4th edn (Toronto: Between the Lines, 2000); D. Gil, *Confronting Injustice and Oppression: Concepts and Strategies for Social Workers* (New York: Columbia University Press, 1998); B. Mullaly, *Structural Social Work: Ideology, Theory and Practice*, 2nd edn (Toronto: Oxford University Press, 1997); and B. Mullaly, *Challenging Oppression: A Critical Social Work Approach* (Toronto: Oxford University Press, 2002).

3. For conflicting views on the role of professionals in building a caring community, see B. Wharf, ed., *Community Work Approaches to Child Welfare* (Toronto: Broadview Press, 2002), and J. McKnight, *The Careless Society: Community and Its Counterfeits* (New York: Basic Books, 1995).

Questions for Reflection

A. *Connecting Policy to Practice in the Human Services* takes the position that an élite few, mainly men with a conservative ideology, exercise a disproportionate amount of influence in Canada and how the country is governed.

1. Do you agree with this statement?
2. If yes, can you give some examples of élite influence?
3. If no, identify your reasons for disagreeing.

B. In a small group of fellow students or friends discuss Lemann's proposition identified in Chapter 9 that 'it is not what we know but what we believe in that makes all the difference'.

4. Is there agreement in the group about this proposition? Why?
5. Can participants identify examples of changing their beliefs because of new knowledge?
6. How are ideologies (belief systems) formed?

C. Identify a recent policy or legislative act at the federal, provincial, or agency level.

7. What alternatives were available to the policy-makers before making the final choice?
8. Why did they choose this alternative?
9. Who were the most influential people making the decision.
10. Who benefited from the policy?

D. Return to the above example.

11. Do any of the policy-making models described in Chapter 2 capture what happened in the policy making process?
12. Do any of these models capture what happens in practice between human service workers and the people they serve?

E. Chapter 3 argues that provincial governments are the most important level of government in providing health and social services.

13. In your view, should the federal government be awarded more authority and responsibility for health and social service programs? Why?
14. In your view, should municipal/regional governments take on increased responsibilities? Why?

15. In your view, should agencies in the voluntary sector take on increased responsibilities? Why?

F. Chapter 3 also discusses the impact of globalization on social policy in Canada. In your small group address the following.

16. Has globalization had a positive or negative impact on social policies in Canada?

17. If the group concluded that the impact had been negative suggest some ways in which the impact might be changed.

E. Chapter 5 contends that local offices of provincial departments/ministries, first line practitioners and service users should be more involved in the policy process than they are at the present time.

18. Is this contention realistic?

19. Are there barriers that stand in the way of increased involvement?

20. What are these barriers?

21. How might they be overcome?

22. Alternatively, should first-line practitioners focus on providing services and eschew any responsibility for policy making?

F. Chapters 6, 7, and 8 argue the case for more inclusive approaches to policy-making.

23. Can you think of other inclusive approaches not identified in these chapters?

24. Are inclusive approaches feasible and realistic?

G. In your small group, discuss the pros and cons of community governance and address the following questions.

25. Is the condition of 'acute localitis' an inevitable consequence of community governance? If so how might it be prevented?

26. Is off-loading an inevitable consequence of community governance? If so, how might it be prevented?

27. Suggest some ways in which communities can be strengthened. Are there some key community institutions?

H. The final chapter presents the argument that social and other human service workers should take an increased role in transforming society. Again in your small group address the following.

28. Is societal transformation an appropriate role for human service workers?

29. If yes, are there barriers that stand in the way of them taking on this role?

30. Can these barriers be overcome? How?

31. If no, should first line practitioners focus on providing services?

Appendix B

Annotated Websites and Selected Canadian Journals

Social Policy Sites

C.D. Howe Institute/Institut C.D. Howe
www.cdhowe.org
Provides policy analysis based on 'objectivity, professionalism and relevance', but is widely known as the conservative research institute recommended by the Canadian Taxpayers Federation.

Caledon Institute
www.caledoninst.org/
The Caledon Institute 'does rigorous, high-quality research and analysis and promotes practical proposals for the reform of social policy at the government and non-government sector.' The Institute is a private, non-profit organization focusing on social and economic inequalities in a broad range of social policy areas.

Canadian Centre for Policy Alternatives
www.policyalternatives.ca
The Canadian Centre for Policy Alternatives undertakes and promotes research on a wide range of issues pertaining to social and economic justice. In addition to reports and books on particular issues, the centre publishes a monthly newsletter, *The Monitor*, which is available free to members.

Canadian Health Coalition
www.healthcoalition.ca
The Canadian Health Coalition is dedicated to preserving and enhancing Canada's public health coalition. The coalition includes groups representing unions, seniors, women, students, consumers, and health care professionals.

Canadian Health Network
www.canadian-health-network.ca
This site contains information and links to organizations, including Aboriginal health, minority groups, HIV/AIDS in Canada, environmental health, gender and health, people with disabilities, and violence prevention.

Canadian Policy Research Networks Inc.
www.cprn.ca

Established in 1995 the Canadian Policy Research Networks is a non-profit think-tank that coordinates three networks focusing on work, family, and health. These networks involve collaboration by researchers in universities and government agencies across the country. The research is funded by a number of federal, provincial, and private-sector agencies.

Canadian Research Institute for the Advancement of Women
www.criaw-icref.ca
The institute is a non-governmental organization devoted to advancing gender equality through research and action. On-line resources include fact sheets about violence against women in Canada, and women and poverty.

Campaign 2000
www.campaign2000.ca
Campaign 2000 was established in 1991 by four national organizations to bring pressure on the federal government to implement the all-party resolution of 1989 to eliminate child poverty by the year 2000. Campaign 2000 is now supported by 87 national, provincial, and local partners. The principle strategy used by Campaign 2000 is the annual report card released on the anniversary of the all-party resolution. This report card documents the extent of child poverty in Canada.

Council of Canadians with Disabilities
www.ccdonline.ca
The Council of Canadians with Disabilities focuses on disability rights including access to job, housing, and democracy.

Fraser Institute
www.fraserinstitute.ca
The Fraser Institute is a think-tank dedicated to 'competitive market solutions to public policy problems'. It is funded mainly through corporate contributions.

Human Rights Education Associates
www.hrea.org/
Human Rights Education is an Ottawa-based organization dedicated to the empowerment of human rights activists and organizations and to the education of people on human rights issues and the role of civil society. It includes databases, publications, and news items.

International Centre for Human Rights and Democratic Development
www.ichrdd.ca/splash.html
This is the site of a non-partisan Montreal-based organization created by the Parliament of Canada to work with citizens' groups and governments in Canada and abroad to promote human and democratic rights. It focuses on four themes: democratic development and justice, women's rights, indigenous people's rights, and globalization and human rights.

National Anti-Poverty Organization
www.napo-onap.ca
The National Anti-Poverty Organization is a voluntary organization committed to advocacy on behalf of low-income Canadians.

National Council of Welfare
www.ncwcnbes.net
The National Council of Welfare (NCW) was established in 1969 as a citizen's advisory body. It advises the Minister of Human Resources Development on matters of concern to low-income Canadians. The council consists of representatives from across Canada and appointed by the Governor-in-Council. Reports by the NCW deal with a range of issues on poverty and social policy in Canada including income security programs, welfare reform, medicare, and taxation. These reports are free of charge to individuals who are on the mailing list. The address is: National Council of Welfare, 9th floor, 112 Kent Street, Place de Ville, Tower B, Ottawa, ON K1A OJ9.

PovNet
www.povnet.org/
PovNet is an Internet site for advocates, people on welfare, and community groups and individuals involved in antipoverty work. Up-to-date information on welfare and related matters in British Columbia is provided, but there are links to current antipoverty issues elsewhere.

Social Administration and Planning Links
www.geocities.com/john_g_mcnutt/administ.htm
Links are provided courtesy of John G. McNutt, Graduate School of Social Work, Boston College, Chestnut Hill, MA 02467.

Status of Women Canada
www.swc-cfc.gc.ca
This site contains resources for gender-based analysis of public policy.

The Canadian Council on Social Development
www.ccsd.ca
The Canadian Council on Social Development (CCSD) is a voluntary, non-profit organization that 'aims to develop and promote progressive social policies inspired by social justice, equality and the empowerment of individuals and communities through research, consultation, public education and advocacy'. CCSD is supported by membership fees and contracts with government. It publishes a quarterly magazine *Perception* that is free to members.

The Council of Canadians
www.canadians.org

The Council of Canadians 'is an independent, non-partisan public interest organization established in 1985. The Council provides a critical voice on key national issues: safeguarding our social programs, promoting economic justice, renewing our democracy, asserting Canadian sovereignty, promoting alternatives to corporate-style free trade and preserving our environment'. The council is supported solely by membership dues.

Government Research Sites

Canadian Social Research Links
www.canadiansocialresearch.net/
This is a social-research clearinghouse with links to national and international research focused on employment and evaluation.

Government of Canada Main Site
www.gc.ca/main_e.html
This site provides access to all federal departments and agencies and official information about Canada. Links to provincial governments are provided.

How Government Works: A Primer
www.edu.psc-cfp.gc.ca/tdc/index_e.htm
This is an on-line program created by the Institute on Governance. It includes information on the structures of government and much more.

Statistics Canada
www.statcan.ca/
This is a general site with links to databases collected by Statistics Canada.

Child Welfare and Family Support Sites

Centre of Excellence for Child Welfare
www.cecw-cepb.ca/
This site provides information on research and activities undertaken by the Centre of Excellence for Child Welfare with links to the First Nations Research site at www.fncfcs.ca

The Canadian Association of Family Resource Programs
www.frp.ca/
Family Resource Programs Canada is a national, not-for-profit organization representing more than 20,000 family resource programs, centres, and related services across Canada. Its mission is to promote the well-being of families by providing national leadership, consultation, and resources to those who care for children and support families.

The Canadian Child Care Federation
www.cccf-fcsge.ca/

The mission of the Canadian Child Care Federation is to improve the quality of child care services for Canadian families. Research results and advocacy positions are provided.

The Child Welfare League of Canada
www.cwlc.ca/
The Child Welfare League (CWL) is a national, voluntary organization dedicated to promoting the well-being of 'at risk' children, youth, and their families. It is governed by a board of directors from child welfare and family-serving agencies across the country.

The Vanier Institute of the Family
www.vifamily.ca/
Established in 1965, the Vanier Institute of the Family provides important information on Canada's 8.4 million families. The Institute is an advocate for policies that can support the well-being of families.

Selected Journals

Canada's Children
Canada's Children is published by the Child Welfare League of Canada three times a year. Articles are focused on policy and practices in child welfare and family services.

Canadian Journal of Community Mental Health
www.wlu.ca/cjcmh/
This interdisciplinary journal is published twice a year. Areas of priority interest include program evaluation in the human services, community needs assessment, and community development with a broad focus on community mental health. Subscriptions in 2003 were $25 for individuals and $20 for students.

Canadian Public Policy
www.economics.ca/
The aim of this interdisciplinary journal is to stimulate research and discussion of public policy problems in Canada. The journal publishes four issues each year.

Canadian Review of Social Policy
The *Canadian Review of Social Policy* is published twice yearly under the direction of an editorial working group. The articles cover a wide range of social policy issues. The annual cost in 2003 was $30 for individuals and $15 for students and low-income households.

Canadian Social Work
Canadian Social Work is the journal of the Canadian Association of Social Workers. It is free to members of CASW, and the cost to non-members was $43.00 plus

GST in 2003. Subscriptions are available from: Canadian Social Work, 383 Parkdale Ave, Ottawa, ON K1Y 4R4. E-mail: casw@casw-acts.ca.

Canadian Social Work Review
The *Canadian Social Work Review* is published twice yearly by the Canadian Association of Schools of Social Work. The subscription rate for individuals was $33, and the student rate was $16 in 2003. Subscriptions are available from Wilfrid Laurier University Press, Wilfrid Laurier University, Waterloo, ON N2L 3C5.

ISUMA: Canadian Journal of Policy Research
ISUMA is a bilingual journal published by Les Presses de l'Université à Montréal on behalf of the Policy Research Secretariat.

Useful Tools for Community-Based Practice

Centre for Community Enterprise
www.cedworks.com
This website includes a resource booklet for Community Economic Development (CED) called *The Community Resilience Manual.* A separate publication called *Tools and Techniques for Community Recovery and Renewal* is also available at this site to provide further assistance to citizens wanting to strengthen or revitalize their local economies. The site lists important CED links and publications.

Community Development Handbook
www.hrdc-drhc.gc.ca/community/menu/index.shtml
This handbook provides a practical guide to community development.

Community Tool Box
ctb.ku.edu/
This site provides resources for all types of community work including how-to sections on many topics such as community assessment, advocacy, planning, grant applications, and much more.

The Partnership Handbook
www.hrdc-drhc.gc.ca/common/partners/partner.shtml
This handbook provides a step-by-step guide to developing partnerships for community-based action.

World Wide Web Resources for Social Workers
www.nyu.edu/socialwork/wwwrsw/
This site provides links to full-text articles from professional journals and a range of other links to government agencies, educational institutions, and professional organizations. The site is updated regularly.

References

Abelson, D.E. (2002). *Do Think Tanks Matter? Assessing the Impact of Public Policy Institutes*. Kingston, ON: McGill Queen's University Press.

Aboriginal Corrections Policy Unit (1997). *The Four Circles of Hollow Water*. Ottawa: Supply and Services Canada.

Alexander, E.R. (1985). 'From Idea to Action: Notes for a Contingency Theory of the Policy Implementation Process', *Administration and Society* 16 (4), 403–26.

—— (2002). E-mail to L. Pierson forwarded to B. Wharf.

Armitage, A. (2003). *Social Welfare in Canada*, 4th edn. Toronto: Oxford University Press.

Arnstein, S.R. (1969). 'A Ladder of Citizen Participation', *Journal of the American Institute of Planners* 4, 216–24.

Assembly of First Nations (2000). *First Nations and Inuit Regional Health Survey*. Ottawa: Author.

Attridge, C., and M. Callahan (1990). 'Nurses' Perspectives of Quality Work Environments', *Canada's Journal of Nursing Administration* 3 (3), 18–24.

Auditor General of Canada (1988). 'Attributes of Well-Performing Organizations', in *Annual Report*. Ottawa: Author.

Bardach, E. (1977). *The Implementation Game*. Cambridge, MA: MIT Press.

—— (2000). *A Practical Guide to Policy Analysis*. New York: Chatham House.

Barlow, M. (2002). 'Stop the Government's Drive to Let More Corporations Sue Our Country', *Letter to Members of the Council of Canadians*, 25 November. Ottawa: Council of Canadians.

Battle, K. (2003). Correspondence to B. Wharf.

BC Ministry of Social Services (1993). *Making Changes: Next Steps*. A White Paper for Public Review. Victoria, BC: Author.

BC Ministry of Women's Equality (1994). *Gender Lens: A Guide to Gender-Inclusive Policy and Program Development*. Victoria, BC: Author.

Bear, S., with the Tobique Women's Group (1991). 'You Can't Change the *Indian Act*', in J.D. Wine and J.L. Ristock, eds, *Women and Social Change: Feminist Activism in Canada*. Toronto: James Lorimer and Company.

Berman, P. (1980). 'Thinking About Programmed and Adaptive Implementation', in H. Ingram and D. Mann, eds, *Why Policies Succeed or Fail*, pp. 205–27. Beverly Hills, CA: Sage.

Bok, S. (1984). *Secrets*. New York: Vintage Books.

Boulding, K. (1964). 'Book Review: *A Strategy of Decision* by D. Braybrooke and C. Lindblom', *American Sociological Review* 25 (5), 29.

Bregha, F. (n.d.). *Public Participation in Planning, Policy and Program*. Toronto: Ministry of Community and Social Services.

Briskin, L., and M. Eliasson, eds (1999). Women's Organizing and Public Policy in Canada and Sweden. Kingston, ON: McGill-Queen's University Press.

Brodie, J. (1995). *Politics on the Margins*. Halifax: Fernwood Publishing.

Brodtrick, O. (1991). 'A Second Look at the Well-Performing Organization', in J. McDavid and B. Marson, eds, *The Well-Performing Organization*, pp. 16–22. Toronto: Institute of Public Administration of Canada.

Brooks, S. (1998). *Public Policy in Canada*. Toronto: Oxford University Press.

Brown, L., L. Haddock, and M. Kovach (2002). 'Watching Over Our Families: Lalum'utul'

Smun'een Child and Family Services', in B. Wharf, ed., *Community Work Approaches to Child Welfare*, pp. 131–51. Peterborough, ON: Broadview Press.

Bryson, J.M. (1988). *Strategic Planning for Public and Non-profit Organizations: A Guide to Strengthening and Sustaining Organization Achievement*. San Francisco: Jossey-Bass.

Buchbinder, H. (1979). 'The Just Society Movement', in B. Wharf, ed., *Community Work in Canada*, pp. 129–52. Toronto: McClelland and Stewart.

Burford, G., and J. Pennell (1995). 'Family Group Decision Making: An Innovation in Child and Family Welfare', in J. Hudson and B. Galaway, eds, *Child Welfare in Canada*, pp. 140–152. Toronto: Thompson Educational Publishing.

Callahan, M. (1993). 'Feminist Approaches to Child Welfare', in B. Wharf, ed., *Rethinking Child Welfare*, pp. 172–209. Toronto: McClelland and Stewart.

——, B. Field, C. Hubberstey, and B. Wharf (1998). *Best Practice in Child Welfare: A Report to the BC Ministry of Children and Families*. Victoria, BC: School of Social Work, University of Victoria.

——, and C. Attridge (1990). *Women in Women's Work: Social Workers Talk About Their Work in Child Welfare*. Victoria, BC: School of Social Work, University of Victoria.

——, and C. Lumb (1995). 'My Cheque or My Children', *Child Welfare* 74 (3), 795–819.

——, D. Rutman, S. Strega, and L. Dominelli (2003). 'Undeserving Mothers: The Lived Experiences of Young Mothers in Care', in K. Kufeldt and B. McKenzie, eds, *Child Welfare: Connecting Research, Policy and Practice*. Waterloo: Wilfrid Laurier University Press.

——, L. Hooper, and B. Wharf (1998). *Protecting Children by Empowering Women*. Victoria, BC: School of Social Work, University of Victoria.

——, C. Lumb, and B. Wharf (1995). *Strengthening Families Through Empowering Women*. Victoria, BC: School of Social Work, University of Victoria.

Cameron, D., and E. Finn (1996). *10 Deficit Myths: The Truth About Government Debts and Why They Don't Justify Cutbacks*. Ottawa: Canadian Centre for Policy Alternatives.

Cameron, G. (1995). 'The Nature and Effectiveness of Parent Mutual Aid Organizations in Child Welfare', in J. Hudson and B. Galaway, eds, *Child Welfare in Canada*, pp. 66–82. Toronto: Thompson Educational Publishing.

——, J. Karabanow, M-C. Laurendeau, and C. Chamberlain (2001). 'Program Implementation and Diffusion', in G. Prilleltensky, G. Nelson, and L. Peirson, eds, *Promoting Family Wellness and Preventing Child Maltreatment*, pp. 318–48. Toronto: University of Toronto Press.

Campaign 2000 (2002). *Sustaining Momentum and Maximizing Opportunities*. Submission to the Laidlaw Foundation. Toronto: Author.

—— Website (2002). 'Poverty Amidst Prosperity: Building a Canada for All Children: 2002 Report Card', 29 December, at www.campaign2002.ca/rc/rc02/1.html.

Campbell, M. (1999). 'Harris Slams Child Poverty Report Card', *Globe and Mail*, 25 November, p. A3.

'Can the Gun Registry Be Saved?' (2003). *Globe and Mail*, 4 January, p. A14.

Canadian Centre for Policy Alternatives (1997). *1997 Alternative Federal Budget*. Ottawa: Author.

—— (1999). 'UN Committee Finds Poverty, Inequality Too High in Canada', *The CCPA Monitor* 5 (9), 24–5.

—— (2000). 'Income Disparities', *The CCPA Monitor* 7 (6), 3.

—— Website (2002). 'UI Cuts Discriminate Against Women', 29 December, at www.policyalternatives.ca/publications/articles/article225.html.

Canadian Council on Social Development Website (2002). 'Percentage and Number of Persons in Low Income/Poverty by Age, Sex and Family Characteristics, Canada, 1990 and 1999,' 10 December, at www.ccds.ca/factsheets/fs-pov9099.htm.

Carley, M. (1980). *Rational Techniques in Policy Analysis*. London: Heinemann.

Carniol, B. (1995). 'Social Work and the Labour Movement', in B. Wharf, ed., *Social Work and Social Change*, pp. 114–43. Toronto: McClelland and Stewart.

—— (2000). *Case Critical*, 4th edn. Toronto: Between the Lines.

Carroll, B., and D. Siegel (1999). *Service in the Field*. Kingston, ON: McGill-Queen's University Press.

Cassidy, F. (1991). 'Organizing for Community Control', *The Northern Review* 11, 17–34.

Chambers, D.E. (1986). *Social Policy and Social Programs: Method for the Practical Public Policy Analyst*. New York: Macmillan.

Chase, G. (1979). 'Implementing a Human Service Program: How Hard Will It Be?', *Journal of Public Policy* 27 (4).

Child Care Advocacy Association of Canada (2003). '90% of Canadians Support National Child Care Plan, 86% Want Publicly Funded System', 27 January, at www.childcareadvocacy.ca.

Clague, M., R. Dill, R. Seebaran, and B. Wharf (1984). *Reforming Human Services: The Experience of the Community Resource Boards in B.C.* Vancouver: University of British Columbia Press.

Clark, C. (2002). 'Martin's Plan Gives Back-Benchers More Clout'.

Clement, W. (1975). *The Canadian Corporate Elite: An Analysis of Economic Power*. Toronto: McClelland and Stewart.

—— (1983). *Class, Power and Property*. Toronto: Methuen. The *Globe and Mail*. 22 Oct, p. 1.

Cohen, M., J. March, and J. Olsen (1972). 'A Garbage Can Model of Organizational Choice', *Administrative Science Quarterly* 17, 1–25.

Coleman, W., and G. Skogstad, eds (1990). *Policy Communities and Public Policy in Canada*. Toronto: Copp Clark Pitman.

'College Vindicates Oliveri, Rejects HSC's Allegations' (2002). CAUT *Bulletin* 49 (1), January, p. 1.

Connors, E., and F. Maidman (2001). 'A Circle of Healing: Family Wellness in Aboriginal Communities', in I. Prilleltensky, G. Nelson, and L. Pierson, eds. *Promoting Family Wellness and Preventing Child Maltreatment*, pp. 349–416. Toronto: University of Toronto Press.

Council of Canadians (1997). *Canadian Perspective* (Fall). Ottawa: Author.

Cruise D., and A. Griffiths (1997). *On South Mountain: The Dark Secrets of the Goler Clan*. Toronto: Penguin.

Dahl, R. (1970). *After the Revolution*. New Haven: Yale University Press.

Dobbin, M. (2001). 'More and More, Our Lives are Dominated by the TNCs', *The CCPA Monitor* 7 (10), 17–20.

Dobelstein, A.W. (1990). *Social Welfare: Policy and Analysis*. Chicago: Nelson-Hall.

Domhoff, C.W. (1967). *Who Rules America?* Englewood Cliffs, NJ: Prentice Hall.

—— (1971). *The Higher Circles*. New York: Vintage.

Durie, H., and A. Armitage (1996). *Planning for Implementation of B.C.'s Child, Family, and Community Service Act*. Victoria, BC: School of Social Work, University of Victoria.

Durst, D. 1999. *Canada's National Child Benefit: Phoenix or Fizzle?* Halifax: Fernwood Publishing.

Dwivedi, O., and G. Gow (1999). *From Bureaucracy to Public Management*. Peterborough, ON: Broadview Press.

Ehrenreich, B. (1987). 'The New Right Attack on Social Welfare', in F. Block et al., eds, *The Mean Season: The Attack on the Welfare State*. New York: Pantheon.

Ellsberg, D. (2002). *Secrets: A Memoir of Vietnam and the Pentagon Papers*. New York: Viking.

Elmore, R. (1979a). 'Complexity and Control: What Legislators and Administrators Can Do About Implementation'. Public Policy Paper 11. Seattle: University of Washington Institute of Governmental Research.

—— (1979b). 'Organizational Models of Social Program Implementation', *Public Policy* 2 (2), 185–228.

—— (1982). 'Backward Mapping: Implementation Research and Policy Decisions', in W. Williams, ed., *Studying Implementation: Methodological and Administrative Issues*, pp. 18–35. Chatham, NJ: Chatham House.

Etzioni, A. (1967). 'Mixed Scanning: A "Third" Approach to Decision-Making', *Public Administration Review* 27, 385–92.

——— (1976). *Social Problems*. Englewood Cliffs, NJ: Prentice Hall.

Fabricant, M. (1985). 'The Industrialization of Social Work Practice', *Social Work* 30 (5), 389–402.

Fagan, T., and P. Lee (1997). 'New Social Movements and Social Policy: A Case Study of the Disability Movement', in M. Lavalette and A. Pitt, eds, *Social Policy: A Conceptual and Theoretical Introduction*, pp. 140–62. London, UK: Sage.

Federal, Provincial and Territorial Advisory Committee on Population Health (1999). *Toward a Healthy Future*. Second Report on the Health of Canadians. Ottawa: Government Services Canada.

Fetterman, D., S. Kaftarian, and A. Wandersman, eds (1996). *Empowerment Evaluation*. Thousand Oaks, CA.: Sage.

Fisher, R., and W. Ury (1983). *Getting to Yes*. New York: Penguin.

Fleras, A., and J.L. Elliott (1999). *Unequal Relations: An Introduction to Race, Ethnic and Aboriginal Dynamics in Canada*, 3rd edn. Scarborough, ON: Prentice Hall.

Flynn, J.P. (1992). *Social Agency Policy*. 2nd edn. Chicago: Nelson-Hall.

Ford, R., and D. Zussman, eds (1997). *Alternative Service Delivery: Sharing Governance in Canada*. Toronto: IPAC and KPMG for Government Foundation.

Frankel, H., B. McKenzie, D. Fuchs, I. Guberman, and S. Taylor-Henley (1996). *An Evaluation of the Family Aide and Family Support Programs at Child and Family Services of Western Manitoba*. Winnipeg: Child and Family Services Research Group, Faculty of Social Work, University of Manitoba.

Frideres, J. (1998). *Aboriginal Peoples in Canada: Contemporary Conflicts*, 5th edn. Scarborough, ON: Prentice Hall.

Fuchs, D. (1995). 'Preserving and Strengthening Families and Protecting Children: Social Network Intervention, A Balanced Approach to the Prevention of Child Maltreatment', in J. Hudson and B. Galaway, eds, *Child Welfare in Canada*, pp. 113–23. Toronto: Thompson Educational Publishing.

Gallagher, J., and R. Haskins (1984). *Policy Analysis*. New York: Ablex.

Gil, D.G. (1990). *Unravelling Social Policy*, 4th edn. Rochester, VT: Schenkman.

——— (1998). *Confronting Injustice and Oppression: Concepts and Strategies for Social Workers*. New York: Columbia University Press.

Globe and Mail Website (2002). '50 Best Paid Executives', *Report on Business Magazine*, 12 December, at http://top1000.robmagazine.com/2002/executives/executives.htm.

Goldstein, H. (1992). 'Should Social Workers Base Practice Decisions on Empirical Research? No', in E. Gambrill and R. Pruger, eds, *Controversial Issues in Social Work*, pp. 107–23. Boston: Allyn & Bacon.

Graham, J., K. Swift, and R. Delaney (2000). *Canadian Social Policy: An Introduction*. Scarborough, ON: Prentice Hall/Allyn & Bacon.

Graveline, F.J. (1998). *Circle Works: Transforming Eurocentric Consciousness*. Halifax: Fernwood Publishing.

Gregg, A.R. (2002). 'Strains Across the Border: The Year-End Poll', *Maclean's*, 30 December, pp. 32–6.

Gwyn, R. (1995). 'Two Cheers, One Boo for Ontario Cutbacks', *Times Colonist*, 27 July, p. 8.

Haddow, R. (1990). 'The Poverty Policy Community in Canada's Liberal Welfare State', in W. Coleman and G. Skogstad, eds, *Policy Communities and Public Policy in Canada*, pp. 213-37. Toronto: Copp Clark Pitman.

——— (1993). *Poverty Reform in Canada, 1958–1978*. Kingston, ON: McGill-Queen's University Press.

Hamilton, A.C., and C.M. Sinclair (1991). Report of the Aboriginal Justice Inquiry of Manitoba, Vol. 1: *The Justice System and Aboriginal People*. Winnipeg: Queen's Printer.

Hargrove, E. (1975). *The Missing Link: The Study of the Implementation of Social Policy*. Washington, DC: The Urban Institute.

Hart, M.A. (2002). *Seeking Mino-Pimatisiwin: An Aboriginal Approach to Helping*. Halifax: Fernwood Publishing.

Hart, R. (2001). 'The National Report', *Perspectives* 23 (1), 17.

Herman, J., L. Morris, and C. Fitz-Gibbon (1987). *Evaluator's Handbook*. Newbury Park, CA: Sage.

Howlett, M., and M. Ramesh (1995). *Studying Public Policy*. Toronto: Oxford University Press.

Hume, M. (1996). 'DFO: The Decline of a Federal Empire', *Vancouver Sun*, 21 December, p. B1.

Ismi, A. (2002). 'Western Neo-Colonialism Fuels Wars, Plundering of Resources', *The CCPA Monitor* 9 (5), 14–17.

Jansson, B.S. (1994). *Social Policy: From Theory to Policy Practice*, 2nd edn. Belmont, CA: Brooks/Cole.

—— (2003). *Becoming an Effective Policy Advocate*, 4th edn. Pacific Grove, CA: Brooks/Cole/Thomson Learning.

Johnston, P. (1983). *Native Children and the Child Welfare System*. Toronto: James Lorimer.

Joint Management Committee (2001). *Aboriginal Justice Inquiry Child Welfare Initiative: Promise of Hope, Commitment to Change*. Winnipeg: Author.

Kahn, A.J. (1969). *Theory and Practice of Social Planning*. New York: Russell Sage Foundation.

Kernaghan, K., and D. Siegel (1995). *Public Administration in Canada: A Text*, 3rd edn. Scarborough, ON: Nelson Canada.

Kerstetter, S. (2002). *Rags and Riches: Wealth Inequality in Canada*. Ottawa: Canadian Centre for Policy Alternatives.

Kettner, P.M., R.M. Moroney, and L.L. Martin (1999). *Designing and Managing Programs: An Effectiveness-Based Approach*, 2nd edn. Thousand Oaks, CA: Sage.

Kingdon, J.K. (1995). *Agendas, Alternatives, and Public Policies*, 2nd edn. New York: HarperCollins.

Kitchen, B., A. Mitchell, P. Clutterbuck, and M. Novick (1991). *Unequal Futures*. Toronto: The Child Poverty Action Group and The Social Planning Council of Metropolitan Toronto.

Klein, N. (2001). *No Logo*. London: HarperCollins.

Kouzes, J.M., and P.R. Mico (1979). 'Domain Theory: An Introduction to Organizational Behaviour in Human Service Organizations', *The Journal of Applied Behavioural Science* 15 (4), 449–69.

Labonte, R., and J. Feather (1996). *Handbook on Using Stories in Health Promotion Practice*. Ottawa: Health Canada.

Lacayo, R., and A. Ripley (2002). 'Persons of the Year', *Time*, 30 December/6 January 2003, pp. 26–7.

Lancaster House (2002). *Government Muzzles of Social Workers' Criticism Unjustified, Appeal Court Finds*, 24 September, at www.lancasterhouse.com/about/headlines_1.asp.

Lapham, L.H. (1988). *Money, Class and Power in America*. New York: Random House.

Lemann, N. (2002). 'Paper Tiger: Daniel Ellsberg's War', *The New Yorker*, 4 November, pp. 96–9.

Lightman, E. (2003). *Social Policy in Canada*. Toronto: Oxford University Press.

Lind, M. (1995). 'To Have and Have Not: Notes on the Progress of the American Class War', *Harpers*, 290 (1741), 35–49.

Lindblom, C.E. (1959). 'The Science of Muddling Through', *Public Administration Review* 19, 79–88.

—— (1968). *The Policy-Making Process*. Englewood Cliffs, NJ: Prentice Hall.

—— (1979). 'Still Muddling, Not Yet Through', *Public Administration Review* 39 (6), 517–26.

Linder, S.H., and B.G. Peters (1987). 'A Design Perspective on Policy Implementation: The Fallacies of Misplaced Prescription', *Policy Studies Review* 61 (3), 459–76.

Lindquist, E.A. (1998). 'A Quarter Century of Think Tanks', in D. Stone, A. Denham, and M. Garnett, eds, *Think Tanks Across Nations: A Comparative Approach*, pp. 27–144. Manchester, UK: Manchester University Press.

Lippitt, R., J. Watson, and B. Westley (1958). *The Dynamics of Planned Change*. New York: Harcourt, Brace and World.

Lipsky, M. (1980). *Street-Level Bureaucracy*. New York: Russell Sage.

Little, B. (2002). 'Romanow's $15-Billion Cure', *Globe and Mail*, 29 November.

Little, M. (1999). 'The Limits of Canadian Democracy: The Citizenship Rights of Poor Women', *Canadian Review of Social Policy* 42, 59–76.

Love, A. (1992). 'The Evaluation of Implementation: Case Studies', in J. Hudson, J. Mayne, and R. Thomlison, eds, *Action-Oriented Evaluation in Organizations*, pp. 135–59. Toronto: Wall & Emerson.

Lundberg, F. (1968). *The Rich and the Super Rich*. New York: Bantam.

Lysack, C., and J. Kaufert (1994). 'Comparing the Origins and Ideologies of the Independent Living Movement and Community Based Rehabilitation'. Presentation to Progress through Partnerships, National Independent Living Conference, Winnipeg, Manitoba, 24 August.

MacBeath, A. (1957). *Can Social Policies be Rationally Tested?* (The L.T. Hobhouse Memorial Trust Lecture). London: Oxford University Press.

McCarthy, S. (2003). 'Social Spending Preferable to Tax Cuts, Poll Finds', *Globe and Mail*, 17 February, pp. A1, A4.

McDonald, R.J., P. Ladd et al. (2000). *First Nations Child and Family Services Joint National Policy Review*. Final Report. Ottawa: The Assembly of First Nations and Department of Indian Affairs and Northern Development.

McGrath, S. (1997). 'Child Poverty Advocacy and the Politics of Influence', in J. Pulkingham and G. Ternowetsky, eds, *Child and Family Policies*, pp. 248–72. Halifax: Fernwood Publishing.

McKeen, W. (1999). 'Vertical Equity Versus Women's Autonomy: The Politics of Feminism in Canadian Income Security Policy in the 1970s', *Canadian Review of Social Policy* 42, 77–100.

—— (2001). 'Shifting Policy and Politics of Federal Child Benefits in Canada', *Social Politics* (Summer), 186–90.

McKenzie, B. (1989). *Decentralizing Child Welfare Services: Effects on Service Demand and the Job Morale of Street-Level Bureaucrats*. PhD diss., Arizona State University, Tempe.

—— (1991). 'Decentralization in Winnipeg: Assessing the Effects of Community-Based Child Welfare Services', *Canadian Review of Social Policy* 27, 57–66.

—— (1994). *Evaluation of the Pilot Project in Block Funding for Child Maintenance*. Winnipeg: West Region Child and Family Services.

—— (1997). 'Developing First Nations Child Welfare Standards: Using Evaluation Research Within a Participatory Framework', *The Canadian Journal of Program Evaluation* 12 (1), 133–48.

—— (1999). Evaluation of the Pilot Project on Block Funding in West Region Child and Family Services: A Second Look (Final Report). Winnipeg: Faculty of Social Work. University of Manitoba.

—— (2002a). *Block Funding Child Maintenance in First Nations Child and Family Services: A Policy Review Final Report*. Winnipeg: Faculty of Social Work, University of Manitoba.

—— (2002b). 'Building Community in West Region Child and Family Services', in B. Wharf, ed., *Community Work Approaches to Child Welfare*, pp. 152–62. Peterborough, ON: Broadview Press.

——, and I. Guberman (1997). 'For the Sake of the Children: A Program for Separating and Divorcing Parents', *The Social Worker* 65 (3), 107–18.

——, and P. Hudson (1985). 'Native Children, Child Welfare, and the Colonization of Native People', in K. Levitt and B.Wharf, eds, *The Challenge of Child Welfare*, pp. 125–41. Vancouver: University of British Columbia Press.

——, and V. Morrissette (2003). 'Social Work Practice with Canadians of Aboriginal Background: Guidelines for Respectful Social Work', in A. Al-Krenawi and J. R. Graham, *Multicultural Social Work in Canada*, pp. 251–82. Toronto: Oxford University Press.

Mackintosh, M. (1993). 'Creating a Developmental State: Reflections on Policy as Process', in G. Albo, D. Langille, and L. Panitch, eds, *A Different Kind of State? Popular Power and Democratic Administration*, pp. 51–65. Toronto: Oxford University Press.

Macklem, K. (2002). 'Canada's Top 100 Employers', *Maclean's*, 28 October, pp. 26–34.

McKnight, J. (1995). *The Careless Society: Community and Its Counterfeits*. New York: Basic Books.

——, and J. Kretzmann (1992). 'Capacity Mapping', *New Design* (Winter), 9–15.

McQuaig, L. (1987). *Behind Closed Doors*. Toronto: Viking.

—— (1991). *The Quick and the Dead*. Toronto: Viking.

—— (1993). *The Wealthy Banker's Wife*. Toronto: Penguin.

—— (1995). *Shooting the Hippo*. Toronto: Viking.

Maluccio, A. (1997). *Assessing Child Welfare Outcomes: The North American Perspective*. Presentation to Third International Conference on The Looking After Children Initiative, Oxford, England, 17–18 March.

Manitoba Joint Committee on Residential Schools (1994). *Proposal for a Manitoba Healing and Resource Centre for First Nations Affected by Residential Schools*. Winnipeg: Assembly of Manitoba Chiefs.

Marchak, M.P. (1991). *The Integrated Circus: The New Right and the Restructuring of the Global Economy*. Kingston, ON: McGill-Queen's University Press.

Marris, P. (1986). *Loss and Change*, rev. edn. London: Routledge and Kegan Paul.

——, and M. Rein (1967). *The Dilemmas of Social Reform*. New York: Russell Sage.

Maslow, A. (1954). *Motivation and Personality*. New York: Harper & Row.

Maxwell, G., and A. Morris (1995). 'Deciding about Justice for Young People in New Zealand', in J. Hudson and B. Galaway, eds, *Child Welfare in Canada*, pp. 168–86. Toronto: Thompson Educational Publishing.

May, K. (2002). 'Recipe for Disaster', *Times Colonist*, 25 August, pp. 1–2.

Miller, J.R. (1996). *Shingwauks' Vision: A History of Native Residential Schools*. Toronto: University of Toronto Press.

Mills, C.W. (1956). *The Power Elite*. New York: Oxford University Press.

—— (1959). *The Sociological Imagination*. London: Oxford University Press.

Milne, G. (2000). *Making Policy: A Guide to the Federal Government's Policy Process*, 8th edn. Ottawa: Author.

Mimoto, H., and P. Cross (1991). 'The Growth of the Federal Debt', *Canadian Economic Observer* 4 (6), 3.1–3.18.

Mintzberg, H. (1983). *Structure in Fives: Designing Effective Organizations*. Englewood Cliffs, NJ: Prentice Hall.

Mishra, R. (1984). *The Welfare State in Crisis: Social Thought and Social Change*. New York: St Martin's Press.

Montgomery, J. (1979). 'The Populist Front in Rural Development: Or Shall We Eliminate Bureaucracies and Get On With the Job', *Public Administration Review* (January/February), 58–65.

Moran, B. (2001). *A Little Rebellion*. Vancouver: Arsenal Pulp Press.

Moroney, R.M. (1991). *Social Policy and Social Work*. New York: Aldine de Gruyter.

Morris, N. (1995). 'Kids at Work', *Maclean's*, 11 December, pp. 28–30.

Morse, J., and A. Bower (2002). 'The Party Crasher', *Time*, 30 December/6 January 2003, pp. 43–6.

Mullaly, B. (1997). *Structural Social Work: Ideology, Theory and Practice*, 2nd edn. Toronto: Oxford University Press.

—— (2002). *Challenging Oppression: A Critical Social Work Approach*. Toronto: Oxford University Press.

Mullen, E. (1992). 'Should Social Workers Base Practice Decisions on Empirical Research? Yes', in E. Gambrill and R. Pruger, eds, *Controversial Issues in Social Work*, pp. 107–23. Boston: Allyn & Bacon.

Murray, R. (1993). 'Transforming the "Fordist" State', in G. Albo, D. Langille, and L. Panitch, eds, *A Different Kind of State? Popular Power and Democratic Administration*, pp. 51–65. Toronto: Oxford University Press.

Nairne, D. (1997). 'Teens Demand Help', *Winnipeg Free Press*, 23 March, p. A1.

Nakamura, R.T. (1987). 'The Textbook Policy Process and Implementation Research', *Policy Studies Review* 7 (1), 142–55.

National Council of Welfare (1994). *A Blueprint for Social Security Reform*. Ottawa: Ministry of Supply and Services Canada.

National Youth in Care Network. (1998). *About Us?*, at www.youthincare.ca.

Newman, P. (1975). *The Canadian Establishment*. Toronto: McClelland and Stewart.

——— (1981). *The Canadian Establishment*. Vol. 2: *The Acquisitors*. Toronto: McClelland and Stewart.

——— (1998). *The Titans: How the New Canadian Establishment Seized Power*. Toronto: Penguin.

Nyp, G. (2002). *Reaching for More: The Evolution of the Independent Living Centre of Waterloo Region*. Waterloo, ON: Independent Living Centre of Waterloo Region.

O'Donnell, S. (1993). 'Involving Clients in Welfare Policy-Making', *Social Work* 38 (5).

Ontario Association of Children's Aid Societies (1973). 'Brief to the Task Force on Family and Children's Services'. Toronto: Author.

Owen, S. (1998). 'Shared Decision Making: A Case Study', in B. Wharf and B. McKenzie, *Connecting Policy to Practice in the Human Services*, pp. 81–96. Toronto: Oxford University Press.

Pal, L.A. (1992). *Public Policy in Canada: An Introduction*. Toronto: McClelland and Stewart.

Palumbo D.R. (1987). 'Introduction', *Policy Studies Review* 7 (1), 97–101.

Panitch, L., ed. (1977). *The Canadian State*. Toronto: University of Toronto Press.

Pateman, C. (1970). *Participation and Democratic Theory*. Cambridge, UK: Cambridge University Press.

Peirson, L. (2002). E-mail to B. Wharf, 23 November.

Pence, E., and W. Shepard (1999). *Coordinating Community Response to Domestic Violence*. Newbury Park, CA: Sage.

Peters, T.J., and R.H. Waterman (1982). *In Search of Excellence*. New York: Basic Books.

Phillips, S.D., and M. Orsini (2002). *Mapping the Links: Citizen Involvement in Policy Processes*. Ottawa: Canadian Policy Research Networks.

Piven, F.F. (1993). 'Reforming the Welfare State: The American Experience', in G. Albo, D. Langille, and L. Panitch, eds, *A Different Kind of State? Popular Power and Democratic Administration*, pp. 66–74. Toronto: Oxford University Press.

———, and R.A. Cloward (1997). *Poor People's Movements: Why They Succeed, How They Fail*. New York: Pantheon.

Pizzey, E. (1997). *Scream Quietly or the Neighbors Will Hear*. Short Hills, NJ: Ridley Enslow.

Popham, R., D. Hay, and C. Hughes (1997). 'Campaign 2000 to End Child Poverty: Building and Sustaining a Movement', in B. Wharf and M. Clague, eds, *Community Organizing: Canadian Experiences*, pp. 248–72. Toronto: Oxford University Press.

Porter, J. (1965). *The Vertical Mosaic: An Analysis of Class and Power in Canada*. Toronto: University of Toronto Press.

Pressman, J., and A. Wildavsky (1973). *Implementation*. Berkeley, CA: University of California Press.

Prigoff, A. (2000). *Economics for Social Workers: Social Outcomes of Economic Globalization with Strategies for Community Action*. Belmont, CA: Wadsworth/Thomson Learning.

Rankin P., and J. Vickers, with the research assistance of A-M Field (2001). *Women's Move-*

ments and State Feminism: Integrating Diversity into Public Policy. Ottawa: Status of Women Canada.

Rawls, J. (1971). *A Theory of Justice*. Cambridge, MA: Harvard University Press.

Reid, A. (1996). *Shakedown*. Toronto: Doubleday.

Rein, M. (1970). *Social Policy: Issues of Choice and Change*. New York: Random House.

—— (1972). 'Decentralization and Citizen Participation in Social Services', *Public Administration Review* 32, 687–701.

—— (1983). *From Policy to Practice*. New York: M.E. Sharpe.

——, and F. Rabinowitz (1978). 'Implementation: A Theoretical Perspective', in W.D. Burnham and M.W. Weinberg, eds, *American Polities and Public Policy*, pp. 307–55, Cambridge, MA: MIT Press.

Report of the Aboriginal Committee (1992). *Liberating Our Children: Liberating Our Nation*. Victoria, BC: Ministry of Social Services.

Report of the Committee on Local Authority and Allied Social Services (1968). London: Her Majesty's Stationery Office.

Report of the Community Panel, Family and Children's Services Legislative Review (1992). *Making Changes: A Place to Start*. Victoria, BC: Ministry of Social Services.

Report of the Gove Inquiry into Child Protection (1995). *Matthew's Story*. Victoria, BC: Queen's Printer.

Rice, J., and M. Prince (2000). 'Life of Brian: A Social Policy Legacy', *Perception* 17 (2), 6–9.

—— (2000). *Changing Politics of Canadian Social Policy*. Toronto: University of Toronto Press.

Ripley, A. (2002). 'The Night Detective', in *Time*, 30 December/6 January 2003, pp. 37–41.

Ristock, J., and J. Pennell (1996). *Community Research as Empowerment*. Toronto: Oxford University Press.

Rittel, H.W., and M.W. Webber (1973). 'Dilemmas in a General Theory of Planning', *Policy Sciences* 4, 155–68.

Robinson, D. (1999). 'Canada's Real Jobless Rate Could Still Be as High as 17.9%', *The CCPA Monitor* 6 (2), 14.

Romanow, R. (2002). *Building on Values: The Future of Health Care in Canada*. Final Report. Ottawa: Commission on the Future of Health Care in Canada, at www.health-carecommission.ca

Roulston, J. (2003). Correspondence to B. Wharf.

Royal Commission on Aboriginal Peoples (RCAP) (1996). *Report Summary*. Report of the Royal Commission on Aboriginal Peoples, at www.ainc-inac.gc.ca

Rutman, D. (1998). 'A Policy Community: Developing Guardianship Legislation', in B. Wharf and B. McKenzie, *Connecting Policy to Practice in the Human Services*, pp. 97–113. Toronto: Oxford University Press.

——, M. Callahan, A. Lundquist, S. Jackson, and B. Field (1999). *Substance Use and Pregnancy: Conceiving Women in the Policy Process*. Ottawa: Status of Women Canada.

Sabatier, P.A. (1986). 'Top-down and Bottom-up Approaches to Implementation Research: A Critical Analysis and Suggested Synthesis', *Journal of Public Policy* 1 (1), 21–48.

Saleebey, D. (1990). 'Philosophical Disputes in Social Work: Social Justice Denied', *Journal of Sociology and Social Welfare* 17 (2), 29–40.

Sancton, A. (1997). 'Reducing Costs by Consolidating Municipalities: New Brunswick, Nova Scotia and Ontario', *Canadian Public Administration* 39 (3), 267–90.

Shapiro, J.P. (1994). *No Pity*. New York: Three Rivers Press.

Schon, D., and M. Rein (1994). *Frame Reflection: Toward the Resolution of Intractable Policy Controversies*. New York: Basic Books.

Schram, B. (1997). *Creating Small Scale Social Programs*. Thousand Oaks, CA: Sage.

Schroedel, J., and P. Peretz (1994). 'A Gender Analysis of Policy Formation: The Case of Fetal Abuse', *Journal of Health Politics, Policy and Law* 19 (2), 335–60.

Schur, N. (1987). *A to Zed*. New York: Harper Perennial.

Shragge, E. (1990). 'Community-Based Practice: Political Alternatives or New State Forms?', in L. Davies and E. Shragge, eds, *Bureaucracy and Community*, pp. 137–73. Montreal: Black Rose Books.

Smale, G. (1995). 'Integrating Community and Individual Practice: A New Paradigm for Practice', in P. Adams and K. Nelson, eds, *Reinventing Human Services*, pp. 59–86. Hawthorne, NY: Aldine de Gruyter.

—— (1996). *Mapping Change and Innovation*. London: Her Majesty's Stationery Office.

Smith, D. (1987). *The Everyday World as Problematic*. Toronto: University of Toronto Press.

Social Planning Council of Metropolitan Toronto (1976). *In Search of a Framework*. Toronto: Author.

Sower, C., J. Holland, K. Tiedke, and W. Freeman (1957). *Community Involvement: The Webs of Formal and Informal Ties That Make for Action*. Glencoe, IL: Free Press.

Spakes, V. (1984). 'Family Impact Analysis as a Framework for Teaching Social Policy', *Journal of Education for Social Work* 20 (1), 59–73.

Statistics Canada Website (2002). 'Labour Force, Employed and Unemployed, Numbers and Rates', 29 December, at www.statcan.ca/english/Pgdb/labor07a, htm.

Status of Women Canada (1996). *Gender-Based Analysis: A Guide for Policy Making*. Ottawa: Author.

Strega, S. (2000). 'Efforts at Empowering Youth: Youth-in-Care and the Youth-in-Care Networks in Ontario and Canada', in M. Callahan, S. Hessle, and S. Strega, eds, *Valuing the Field: Child Welfare in an International Context*, pp. 43–63. Aldershot, UK: Ashgate Press.

Stringer, E. (1996). *Action Research*. Thousand Oaks, CA: Sage.

Swift, K.J. (1995a). *Manufacturing 'Bad Mothers', a Critical Perspective on Child Neglect*. Toronto: University of Toronto Press.

—— (1995b). 'Missing Persons: Women in Child Welfare', *Child Welfare* 74 (3), 486–503.

——, and M. Birmingham (2000). 'Location, Location, Location: Restructuring and the Everyday Lives of "Welfare Moms"', in S. Neysmith, ed., *Restructuring Caring Labour: Discourse, State Practice and Everyday Life*, pp. 93–115. Toronto: Oxford University Press.

Teeple, G. (1995). *Globalization and the Decline of Social Reform*. Toronto: Garamond Press.

—— (2000). *Globalization and the Decline of Social Reform into the Twenty-First Century*. Aurora, ON: Garamond Press.

Thayer, F. (n.d.). 'Participation and Liberal Democratic Government'. Unpublished paper prepared for the Committee on Government Productivity. Toronto: Government of Ontario.

Titmuss, R. (1968). *Commitment to Welfare*. London: George Allen and Unwin.

—— (1974). *Social Policy*. London: George Allen and Unwin.

Torjman, S., and K. Battle (1995). 'Cutting the Deficit in Child Welfare', *Child Welfare* 74 (3), 459–85.

Valentine, F. (1994). *The Canadian Independent Living Movement: An Historical Overview*. Ottawa: The Canadian Association of Independent Living Centres.

Warren, D. (1981). 'Support Systems in Different Kinds of Neighbourhoods', in J. Garbarino and S. Holly Stocking, eds, *Protecting Children from Abuse and Neglect*, pp. 61–93. San Francisco: Jossey-Bass.

Weller, F., and B. Wharf (1995). *From Risk Assessment to Family Action Planning*. Victoria, BC: School of Social Work, University of Victoria.

Wharf, B. (1984) *From Initiation to Implementation: The Role of Line Staff in the Policy-Making Process*. Victoria, BC: School of Social Work, University of Victoria.

——, ed. (2002). *Community Work Approaches to Child Welfare*. Peterborough, ON: Broadview Press.

——, and M. Callahan (1984). 'Connecting Policy and Practice', *Canadian Social Work Review*, 30–52.

——, and M. Clague, eds. (1997). *Community Organizing: Canadian Experiences*. Toronto: Oxford University Press.

Wharf, B., J. Cossom, R. Hern, and D. Thomson (2003). 'Neighbourhood Houses and More Funding'. *Perspective* 25.2, pp. 20–1.

Wharf Higgins, J.S. (1997). 'Who Participates: Citizen Participation in Health Reform in B.C.', in B. Wharf and M. Clague, eds, *Community Organizing: Canadian Experiences*, pp. 273–302. Toronto: Oxford University Press.

————, J. Cossom, and B. Wharf (2003). 'Citizen Participation in Social Policy', in A. Westhues, ed., *Canadian Social Policy*, pp. 301–18. Waterloo, ON: Wilfrid Laurier University Press.

Williams, W. (1976). 'Implementation Analysis and Assessment', in W. Williams and R. Elmore, eds, *Social Program Implementation*, pp. 280–93. New York: Academic Press.

———— (1980). *The Implementation Perspective*. Berkeley, CA: University of California Press.

Witkin, S.L., and S. Gottschalk (1988). 'Alternative Criteria for Theory Evaluation', *Social Service Review*, 211–24.

Wyers, N.L. (1991). 'Policy-Practice in Social Work: Models and Issues', *Journal of Social Work Education* 27 (3), 241–50.

Yanow, D. (1987). 'Toward a Policy Culture Approach to Implementation', *Policy Studies Review* 7 (1) 103–15.

Yeatman, A., and S. Gunew. (1993). *Feminism and the Politics of Difference.* Sydney: Allen & Unwin.

Index

release results, she published her findings in a medical journal in 1996. The hospital promptly fired her, but because of widespread public indignation subsequently revoked the firing.

Oliveri's findings were supported by some colleagues and peers but questioned by others. The dispute as to the accuracy of her findings and of her right to break the contract by blowing the whistle raged on both national and international fronts for six years. During this time, Oliveri was maligned both professionally and personally. She was accused of having dealt with patients in an unethical fashion and of having stolen from her research grants. In addition, Apotex lashed out by accusing her of rude and intemperate behaviour. In late 2001, the College of Physicians and Surgeons of Ontario fully vindicated Oliveri, indicating that she acted in a manner that was in the best interests of her patients ('College Vindicates Oliveri', 2002). Although a settlement between Oliveri, four colleagues who supported her, and the hospital was reached, the terms of the settlement have not been made public.

Three whistle-blowers in the United States received so much public attention in 2002 that they were named as *Time*'s Persons of the Year for 2002. The three women are Cynthia Cooper of WorldCom, Sherron Watkins of Enron, and Colleen Rowley of the Federal Bureau of Investigation (FBI). Both Cooper and Watkins became aware of dishonest auditing practices in their organizations and drew these to the attention of the chief executive officers. When no action was taken by these executives, Cooper and Watkins blew the whistle. Rowley identified such serious weaknesses in the data-gathering systems of the FBI that information about potential terrorist acts went unnoticed. Her immediate superiors dismissed her claims and Rowley then communicated directly with the head of the FBI and with two Senators.

All these whistle-blowers were treated with disdain and anger by their colleagues. Rowley was compared to a spy convicted of treason; Cooper 'has been screamed at and she has been patronized' (Ripley, 2002, p. 37) and the 'atmosphere at Enron had grown so tense that Watkins called office security for advice on self defense' (Morse and Bower, 2002, p. 43). The introduction to the article on these three women summarizes both the significance and consequences of their actions:

> These women were for the 12 months just ending what New York firefighters were in 2001: heroes at the scene anointed by circumstance. They were people who did right just by doing their jobs rightly—which means ferociously, with eyes open and with the bravery the rest of us always hope we have and may never know if we do. Their lives may not have been at stake, but Watkins, Rowley and Cooper put pretty much everything else on the line. Their jobs, their health, their privacy, their sanity—they risked all of them to bring us badly needed word of trouble inside crucial institutions. (Lacayo and Ripley, 2002, p. 26)

All the foregoing examples of whistle-blowing have received a great deal of public attention, but whistle-blowers in the social services have remained rela-